CAMBRIDGE IBERIAN AND
LATIN AMERICAN STUDIES

GENERAL EDITOR

PROFESSOR P. E. RUSSELL F.B.A.

EMERITUS PROFESSOR OF SPANISH STUDIES,
THE UNIVERSITY OF OXFORD

The love poetry of
Francisco de Quevedo

The love poetry of
Francisco de Quevedo

An aesthetic and existential study

JULIÁN OLIVARES, JR

UNIVERSITY OF HOUSTON

CAMBRIDGE UNIVERSITY PRESS

CAMBRIDGE

LONDON   NEW YORK   NEW ROCHELLE

MELBOURNE   SYDNEY

Published by the Press Syndicate of the University of Cambridge
The Pitt Building, Trumpington Street, Cambridge CB2 IRP
32 East 57th Street, New York, NY 10022, USA
296 Beaconsfield Parade, Middle Park, Melbourne 3206, Australia

First published 1983

Printed in Great Britain at the University Press, Cambridge

Library of Congress catalogue card number: 81-14702

British Library Cataloguing in Publication Data
Olivares, Julián
The love poetry of Francisco de Quevedo.—
(Cambridge Iberian and Latin American studies)
1. Quevedo, Francisco de—Criticism and interpretation
I. Title
861'.3 PQ6424.Z5
ISBN 0 521 24362 9

To Kathy

Contents

Preface and Acknowledgments

Francisco Gómez de Quevedo y Villegas (1580–1645) led an active and turbulent life. He was famous for his religious and moral prose, his picaresque novel, the *Buscón* (*The Sharper*), and his satirical *Sueños* (*Dreams*). Following the practice of the period, he published no books of his own poetry. With the exception of some anthologized poetry, he gained the reputation as a brilliant and provocative poet mainly from the circulation of his poetry in manuscripts. He was a noted polemicist and wit, a protean, complex individual both praised and censured. He was a Knight of the Order of Santiago (St James), and spent much of his life in the service of His Majesty and royal favorites. In his political activities he made many enemies. He was incarcerated four times, the last contributing to poor health and his death. Most of his poetry was published posthumously in 1648 and 1670.

This book studies a corpus of Quevedo's poetry commonly regarded as his serious love poetry. Within this context I have limited the study to sonnets in the range of the High Style, taking into consideration the poet's tendency to blur the distinction by introducing into this category 'indecorous' elements. I do not wish to give the impression that I have arranged the sonnets in a chronological sequence. Although valuable work has been done in this regard (J. Crosby, H. Ettinghausen, R. Moore), the dating of Quevedo's poetry is still far from conclusive. Rather, I have attempted to discover a trajectory of intensity in this love poetry indicating his philosophical concern with, and personal reaction to, courtly love. The term 'existential' in the title is not to be taken as reflecting a modern philosophy or attitude, but as the attempt to see the love poetry, and his involvement with the courtly tradition, as an expression related to the poet's experience and existence.

This study is a revised and shortened version of a doctoral dissertation submitted at The University of Texas, Austin, 1977. I wish to acknowledge my gratitude to A. A. Parker for inducing me to write the dissertation on Quevedo and his patient supervision of it, for reading the first draft of the manuscript and his invaluable suggestions; to my colleague Harold Jones who read a portion of the manuscript and gave me critical assistance; to my wife Kathleen for her diligent reading of the typescript and for assistance in the clarification of stylistic obscurities. A special acknowledgment and thanks go to my friends and colleagues who graciously gave time and effort to the demanding task of translating: to Lenore Padula, Bridgewater State College, and to James A. Anderson, The University of Texas, Austin, for their assistance in translating parts of Flaminio Nobili's *Il trattato dell'amore humano*; to the latter again for the translation of Quevedo's prose; and to Bernard P. E. Bentley, University of St Andrew's, for the translation of most of Quevedo's poetry. I also thank Elias L. Rivers, State University of New York, Stony Brook, for allowing me to use the translations of Quevedo from his anthology, and for providing me with the translation of sonnet 451. My gratitude goes as well to the Ford Foundation Fellowships for Mexican Americans, and to its Director, Arturo Madrid, for the fellowship that allowed me to complete the dissertation; to the National Endowment for the Humanities and to the American Council of Learned Societies for the grant to revise the dissertation for book publication; and to the University of Houston for the funds to prepare the typescript. I acknowledge the cooperation of the following who gave permission to quote from copyright material: from *Gli Asolani* by Pietro Bembo, Rudolph B. Gottfried, translator, Indiana University Publications, 1954; excerpts from *The Book of the Courtier* by Baldesar Castiglione (translated by Charles S. Singleton), copyright © 1959 by Charles S. Singleton and Edgar de N. Mayhew, reprinted by permission of Doubleday & Company, Inc.; from 'Baltasar Gracián's *The Mind's Wit and Art*,' Leland H. Chambers, translator, Dissertation, University of Michigan, 1962; from *Petrarch's Lyric Poems*, Robert M. Durling, translator and editor, Harvard University Press, 1976; from *Renaissance and Baroque Poetry of Spain*, with English Prose Translations, Elias L. Rivers, translator and editor, copyright © 1973 by Elias L. Rivers (New York: Charles Scribner's Sons, 1966), reprinted with the permission of Charles Scribner's Sons.

I

Introduction

Spain had declined as a world power by the seventeenth century. A political and economic decay accentuated a spiritual and moral turmoil, causing the country's optimism to yield to bitterness, cynicism and resignation. A mood of *desengaño*, disillusionment, now prevailed. Yet, if on the one hand this spirit of disillusion encouraged a confrontation with the realities of the Spanish situation, on the other there was still the illusion that the glory of the past would return.[1] A parallel situation occurs in literature with regard to the role of courtly love as the thematic basis of nearly all love poetry. The idealistic social and literary phenomenon of courtly love, now pervaded by reality, was on the verge of dissolution, maintained only by its form and the determination of a few idealists.[2]

A prime social reason for the duration of courtly love was, as Leonard Forster sustains, that it was a game which could be taken seriously or frivolously:

what for Petrarch himself was deadly serious became for his successors a game, which like all games can be serious or not as circumstances require . . . But though it was a game – perhaps because it was a game – it provided the framework within which genuine love-making and courtship leading to a marriage could be . . . conducted. On the other hand, it need be no more than a game – it could be serious or as frivolous as you wanted. It was surely this flexibility which accounted for its enormous popularity for so long (*The Icy Fire*, pp. 66–7).

In this 'game' one could carry on a virtuous relationship with one person, suspend the rules with another and indulge the flesh. Poets participated in this social aspect of courtly love. In a society where love was an important topic of conversation, poetry, operating through a conventional framework and conventional idiom, became a kind of heightened social small talk (Forster, p. 62).

With the waning of the sixteenth century, this courtly game was going out of fashion, and was even held up to ridicule. Flaminio Nobili, in his *Il trattato dell'amore humano* (1567), points to the hypocrisy of the courtly aspirant who, restricted by the convention's rules and seeking no higher guerdon than an embrace and a spiritual kiss, curses his fortune if his lady gives herself to another: 'Now when the body of the beloved Woman cannot be entirely enjoyed without violation of the laws, he who seeks to enjoy at least her soul, through an exchange of Love, and to see her, and to hear her, and to think of her, most certainly shall experience human love; but he will curse fortune more than once if it grants another the possession of her body.'[3]

In the Golden Age of courtly love, it is doubtful if the courtier saw any contradiction in oscillating between *amor purus* and *amor mixtus* (soul and body) or even *amor ferinus* (bestial love). He satisfied the spirit on one level and the flesh on another; indeed, sexual relief on the 'lower' levels was a real safety valve from the rigors of virtuous love. In the seventeenth century this practice was seen as hypocritical; reality and morality demanded the abandonment of the 'pretense' to love a woman virtuously when the lover really hankered for her body. Courtly love was ridiculed, and no one was more critical of it than Francisco de Quevedo. Familiar with Nobili's treatise, Quevedo caustically echoes the former's observation of the absurd and hypocritical behaviour of lovers in *El alguacil endemoniado* ('The alguazil or catchpole possessed'), where the devil describes them in hell:

Son de ver los que han querido doncellas, enamorados de doncellas con las bocas abiertas y las manos extendidas, destos unos se condenan por tocar sin tocar pieza, hechos bufones de los otros, siempre en vísperas del contento, sin tener jamás el día, y con sólo el título de pretendientes. Otros se condenan por el beso como Judas, brujuleando siempre los gustos, sin poderlos descubrir. Detrás destos en una mazmorra están los adúlteros; éstos son los que mejor viven y peor lo pasan, pues otros les sustentan la cabalgadura y ellos la gozan.[4]

[You really must see those lovers of young maidens with their mouths agape and their arms outstretched; of these some are damned for feeling without ever coming to the touch, seen by others as clowns, ever present on the eve of happiness, but never there when its day dawns, only achieving the title of place-seekers. Others allow themselves to be damned for a kiss, like Judas, always shuffling their desires like a pack of cards but never disclosing any particular suit. Behind these, imprisoned in an underground dungeon, are the adulterers; these are the ones who live the best but sin the worst, for others maintain their mounts and they enjoy the ride.]

Because of his protean nature and the diversity of his work, Quevedo would seem a paragon of contradictions. It would appear that he also participated in the 'hypocrisy' of courtly love, oscillating between the joy of the flesh and the noble love of the spirit. Among his contemporaries he was known to have been rather lusty and scandalous. In *El tribunal de la justa venganza* ('The court of just revenge'), Quevedo is called a 'Doctor en Desvergüenzas,' a 'Bachiller en Suciedades,' and a 'Catedrático de Vicios y Proto-Diablo entre los hombres' ('Doctor of Shamelessness,' 'Bachelor of Smut,' 'Professor of Vice and Proto-Devil among men'). Among its many censures, the *Tribunal* reprehends 'La celebridad que hace de los vicios y torpes deleites carnales y a la libertad de su lengua y pluma con que ofende y deshonra a toda esta Monarquía' ('The ostentation he makes of vices and obscene carnal delights, and his unrestrained tongue and pen with which he offends and dishonors the entire Monarchy'; in *Verso*, 1932, pp. 1099–100). His burlesque description of himself would have corroborated the charges:

Don Francisco de Quevedo, hijo de sus obras y padrastro de las ajenas, dice
. . . que es hombre de bien, nacido para mal, hijo de algo para ser hombre de muchas fuerzas y de otras tantas flaquezas . . . señor del valle de lágrimas; que ha tenido y tiene . . . muy grandes cargos de conciencia; dando de todos muy buenas cuentas, pero no rezándolas; ordenado de corona, pero no de vida; que es de buen entendimiento, pero no de buena memoria; es corto de vista, como de ventura; hombre dado al diablo y prestado al mundo y encomendado a la carne; rasgado de ojos y de conciencia; negro de cabello y de dicha; largo de frente y de razones, quebrado de color y de piernas, blanco de cara y del todo, falto de pies y de juicio, mozo amostachado, y diestro en jugar las armas, a los naipes y otros juegos; y poeta sobretodo (*Memorial que dio en una Academia, Prosa*, 1958, pp. 88–9).
[Don Francisco de Quevedo, child of his own deeds and stepfather of others, declares . . . that he is a good man, born to do ill and in [of] position to be a man of many strengths and as many debilities . . . master of the valley of tears, who has had, and still has, many heavy loads of guilt – confessing them well but not as a litany; his papers in order, but not his living; quick-witted, but short of memory; as poor of vision as of fortune; a man committed to the devil, on loan to the world and given to the flesh; slant eyed and slant conscienced; black of hair and fortune; short on hair and morals; neither his color nor his legs quite right; fair looking and fair game for all; his feet as bad as his judgment; a mustachioed young man, clever at arms, cards and other games; and a poet, above all.]

He was known to have had a mistress with whom he 'lived in sin.' On March 24, 1624, the Junta de Reformación[5] (Council of Reform-

3

ation) investigated the morals of two sisters. On the report's margin there is this notation:

Las Ledesmas, la una está casada con un músico, no da escándalo de vivir mal, y por esto y ser casada no se puede tocar en ella. La otra está amancebada con don Francisco de Quevedo y tienen hijos. Esta amistad, en cuanto a comunicación de pecado, está dejada, en particular ahora que él vive de asiento en la Torre de Juan Abad, y de presente está ausente en jornada de su Magestad. Tendráse cuidado, en volviendo, con ver si reinciden (González de Palencia, p. 290).
[The Ledesma sisters: one is married to a musician, no evidence of bad habits, therefore, and being married, she cannot be faulted. The other is living with Don Francisco de Quevedo, and they have children. This friendship, insofar as its sinfulness is concerned, is over, particularly now that he resides in the Torre de Juan Abad, and at the present time is absent on a journey for His Majesty. When he returns, it will be observed if they take up again.]

In the light of Quevedo's 'lusty' nature and his criticism of courtly love, as seen in his satirical and burlesque poetry, the pursuit of the courtly ideal in his serious love poetry is particularly significant. In an age in which the ideal is collapsing, its last stand can be attributed to a special appeal on the personal level. Doris L. Baum says of Quevedo, 'The fact that he was one of the last Spanish poets to follow the tradition of courtly love . . . is significant in the history of Spanish literature, as it indicates the last vestiges of idealism in an era which was moving toward the cult of reason' (p. 152). The attempt to follow this idealistic tradition may be seen as an intense need for spiritual fulfillment. In his *Virtud militante* (*Militant Virtue*), Quevedo instructs the reader of the perpetual battle waged by the spirit and the flesh: 'El Apóstol dijo que el espíritu militaba contra la carne y la carne contra el espíritu. Luego tú, que eres compuesto de estas dos cosas, eres una perpetua milicia y tu combate, continuo; campo de batallas, eres dichoso, si en ti vence la mejor parte' ('The Apostle said that the spirit warred against the flesh, and the flesh against the spirit. You, then, who are made up of these two things, are a perpetual militia, and your battles are constant; battlefield that you are, you are fortunate if the better part of you shall conquer'; *Prosa*, 1958, p. 1229). Perhaps in an attempt to conquer the flesh, or at least to atone spiritually for his sensuality, Quevedo may have looked to courtly love as a virtuous counterweight for his carnal excesses, as a release from an era of *desengaño* and an existence eroded by time, from the 'anguish of living death' (Laín Entralgo, p. 37).

4

The principal reason for following the courtly tradition is literary. Quevedo says that he was, above all, a poet, 'poeta sobretodo'; and in the expression of noble love he wrote in the Petrarchan idiom. He had no other choice. Petrarchism, a poetic idiom of great flexibility and expressiveness, had become the language of love and the most popular modality of courtly love. There are two explanations behind this particular stylization of sentiment. First, for the Renaissance intellectual, Petrarch represented the ideal humanist; therefore the humanist imitated Petrarch, and, if he wrote poetry, he adopted the courtly convention. Second, the sixteenth century was a period of literary renewal in nearly all of the countries of western Europe, and this called for the creation of a vernacular with all of the expressiveness and dignity of Latin. Here again the model was Petrarch. Serious love poetry thus began as a Petrarchist exercise, and with the Italianate verse forms came Petrarch's ethos; however, the latter could not be assimilated until the form was acclimatized (Forster, p. 35). When lyrical poetry became a serious craft, then, the genre itself perpetuated the courtly manner. This association of genre and convention would change the style, sensibility and thought of future generations. This change in Spanish lyric poetry took effect in the early sixteenth century with Garcilaso de la Vega's successful acclimatization of the Italianate forms, especially the sonnet.[6] With this we have a curious turn of events. The troubadours created a genre which was a reflection of their society; and this genre, in turn, brought about a change in thought and feeling. As C. S. Lewis notes, 'life and letters are inextricably intermixed. If the feeling came first, a literary convention would soon arise to express it; if the convention came first, it would soon teach those who practised it a new feeling' (1936, p. 22). It is doubtful if the Petrarchists themselves were aware they were writing and conducting themselves according to a convention or system: 'The convention was coherent and pervasive, it was invaluable, it was part of the air they breathed, and many of them probably thought very little about it. What we see as a system was for them a natural mode of conventional utterance and conventional behaviour' (Forster, p. 22).

Coming at the end of this tradition, Quevedo had a critical perspective denied to his predecessors. He was aware that courtly love was an abstraction, yet it appealed to his real need for spiritual fulfillment. His conscience surely told him there was something more to love than physical union. By assuming the convention, Quevedo

5

inherited its style and code of conduct; but in the long run he found himself compelled to react against the very ethos which the genre was propagating. The alluring presence of the unattainable woman caused him agony; yet his greatest torment was his subjection to what he came to realize was an absurd code. It is this tension between the demands of the courtly genre and his reaction to it that we shall find especially compelling and significant.

On the verge of the collapse of the courtly tradition, Quevedo's love lyrics are important because of the portrayal of an arduous conflict between idealism and reality. This conflict has not been appreciated by many of his critics. Even in his lifetime the poet's reputation loomed unfavorably over his writings: 'Yo . . . malo y lascivo, escribo cosas honestas, y lo que más siento es que han de perder por mí su crédito, y que la mala opinión que yo tenga merecida, ha de hacer sospechosos mis escritos' ('I . . . evil and lascivious, write honest things, and what I most regret is that they should lose their credit because of me, and that the bad reputation I have earned so well should make my writings suspect'; *Espistolario*, p. 15).

Either because they placed undue emphasis on shaky biographical details or because they took one aspect of his writings as the 'essential' Quevedo, the majority opinion of critics up to the mid-twentieth century was that he was unable to write 'sincere' love poetry.[7] Because he was either a moralist (Carilla, p. 175), a misogynist (Romera-Navarro, p. 301) or a slave of the flesh (Maura y Gamazo, p. 34), Quevedo's love poetry was considered as being 'passionless,' written 'without conviction solely to satisfy the taste of the epoch' (Bouvier, pp. 157, 164).

In most of this criticism there is implicit an unjustifiable criterion for evaluating Quevedo's love poetry. This is made clear in Antonio Papell's comment on these lines from sonnet 358:

> A fugitivas sombras doy abrazos;
> en los sueños se cansa el alma mía;
> paso luchando a solas noche y día
> con un trasgo que traigo entre mis brazos.

[Around fugitive shadows I cast my embrace; in dreams my soul tires itself out; I spend night and day struggling alone with a goblin here within my arms. (BB)]

He remarks: 'Are these sentiments sincere? No, they are not. How far removed he is from the crystalline melancholy of Garcilaso!'[8] As will be demonstrated later, the sonnet does indeed express a significant experience, a reaction against the oppressive burden of courtly love. The main objection of such critics is that Quevedo's poetry is *not like* the courtly and Neoplatonic lyrics of his predecessors. The poet's detractors do not take into consideration the fundamental point that his love poetry ought not to have been like theirs. If it were the same, then a case could be made for insincerity. In such lines as those cited above, we perceive the distance and difference between Garcilaso's 'el dolorido sentir,' the tender or melancholy feeling, and Quevedo's 'dolorido desgarro,' unrestrained suffering.[9] The restrained emotion expressed by Garcilaso in poems of exquisite equilibrium becomes in Quevedo's a flood of passion charging the poetry with extraordinary tension; resigned melancholy erupts in an anguished cry; feelings are now not only profoundly analyzed but also expressed with penetrating wit and intensified verbal inventiveness.

The extremism of Quevedo's nature, his 'dos almas' ('two souls'), disconcerted the poet's critics. They seem not to have been aware of that unique mechanism of sensibility of the metaphysical poet which, according to T. S. Eliot, enabled him to devour and amalgamate disparate experience ('The Metaphysical Poets,' p. 247). What he devoured could be reordered by his mind and sensibility into separate qualitative levels. Traditionally, literature helped toward this by the Theory of the Three Styles, a distinct style or decorum befitting the subject and governing the relation of ornament to it (Tuve, pp. 192–247). In the Low (*bajo*) Style, only reality, and usually coarse, could be treated, and this in a burlesque or satirical manner. In the octave of sonnet 609[10] we note the poet's lampoon of the courtly lover whose only satisfaction comes from contriving mental orgasms out of frustrated desire:

> Quiero gozar, Gutiérrez; que no quiero
> tener gusto mental tarde y mañana;
> primor quiero atisbar, y no ventana,
> y asistir al placer, y no al cochero.
> Hacérselo es mejor que no terrero;
> más me agrada de balde que galana;
> por una sierpe dejaré a Diana,
> si el dármelo es a gotas sin dinero.[11]

[I want to enjoy sex, Guitérrez; I don't want mental pleasure later or tomorrow [never]; I want to gaze at beauty and not at the window, and attend to pleasure and not to the coachman. Doing it is better than wooing her from the streets; I prefer it free than at the price of courtesy: I'll leave Diana for a snake, if I can get it for a penniless swelling. (BB, JO)]

In the Middle (*mediano*) Style, we have this pastoral idyll, a madrigal in which sexual intercourse is still the subject, but without the bawdy jocularity and coarse diction. In contrast with the above expression of *amor ferinus*, in 413 we encounter *amor mixtus*:

> Los brazos de Damón y Galatea
> nueva Troya, torciéndose, formaban
> (que yo lo vi, viniendo de la aldea);
> sus bocas se abrazaban
> y las lenguas trocaban.
> En besos a las tórtolas vencían;
> las palabras y alientos se bebían
> y en suspiros las almas retozaban,
> Mas el, estremeciéndose, decía:
> '¡Ay, muero, vida mía!'
> Y ella, vueltos los ojos, le mostraba
> en su color lo mesmo que le daba.
> Fue tan dulce este paso y de tal suerte,
> que quiso parte dél la misma Muerte,
> pues quedando sin fuerza y sin aliento,
> entrambos despidieron el contento,
> y las niñas hermosas,
> que, al fin, de vergonzosas se escondieron,
> ya tristes, de envidiosas,
> a los divinos ojos se volvieron,
> dando armas a Damón con que venciese
> al arrepentimiento, si viniese.

[The arms of Damon and Galatea shaped, as they entwined, a new Troy (and I saw it, coming from the village); their lips embraced and their tongues enlaced. They outdid the turtle-doves with their kisses; they drank each other's words and breath and their souls frolicked in their sighs. But he, quivering, repeated 'I'm dying, oh [my love and] my life!' And she, her eyes upturned, showed him with their color the same as she was giving him. This transport was so sweet and such that Death itself wanted a share in it, since, losing strength and breath, both dispatched their joy. And her precious pupils which, at the end, bashful, had hidden themselves, and now sad from envy, returned to her divine eyes, giving Damon strength to overcome his remorse, if it should come. (BB)]

Periphrastic language barely cloaks graphic details of the act. Line two contains a conceit. Galatea is a 'nueva Troya' because she has put aside her defenses, allowing herself to be penetrated. Lines 9–12 refer obviously to the climax of the act, but the details may need some elucidation. Galatea's eyes, upturned in the ecstasy of orgasm, show only the white, the color of death (the pale skin drained of blood), at the moment that she is giving Damón his 'erotic death.' The rapture

8

of this death is brief, as it attracts the attention of Death itself. Death destroys their happiness, not out of malice, but because Death shares the lovers' yearning for joy. Death, too, suffers from solitude. The poet, however, doubts that Damón will feel any remorse for love's consummation. If so, he will see in the beloved's 'niñas de los ojos' ('pupils,' but also 'the apple of his eye'), that the experience of possessed beauty can overcome a seizure of the conscience – if he were to have one. Witnessing the love-making of two rustics, portrayed in pastoral innocence, the poet implies that all love should be as guiltless as theirs. Yet as an educated man, framed by the morals of his times, he cannot entirely avoid seizures of his own conscience. Ideologically, if not in style, this madrigal corresponds to two major concerns in Quevedo's love poetry of the High Style: the attempt to make some accommodation for the demands of the flesh within the framework of a genre that glorifies only virtuous love, and the destruction of Eros by Thanatos.

Sonnet 451 is an example of the High Style (*alto* or *sublime*), and of *amor purus*:

> ¿Cómo es tan largo en mí dolor tan fuerte,
> Lisis? Si hablo y digo el mal que siento,
> ¿qué disculpa tendrá mi atrevimiento?
> Si callo, ¿quién podrá excusar mi muerte?
>   Pues, ¿cómo, sin hablarte, podrá verte
> mi vista y mi semblante macilento?
> Voz tiene en el silencio el sentimiento:
> mucho dicen las lágrimas que vierte.
>   Bien entiende la llama quien la enciende;
> y quien los causa, entiende los enojos;
> y quien manda silencios, los entiende.
>   Suspiros, del dolor mudos despojos,
> también la boca a razonar aprende,
> como con llanto y sin hablar los ojos.

[How can I stand such suffering for so long, my lady? If I speak out and tell of the pain I feel, how can my disobedience be excused? But if I am silent, how can I avoid death? For how can my eyes and emaciated countenance behold you without telling you the truth? Intense feeling finds a voice even in silence: the tears that it sheds are most eloquent. The flame is understood by her who ignites it; and she who causes suffering understands it; and she understands silence who imposes it. Sighs, the mute by-products of suffering, the mouth also learns to speak, just as silent tears put words into one's eyes. (ER)]

The sonnet is based on the paradox that virtuous love is the cause of the courtly lover's grief. While in this style sex is not explicit, it is clear

9

that the lover, attempting to keep his love pure, nonetheless suffers from frustrated desire. The problem is that convention demands that suffering be silenced; so, if he speaks, he disobeys the code and his lady. On the other hand, if he remains silent, how will she know he is suffering? The answer is provided by a second paradox, the rhetoric of silence. Since she ignites the flame of his love, since she is the cause of his grief and causes his silence, she should understand, interpret, his obedient silence as a 'voicing' of his affliction. Furthermore, if his eyes, which cannot speak, can communicate his grief by reason of their tears, his lips too are capable of speechless communication. By emitting sighs they discourse (*razonar*), on his affliction. His sighs are the mute spoils of pain. If his beloved can be eloquently silent, inasmuch as she understands why he continues to be her servant at the cost of unmitigated grief – 'elocuente, Lisi, tu hermosura / califica en tu luz mi desatino / y en tus merecimientos mi locura' ('Lisi, your eloquent beauty gives credit by your light to my foolishness and by your merits [gives credit] to my madness,' BB) (480) – conversely his silence can also be eloquent.

It may well be that Quevedo's expression of the entire range of his amatory experience, both real and imagined, in all the levels of style frustrated his early critics, unable to reconcile the differences. The point is that they need not be reconciled, since each corresponds to a distinct facet and quality of experience; first on the level of diction, as in the second quatrain of sonnet 358:

> Cuando le quiero más ceñir con lazos,
> y viendo mi sudor, se me desvía;
> vuelvo con nueva fuerza a mi porfía,
> y temas con amor me hacen pedazos.

[When I most want to capture it with bonds, on seeing my sweat [effort], it slips away; I turn again with renewed strength to my persistence, and my obsession with love shatters me to pieces. (BB)]

With 'sudor' (sweat) and 'pedazos' (pieces), the poet incorporates into the High Style of courtly love diction previously only appropriate to the lower styles.[12] In this way he revitalizes an exhausted convention, and the novelty, the *shock*, produced conveys the turmoil courtly love is generating in his psyche and emotions.

The second aspect of the poet's amalgamation of experience is to be found in *conceptismo*, which in Quevedo as in the English Metaphysicals consists of an operation of the unified sensibility of intellect and emotion in the production of the conceit. The *concepto* (conceit) results from the operation of *agudeza* (wit), and is primarily that particular metaphor cultivated by the Metaphysicals and their continental counterparts which discovers a *correspondencia*, a correspondence or affinity, between things radically disparate.[13] The failure of Quevedo's critics to appreciate this spirit and expression of the Baroque caused them to see his love lyrics as 'more witty than passionate' (Mérimée, 1931, p. 238), and to call them 'insipid' because they contain only *culterano* pomp and *conceptista* artifice.[14]

The final tercet of sonnet 303 contains two light conceits derived from the elaboration of Petrarchan commonplaces. The sonnet concerns a carnation which presumed to compete with the beauty of the poet's lady, but finds itself crushed by the hail of her pearly teeth. In her rage to crush the flower, she bites her lip:

> Sangre vertió tu boca soberana,
> porque, roja victoria, amaneciese
> llanto al clavel y risa a la mañana.

[Blood was spilt by your sovereign mouth, so that, [with this] red victory, [dewy] tears should dawn for the carnation and laughter for the morn. (BB)]

The flow of blood is a red victory over the carnation, causing it to weep; that is, the blood on the petals gives the appearance of a carnation shedding scarlet tears. This conceit, in immediate association with 'amaneciese' (derived from *amanecer*, to dawn), simultaneously expresses a standard topos: the beloved's beauty is as splendid as dawn, in this case the red streaks of dawn. However, the traditional correspondence of this comparison is secondary; what revitalizes this exhausted metaphor is the introduction of a novel correspondence. The correspondence between the lady as dawn and the carnation's defeat is the verb in its meaning of 'to awaken' or 'to dawn on one.' With this meaning the poet dramatizes the experience of *desengaño*, disillusionment. The carnation 'wakes up' to the lady's splendor, dawning to its presumption to rival her beauty. Consequently, if the flower wakes up, finding itself vanquished and humiliated, then the lady must be sunrise itself. At this point the popular metaphor of the laughter of the sun's rays is incorporated into the encomium of the beloved's beauty.[15] The sonnet ends with morning, cosmic beauty, laughing over her victim.

This sonnet manifests a concern of late Petrarchists to overcome the absorption of the speaker's personality by the rhetorical catalogue of beauty (Brown, 1976, pp. 35–9). Instead of lurking passively behind a traditional encomium, Quevedo's procedure often depends on a conceited reworking of amorous commonplaces by which he personalizes a weakened tradition. Aware of the formal and rhetorical limitations, the sensitive reader perceives that the poet is not just paying lip service to a convention, but that by means of wit and verbal dramatization he rehabilitates the commonplaces, discloses afresh the emotions that once informed them. Although the topic of the carnation dominates the metaphorical plane, serving as a competitive yet inadequate analogue of the beloved's lips, it discovers a more important dimension. On this affective level the speaker, the observer, becomes a vicarious participant. The red ('encarnada') carnation is a symbol of the lover's passion. Like the carnation, he presumed to be worth of her beauty and love, but likewise experienced mocking humiliation and icy disillusionment; in short, he suffers from a crushed ego.

The above example of *conceptismo* would have impressed some critics as being pure artifice, and therefore 'insincere.' In the appraisal of Petrarchan sonneteers, and especially their Baroque successors, it would be well to heed C. S. Lewis's admonition: 'They are not trying to communicate faithfully the raw, the merely natural, impact of actual passion. The passion for them is not a specimen of "nature" to be followed so much as a lump of ore to be refined: they ask themselves not "How can I record it with the least sophistication?" but "Of its bones what coral can I make?", and to accuse them of insincerity is like calling an oyster insincere because it makes its disease into a pearl' (1938, p. 145). That Quevedo's sophistication lies more in the area of wit is hardly a basis for calling his love poetry insincere.

Sincerity in poetry does not depend on a correlation between lived experience and the imaginative construction of this experience. The *artifact* does not have to square with a *fact* of the poet's life. This was particularly true in the Renaissance and Baroque periods. If the spread of courtly love began as a Petrarchistic exercise, it need not have been inspired by the love for a real woman. It was common practice to *fingir amores*, pretend love. While a real love, given the poet's talent, could provoke good poetry, serious love poetry was judged, among other things, by its capacity to reveal the poet as a 'representative of love.' About the mid-sixteenth century courtly verse went into a decline. While the reasons for this are too complex to deal with here, we can suspect that some causes were the debilitated commonplaces which could rarely be vitalized, the intrusion of

reality, and the long-term effect of *fingir amores*, which undermined a
sustained degree of artistic imagination. Quevedo noted that love in
his seventeenth century was only skin deep, 'Los amores de este siglo
no pasan de la corteza';[16] and because it was such a deceptive
affection, it could be pretended: 'Engañoso afecto es el amor, y siendo
tan natural, es el que recibe más artificios; porque o por cortesía o por
interés o por engaño, puede llegar a fingirse, y lo que es más peligroso,
por agradecimiento, como el que por no parecer ingrato finge que
dura en amar' ('Love is a deceptive emotion, and being the most
natural thing, it is receptive to the greatest artifice; because either out
of courtesy or self-interest or deceit, it can be feigned; and what is
worst of all, out of gratitude, as in the case of one who, not wishing to
appear ungrateful, pretends that his love endures'; 'Sentencia 972').
With Quevedo, however, love is a profound experience; and in the twilight of its long tradition courtly love again becomes dynamic poetry.

Otis Green, in his *Courtly Love in Quevedo* (1952), maintains that the
impression of insincerity derives, in part, from the failure of critics to
perceive that 'in Quevedo's love poetry . . . there is a hierarchy, from
amor ferino to a love of chaste detachment – *cupiditas sine cupiditate* – and
that only the last had meaning for Quevedo. Courtly love, therefore,
is not to be regarded as *un tema más* [one more theme] within the body
of his amatory verse, but as the central theme – a theme with which he
was deeply and philosophically concerned' (p. 8). From the fourteenth century through the fifteenth, probably the most important
topic discussed among Italian intellectuals concerned the nature of
love; and the question they asked themselves was: 'What is the noblest
way to love?' Love became an area of considerable philosophical
speculation. In the sixteenth century philosophical love treatises were
supplanted in popularity by manuals like Pietro Bembo's *Gli Asolani*
(*The Asolani*) and Baldesar Castiglione's *Il libro del cortegiano* (*The
Book of the Courtier*). As aesthetic responses to philosophical specu-
lations on love, it was mainly these works which influenced amatory
literature. Towards the next century it may be safe to say that, while
courtly love poetry did convey an ethos of ideal love, it became less a
philosophical concern than an area of aesthetic recreation. Quevedo's
serious love poetry, however, reveals a profound concern with both.

It needs emphasizing that one's philosophical formation, the
training of one's conscience and one's literary culture are all *parts of
experience*. In the past, when supreme importance was attached to this
kind of intellectual formation, it constituted an overwhelmingly

important part of one's living. No exploration of experience would have been considered what we now call 'existential' if the mind and the moral conscience did not participate in it, however much they might have been in abeyance in these acts over which the passions and the senses had exercised dominance. The main point is that Quevedo's sonnets to Lisi, for example, do not need to be squared with his real life in order to be accepted as profound and moving poetry. They represent an imaginative construction of experience, which was no less real for not being necessarily lived in that particular form. In dealing with the ethos of the genre, and taking to it his philosophical concern, he undoubtedly asked himself: 'What is the noblest way in which a man can love a woman; is such a love possible; how would I live it if I could; how would it affect me?' Quevedo's imagination, mind and heart, operating on and around experience, learned as well as lived, produced for us a record of human living, existence, more 'real,' certainly more significant, than a truthful autobiography. It is the intention of this study, therefore, to deal with Quevedo's experience of love on the highest level, expressed as 'poetic truth' in the 'High Style.'

Amédée Mas divides the poet's admirers in two camps, the ancients and the moderns. The ancients, behind Green, project Quevedo into the past and see in him the last of the troubadours, the last singer of courtly love; the moderns, headed by Dámaso Alonso, make of him the elder brother of our existential anguish (p. 291). Contrary to the 'ancients,' Mas sustains that courtly love is not Quevedo's central theme but only 'un tema más' (p. 306). Emphasizing his satirical and burlesque verse, Mas holds that Quevedo's characteristic vein lies in the caricature of woman and in the preference for easy women to the imagined love of courtly lovers for noble ladies (p. 300). While this poetry of the Low Style does indeed reveal an anticourtly attitude, one cannot assume the same attitude when dealing with the courtly tradition in the High Style. In order to discover the poet's attitude here, one must arrive at it from within the confines of the genre itself. It is a critical oversight to apply the *persona* disclosed in one type of poetry to poetry of a totally different order. Even so, it could be convincingly argued that courtly love is the central theme of his satirical and burlesque love poetry as well. It is the target of his ire and caricature; and because of the license permitted by the Low Style, the poet's anticourtly posture is patently evident. However, the detection of such a posture within the confines of the tradition in the High Style becomes a complex matter requiring considerable scrutiny. Both types of poetry, then, are the two sides of the same preoccupation.

Green's recognition of the thematic and philosophical importance that courtly love had for Quevedo was a major step in the revaluation of his love poetry; yet this affirmation is not accompanied by sufficient analysis. Rather, taking an historical approach, he attempts to demonstrate that this love poetry is a continuation of the courtly elements of the fifteenth-century *cancioneros*, anthologies (*CLQ*, p. 79). The poet's detractors were correct in noting the differences in Quevedo's love poetry with regard to his predecessors, but erred in assuming this was a basis for a negative evaluation; Green, on the other hand, stresses the similarities and does not take into sufficient consideration the differences. With emphasis on the themes and motifs of courtly love – the beauty of the beloved, the eyes, reason, passion, *engaño* (deception), etc. – he points out parallels in Quevedo but skims their treatment within the poem. He focuses on the convention, and overlooks the manner in which it is utilized. While at times Quevedo does assume a conventional pose, Arthur Terry notes that in many of his poems, 'though many of their details are related to the courtly love tradition, it is important to consider how these are used within the actual poem'; such a consideration will show that they 'are invariably handled critically and with a full awareness of their implications' (*Anthology*, II, pp. xxvi–xxvii).

Mas's criticism of the 'modern camp' is prompted by D. Alonso's perception of unrestrained emotion, 'desgarrón afectivo,' in Quevedo's sonnet 472, 'Cerrar podrá mis ojos' ('My eyes may be closed'), which Alonso declares is the greatest Spanish love sonnet, and by his claim that the Baroque poet expresses an anguish comparable to that of 'our modern poets' and of the 'anguished man of the twentieth century' (pp. 526, 76–77). Taking exception to this 'too modern interpretation,' Mas sees in Quevedo's poetry, particularly sonnet 472, less emotion than conceptual logic and verbal inventiveness (p. 293). In his opinion this is what gives an apparent originality to commonplaces and creates ambiguities which the poet probably did not intend (p. 298). Here we note again a shortsightedness obstructing a keener critical vision of the Spanish literature of the seventeenth century. In separating aesthetics from experience, art from emotion, Mas fails to recognize the Baroque sensibility informing a convention with verve and originality.

The emergence of the conceit as a dominant factor in Baroque poetics can be attributed to a remarkable sensibility. T. S. Eliot has stated that, by this mechanism of sensibility, the English meta-physical poet could feel a thought 'as immediately as the odour of a rose'; it was an experience which 'modified his sensibility.' Around the mid-seventeenth century, however, 'a dissociation of sensibility set in, from which we have never recovered' (p. 247). A. A. Parker has applied Eliot's observation on the Metaphysicals' 'amalgamation of experience' to Quevedo and to Spanish *conceptismo*. Parker discovers in the Baroque dramatist, Pedro Calderón de la Barca, a definition of poetry that defends *conceptismo* and substantiates Eliot's observation: 'The writing of poetry is an adornment of the soul or a skill of understanding,' adding:

In this marvellous formula Calderon fixed his definition of poetry in accordance with the theory and practice of his time. Such a definition could only be formulated at a time when the concept of the essential unity of the human personality still prevailed. It could not be conceived that within the integrated man, of uncorrupted will, there could be a dichotomy between experience and reason, emotions and ideas, logic and imagination, the aesthetic and ethical sensibility. In poetry all human faculties were involved, co-ordinated by the unity of the soul.

With advice for the understanding of this poetry, he continues:

And what was necessary for writing poetry is also necessary for reading it. A certain intellectual agility is also needed by the reader. An intellectual effort in the reading will reveal that very often what seems absurd and whimsical is profound, and an apparent obscurity is astonishing luminosity.[17]

Because many critics have not made this intellectual effort, they have failed to see that in Quevedo's era *conceptismo* was inseparable from a vision which united aesthetics and experience.

The parallels between Quevedo and the English Metaphysicals have been pursued by L. E. Hoover in her comparative study, *John Donne and Francisco de Quevedo* (1978). The metaphysical orientation of these poets, obsessed with the problems of time, death and solitude, invests the traditional love themes inherited from Petrarch and the *amour courtois* tradition with 'greater profundity,' creating a love poetry 'vigorously original' (p. xviii). While both poets seek in love a mode of transcendence, their poetry is permeated by the major Baroque theme of *desengaño*, disillusionment, and discloses

the anguish with which Donne and Quevedo ponder love's mutability, the destructive power of unrequited adoration and the beloved's disdain, the deathlike qualities of the lovers' parting and absence, or the actual death of the beloved herself. Time and death are strong adversaries, capable of destroying love, the lover, and the beloved. Consequently, in Quevedo's Lisi sonnets, as in Donne's love poetry, the Baroque theme of *desengaño* often defines their love, be it requited or non-requited (p. xxi).

This study will concentrate on Quevedo's love poetry of the High Style within the context of courtly love, Petrarchism and Neoplatonism, and with a regard to the poet's metaphysical preoccupations. From his confrontation with the stylistic and ethical limitations of traditions of conventional love there emerges an expression of remarkable aesthetic originality and tension, demonstrating that love was an existential concern. Furthermore, we shall endeavor not only to demonstrate the originality of this poetry with respect to Renaissance and Baroque poetics, but also to determine, in an objective manner, where it approaches modern sensibility and expression.

2

The conception of an ideal

Courtly love can frequently be a source of amusement to modern readers. For the uninitiated it often conjures up the vision of a lavish display of stylized behavior and flowery language. The idea that sentiment can be formalized, made art, may seem strange, and most difficult to accept is the concept that love may be suffering and not pleasure. The notion of a love which, ultimately, does not seek sexual satisfaction may appear to some as unrealistic and even absurd' Courtly love is difficult to take seriously, providing at best escapist literature and entertainment at the cinema. Yet when we do take it seriously, when we look for the ideals that gave it shape, we find that love was conceived as a civilizing force in a barbarous society. In his respites from battle, the medieval knight sought moral and cultural perfection through the pursuit of love. Valor depended not only on courage but also on spiritual refinement. In order to escape or overcome an ambience of barbarity, love needed to be formalized:

To formalize love is the supreme realization of the aspiration to the life beautiful . . . to formalize love is, moreover, a social necessity, a need that is the more imperious as life is more ferocious. Love has to be elevated to the height of a rite. The overflowing violence of passion demands it. Only by constructing a system of forms and rules for the vehement emotions can barbarity be escaped (Huizinga, pp. 108–09).

Love was ideally envisioned, if not as a corrective, at least as a way to offset a crude reality. In a time of barbarity love filled a social need and satisfied the personal desire for spiritual refinement.

The concept of love as a civilizing force is not by any means foreign to the ideals that have inspired other generations. It has recently been proposed in new and frank ways, particularly as an outspoken opposition to war. Popular slogans urged us not long ago to 'Make love not war'; hence love can again be regarded as a means of rescuing society from barbarity. Although such a slogan appeals to

18

man's noble worth, it involves essentially the transference of aggres-sive, destructive behaviour into a life-affirming activity; and this is not unlike one of the purposes of courtly love. However, in our alienated society it is difficult to know what love is. To help overcome this problem, Erich Fromm states that 'The first step to take is to become aware that love is an art . . . if we want to learn how to love, we must proceed in the same way we have to proceed if we want to learn any other art' (p. 4). The learning of this art is divided in two parts: 'one, the mastery of the theory; the other, the mastery of the practice' (p. 4). Like his medieval predecessor, Andreas Capellanus (*The Art of Courtly Love*), Fromm perceives that success in love requires a gentle heart and a noble spirit, and acknowledges that love is not based exclusively on sexual gratification.

When we examine courtly love, we shall find that, to a certain extent, its ideas are shared by contemporary society. These ideas, of course, evolve and are modified by different times and contexts, but one thing remains paramount: love continues to be an aspiration and can be conceived as an ideal, in spite of the configuration given to it or the convention it may become. The purpose of this chapter is to study the courtly ideal in the latter stages of its development and crisis, which includes the attempt to correct a 'confused' ideal and relieve psychic torment and sensual grief through Neoplatonic love. Here we shall include a discussion of representative sonnets, demonstrating the *conventional* Quevedo, with the closest links to the tradition. The decline of the ideal will be seen in the discussion of Nobili's love treatise. In this final stage of the general theory we shall note the break-up of the ideal under the pressure of the reality of passion. This is marked by Nobili, and this is the prelude to the *essential* Quevedo, the poet who penetrates beyond conventional ideas into the heart of the matter.

The ideal that courtly love embraces is human love. One type of this love leads to marriage and procreation; the other is characterized by reason and the spirit. Nobili distinguishes the two types in the following manner:

We take the word 'human' in a double sense, so that sometimes it means that which is the natural behavior of men, and other times it means that which conforms to honesty and to laws; just as we regularly say that all men are possessed of Reason, but on other occasions we mean only those who live by the rule of correct and good reasoning. So in the first sense, all the . . . Loves are human; but in the second, only the last two; that is, for a man to have his beloved as his Wife, and the other to gratify his soul and his sight.[1]

Noble human love is with the heart, mind and soul. It is a virtuous love that delights in the physical and spiritual beauty of the beloved.

In the Middle Ages courtly love was the means by which human love, or 'amor purus' as Andreas calls it (p. 122), was to be attained. This system of love was founded on three basic tenets: first, on the ennobling force of human love; second, on the elevation of the beloved to a place of superiority above the lover; third, on the conception of love as ever-unsatiated and increasing desire.[2] The second and third tenets are not essential to human love, but constitute the distinctive configuration given to it by courtly love. By creating a cult of the beloved, and by fanning the flames of desire but abstaining from sensual satisfaction, a particular modality of human love was established which made its attainment virtually impossible.[3]

In order to ensure that his love would not be consummated, the lover occasionally sought an inaccessible woman, frequently a married one, as Petrarch's Laura seems to have been (Bishop, chap. 5). As he was denied her favors, the lover enjoyed only the contemplation of love, while deprivation caused the senses to agonize. This 'have-and-have-not' situation became a literary convention (Green, 1968, I, p. 74). Yet, whether in life or literature, we find a spiritual reality: the zeal for perfection, the yearning for transcendence which inspires human love. By denying the senses their satisfaction, the body suffered; but this suffering satisfied the spirit. Love was glory for the spirit, an ordeal for the body. Another consequence of the tension between the lover's abstract devotion to a woman of flesh and blood was psychological torment. These corporal and mental afflictions were willingly tolerated as proof of his love.

The principal characteristic of the courtly lover, and one which receives refinement from Petrarch and becomes the fundamental note of Spanish love poetry throughout the sixteenth century, is *el dolorido sentir*, the tender feeling. As Pedro Salinas puts it, his is 'a particular mode of being, self-justified, separate from any end . . . that takes satisfaction in being no more than a lover'; courtly love is 'a pleasure in which there is suffering.' It is worth the pain, *vale la pena*, because it is a road to perfection, *camino de perfección* (pp. 13–14, 22). The tension borne by the courtly lover found its literary correlation in the antitheses which constitute the stylistic essence of courtly love poetry. Both in literature and in life, courtly love became a 'work of art requiring the greatest sensitivity and taste. Concomitantly, the hero became an artist and a gentleman. The art which he professed was called . . . *cortesía*' (Valency, p. 29).

In the early stages of the courtly convention, the lover was not always successful in resisting the craving of the flesh. Andreas's treatise reveals that, while *amor purus* was the aspiration of every good lover, it was not wholly condemnatory to settle for *amor mixtus* (p. 122). This did not disprove the concept of courtly love, for, as Valency notes, 'The concept perhaps had a certain rigidity; the troubadours did not' (p. 142). However, in the late twelfth and early thirteenth centuries, the attempt to overcome sensuality became a major concern of the troubadours (Valency, p. 180). The ideal of true love was refined to the point where the woman of flesh and blood adored by them became ethereal for the *stilnovisti*. With the *dolce stil nuovo*, the sweet new style, she was desexualized; the lady vanished and became a celestial intelligence sojourning on earth. By calling their beloved an angel, the *stilnovisti* were not entertaining a hyperbole but advancing a belief (Valency, pp. 227–33). The ideal of human love appears to have been lost among these poets. In their scheme the lady was not loved for her sake but for the sake of God, and as such they prepared the way for the Neoplatonists. It took Petrarch to bring this angel down to earth.

Petrarch's Laura is not a symbol or signpost to God; rather, she is 'a real woman, whose beauty intoxicates him. Hence he can hymn her various physical attributes . . . and do so with a better conscience in that she represents physical and spiritual perfection' (Forster, p. 3). While the troubadour lamented the withholding of favors which might be granted, the Petrarchist, although aspiring to the consummation of love, knows that it will not be granted, and is resigned to his fate (Forster, pp. 2–3). Petrarch expresses the tension between body and spirit through a poetic idiom of great flexibility, expressiveness, and with a wide range of antitheses. The characteristic tonality of his *Rime* is a pervasive melancholy. The *dolorido sentir* acquires its most profound expression with Petrarch, finding only later a comparable singer in Garcilaso.

In Petrarch's finest poems he achieves a precarious balance between passion and purification. His followers, however, were less interested in such a poetical resolution than in elaborating and exploiting his antitheses for their own purposes (Forster, p. 4). The *Rime* reveal a determination not to resolve the conflict between sensuality and human love. This is what most distinguishes the courtly lover. He is not only resigned to his fate, but content to live in fire and ice: 'The interpenetration of pleasure and pain, and the satisfaction which could be derived from holding these two opposites in an uneasy balance, is basic in Petrarch's works and becomes the fundamental theme of the Petrarchistic convention' (Forster, p. 13). This *dulce martirio*, sweet affliction, is the essential characteristic of the courtly lover, and one which we must bear in mind when we consider the essential Quevedo.

The Petrarchan antithesis of ice and fire, along with the courtly tenets of the beloved's superiority and the lover's unsatiated desire, are dramatized in Quevedo's sonnet 293, probably an early love poem. D. Alonso has commented on the evident Petrarchism of Quevedo's early love poems, which tend towards an excessive use of antitheses, often framed in bipartite lines (pp. 504, 507).

> Ostentas, de prodigios coronado,
> sepulcro fulminante, monte aleve,
> las hazañas de fuego y de la nieve,
> y el incendio en los yelos hospedado.
>   Arde el hibierno en llamas erizado,
> y el fuego lluvias y granizos bebe;
> truena, si gimes; si respiras, llueve
> en cenizas tu cuerpo derramado.
>   Si yo no fuera a tanto mal nacido,
> no tuvieras, ¡oh Etna!, semejante:
> fueras hermoso monstro sin segundo.
>   Mas como en alta nieve ardo encendido,
> soy Encélado vivo y Etna amante,
> y ardiente imitación de ti en el mundo.

[You proudly display, with marvels crowned, exposive tomb and treacherous mountain, the glorious feats of fire and snow, and a blazing furnace lodged in ice. Bristling winter burns in flames, and the fire drinks up raindrops and hail; it thunders when you sigh; when you breathe, it rains in ashes your scattered corpse. If I were not born for such ills, you would have, oh Etna, no equal; you would be, splendid monster, without peer. But since in lofty snows I burn inflamed, I am Enceladus alive and Etna in love, a burning imitation of you in the world. (BB)]

The lover's comparison to a volcano, while traditional, is appropriate: the icy volcano is a monumental correlative of the lover's passion burning in his beloved's coldness.

The quatrains describe an unidentified subject as a fulminating tomb and a treacherous mountain which openly displays its prodigious deeds of fire and snow. Winter is able to burn among bristling flames and the fire drinks rain and hail; if it grieves, it thunders; if it breathes, it consumes itself and showers its ashes. In the tercets the poet exclaims that, if it were not for his misfortune, Etna would be a wonder without equal. The subject is identified as a famous volcano. In the concluding tercet the comparison of the lover with the volcano is completed, and the intention is made clear.[4] His passion burns for a cold lady, and this antithesis makes him an 'Encélado vivo y Etna amante,' a burning imitation in life of the volcano.

The poet's intention is amplified through a witty use of mythology. Enceladus was one of the Giants who rebelled against the Gods. He was struck down by the chaste Athena and buried beneath the volcano, Etna. The witty use of this myth is discovered in the correlation of lines two and thirteen. Etna fulminates because it is a volcano, but it is also a tomb because Enceladus is buried beneath it; furthermore, since the Giant revolted against the Gods, the volcano is a treacherous mountain, whose eruptions manifest the Giant's anger, a connotation of 'fulminante.' These conceits are extended in line thirteen. Since the lover is a live Enceladus, he is a traitor; and his treachery is a consequence of his volcanic passion, making him an 'Etna amante.' Like Enceladus, he too has rebelled against a goddess. His lust has attempted to assault the summit of virtue; therefore, he is also a 'monte aleve.' This conceit has a second part. For his transgression of the courtly code of virtuous love, he is condemned to be, like Etna, a 'sepulcro fulminante.' His punishment is his unconsummated passion, making life a living, fiery death. This metaphor discloses the sonnet's cause as death-in-life, a major theme in the totality of Quevedo's love poetry of the High Style. The comparison with Etna is completed in that, like the volcano which reconciles the dualities of fire and ice, his passion causes him to burn in the icy disdain of the beloved. Similarly, his sighs are like thunder, and his respiration is the exhalation of the fire that consumes him within.

The sonnet's structure is based on the duality afflicting the poet. The Petrarchan antitheses of ice and fire and their variants are quite numerous, as Alonso points out; but here they do not produce 'tedious oppositions' (p. 506). These antitheses are handled with considerable craftsmanship and admirably amplify the sonnet's cause. This is particularly evident in lines five and six, where the antithesis within each line is emphasized by the contrast between these lines. The emphatic hendecasyllable stresses 'arde' and 'llamas,' and the sapphic line accentuates 'lluvias' and 'granizos.'[5] The abundance of the antitheses is dictated by the nature of the things compared. The manner in which these shared characteristics are

23

patterned to reveal the cause justifies the comparison of the lover with a volcano.[6]

We can, however, agree with Alonso that there is no originality in the structural procedure. It was commonplace to develop an image taken from nature – frequently itself a topic, such as a brook or volcano – then in the conclusion compare it to the speaker's psychological state. Nonetheless, Quevedo succeeds in condensing at the poem's end an 'extraordinary affective capacity' (pp. 506–07). This capacity derives from the poet's invigoration of Petrarchan commonplaces and structures. More to the point, the sonnet owes its vigor to the witty nature of the imagery, which compresses meaning and expresses emotion. Alonso seems to have overlooked the role of the imagery in this early love sonnet; indeed, Quevedo's 'extraordinary affective capacity' can often be attributed to the expressive force of the conceit.

Sonnet 335 expresses the courtly tenet of love's ennobling power, which can be achieved only through the 'sweet affliction' of sensual denial:

> Quien no teme alcanzar lo que desea
> da priesa a su tristeza y a su hartura:
> la pretensión ilustra la hermosura,
> cuanto la ingrata posesión la afea.
> Por halagüeña dilación rodea
> el que se dificulta su ventura,
> pues es grosero el gozo y mal segura
> la que en la posesión gloria se emplea
> Muéstrate siempre, Fabio, agradecido
> a la buena intención de los desdenes,
> y nunca te verás arrepentido.
> Peor pierde los gustos y los bienes
> el desprecio que sigue a lo adquirido,
> que el imposible en adquirir, que tienes.

[He who fears not the attainment of his desire hastens his sorrow and his satiety: his entreaty lends a noble light to beauty, as much as unappreciated possession vilifies it. He who obstructs his satisfaction circles around with loving delay, since gross is the pleasure and uncertain the joy of possession. Show yourself, Fabio, grateful for the good intention of her disdain, and you will never see yourself repentant. More readily are pleasures and favors lost by the contempt which follows achievement, than [by what is] impossible to achieve, which is [already] yours. (BB)]

The sonnet argues the virtue of courtly love to a frustrated lover, Fabio. Since Fabio is the poet's *persona*,[7] we can take the poem as advice to himself, or rather a rationalization for frustrated desire.

The sonnet advises against the physical possession of the beloved. The lover who is rash to attain sexual satisfaction will hasten his sadness, because, once satisfied, his desire for the beloved will cease. Thus he should strive for desire itself, or rather unfulfilled desire. In this manner the beloved's beauty is perpetually prized, while satisfaction occasions her debasement. This idea accords with the courtly theory by which consummation brings an end to desire, and, perforce, an end to love.[8] Furthermore, self-denial redounds in the lover's own self-esteem. This sense of worth reflects the courtly tenet of love's ennobling power. By enduring his burning passion, the lover hopes for purification and spiritual perfection. The beloved is thus a means to an end; her perfection is

the measure of the lover's personal distinction. In the superlative worth of the lady, the lover finds the surest guarantee of his own pre-eminence . . . The lover's compliments, like all self-flattery, are therefore utterly sincere. The lady, while he loves her, is for him really the loveliest and best of women, for it is in terms of his own self-love that he sees her (Valency, p. 26).

The rigor of chastity is a 'sweet affliction' which the poet calls 'halagüeña dilación,' a sensuous, stimulating and indefinite delay of love's guerdon. This process of spiritual refinement is preferred to the crudeness of sexual satisfaction. The joy, 'gloria,' based on physical possession will not endure.[9] With this advice, the speaker tells Fabio he should be thankful for the beloved's disdain, for it is well intended. By disdaining him, the beloved maintains their virtuous love and, if he is constant, makes the lover's desire burn more passionately. By persevering in the flames of his passion, he can purify himself and become virtuous; therefore, he would never repent of his gratitude for the lady's disdain. The sonnet ends with the have-and-have-not paradox of courtly love. By having sexual fulfillment, which ends in contempt for the beloved, he would readily lose[10] those pleasures and goods which he possesses by virtue of accepting the impossibility of love's consummation. These 'gustos y bienes' are what the lover enjoys through the only possession permitted by human love: 'beauty cannot be possessed otherwise, except by looking and contemplating. For our eye and mind have no other way than this to possess' (Nobili).[11] Such an ideal possession is pointed to by Quevedo in his *Providencia de Dios*: 'No hay cosa tan grosera para los deleites humanos como la posesión dellos' ('There is nothing so deleterious to human pleasures as the possession of them,' *Prosa*, p. 1403). This sonnet explicitly presents two tenets of courtly love: ever-increasing desire and the ennobling power of love. The third tenet, the beloved's superiority, is implicit. The lady's incomparable beauty and virtue are marks of her superiority; and only through the chaste love of such a beautiful and unattainable lady can the lover aspire to be ennobled. This is the advice the speaker gives himself through his *persona*. In the conflict between the body that yearns to satisfy its needs, and the soul that demands perfection and spiritual union with the beloved, reason and conscience opt for the purity of courtly love. Nonetheless, we get the feeling that this decision is a rationalization; a cover up for frustration on the sensual level. Green, on the contrary, sees in the first two lines a positive statement against physical possession (*CLQ*, p. 8); but he quotes these out of context and disregards the speaker's self-moralizing pose and the undercurrent of frustration perceptible in the initial tercet.

The courtly lover often seeks the beloved's recognition of his pure love. His self-esteem and ennoblement can depend on becoming her recognized courtly suitor. In sonnet 301 the poet begs his beloved to accept him as her courtly servant:

> ¡No sino fuera yo quien solamente
> tuviera libertad después de veros!
> Fuerza, no atrevimiento, fue el quereros,
> y presunción penar tan altamente.
>
> Osé menos dichoso que valiente;
> supe, si no obligaros, conoceros;
> y ni puedo olvidaros ni ofenderos:
> que nunca puro amor fue delincuente.
>
> No desdeña gran mar fuente pequeña;
> admite el sol en su familia de oro
> llama delgada, pobre y temerosa;
>
> ni humilde y baja exhalación desdeña.
> Esto alegan las lágrimas que lloro;
> esto mi ardiente llama generosa.

[If only I were not the only one to lose all freedom after seeing you! It was compulsion, not boldness, to love you, and vanity to suffer for such a noble cause. I was bold, less fortunate than brave; I was able, if not to compel you [to respond], to know you; and I can neither forget nor offend you: since pure love was never delinquent. A vast ocean does not scorn a small stream; the sun admits into its golden family a slight, weak and timorous flame, and it does not scorn a humble and low flash of light. This is adduced by the tears I weep; this [is the claim] of my noble, passionate flame. (BB)]

The sonnet begins with the topic of love's captivation. Although it was compulsion and not choice or daring that caused the poet to love his lady, it was presumptuous to grieve for such a noble personage. The quatrain suggests two elements in the development of courtly love. First, the lady's beauty is not apparent to all; beauty is more than external, thus only those with a sensitive heart and soul can perceive this beauty (Valency, p. 206). Second, once this beauty is perceived, one cannot resist love. The latter is expressed in the epigraph given the sonnet by González de Salas, the poet's first editor: 'No se disculpa, como los necios amantes, de atreverse a amar; antes persuade a ser superior hermosura la que no permite resistencia para ser amada' ('He does not excuse himself, like foolish lovers, for daring to love; rather he argues that it is irresistible to love superior beauty'). Beauty is the cause of love, and for the poet there is no question of volition; he is powerless to resist. In the second quatrain the poet declares that he did dare, but only in requesting that she accept his service; however, he was less fortunate than brave. Although she did not grant his boon, he succeeded in knowing her, and now he cannot forget her, nor can he offend her, because his love is pure, seeking no guerdon other than courtly service.

The poet attempts to persuade his lady to accept his service on the basis of analogy. A great sea does not disdain water from the smallest spring, the sun accepts in its rays the most tenuous and timorous flame, and does not scorn a humble and weak light. The sea and sun are, of course, allusions to the beloved herself. It is worthwhile mentioning that as the rhetoric of beauty became increasingly conventionalized, the lady virtually disappeared. Her particular physical qualities were lost in the process of hyperbole, becoming universal but abstract stereotypes. Furthermore, since the lady dwelled in the lover's heart and soul, there was no need to describe external reality. The accurate description of landscape and the beloved's beauty were passed over for the task of describing the effects of love and beauty on the poet's heart, soul, mind and emotions. We note in these sonnets, then, the pervasiveness of this convention. The poet concludes his rogation with an affirmation of the truth of his statements; as proof that his love is not base but pure, he offers the beloved his tears and his love's noble flame. He hopes that, by this renewed and fervent request, she will accept him. To refuse is cause for grief, as he confirms in 'Sentencia 1074,' 'Reconocer y amar y no poder servir es dolor grande' ('To surrender and love, and not be permitted to serve, is a great sorrow').

Sonnets 293, 335 and 301, we have just seen, demonstrate

Quevedo's recognition of the courtly ideal. While sensuality, in the form of unsatisfied desire, is part of the convention, it is a means to an end: the moral and spiritual perfection of the lover. Only by overcoming the psychological and physical torment of concupiscence can the courtly aspirant prove his worth.

At this stage we must consider Bembo's *Gli Asolani*, which, together with Castiglione's *Il libro del cortegiano*, greatly influenced the love literature of the sixteenth century, and to a lesser degree that of the seventeenth. In conjunction with *Gli Asolani*, we shall consider R. O. Jones's opinion that courtly love *is* sensuality; for him, Perottino, the book's first interlocutor, is the exemplification of such a love, 'disordered' and 'sensual.'[12] With Bembo's treatise we shall note a development overlooked by Jones, the ambivalence with which the former regards courtly love.

Perottino laments, 'The fate of lovers is so pre-eminently wretched that being alive, they cannot die' (Bembo, pp. 33–4). On the basis of this lament, Jones sustains, 'In attacking the conception of love described by these words, Bembo is attacking by implication a literary tradition' (1962, p. 160). Unavoidably couched in courtly rhetoric, Perottino's dialogue is not an exposition of courtly love, but an account of his victimization by *loco amor*, mad love. If the courtly lover holds that love is the source of all virtue, for Perottino it is the cause of every grief: 'I cannot . . . describe . . . this universal plague, this general outrage against mankind, called love . . . And in truth, all who follow him receive no better guerdon for their toils than bitterness and earn no other prize, no other recompense than grief; for that is the coin in which he pays his servants' (pp. 20–1). Perottino's situation is the obverse of the courtly coin; he represents the lover obsessed with the flesh. And this is part of Bembo's point. As we shall see, Bembo approves of the courtly ideal, but he is aware that human love is difficult to sustain. It is much easier to acquiesce in the demands of the flesh. Though he disapproves of Perottino's *loco amor*, he sympathizes with his affliction. It is a mistake to identify only Perottino with courtly love; rather, the three interlocutors represent the potential good to which the courtly lover can ascend, and the potential danger to which he can fall.

Bembo's second interlocutor, Gismondo, sustains that love and desire are not the same, making this distinction: 'Love is a natural affection of our minds and therefore necessarily sober, reasonable, and good. So, whenever an emotion of ours is not sober, not only does it fail to be reasonable and good, but by the same token it cannot be love' (p. 100). As love is always temperate, any emotion causing fire and madness is not love but desire (p. 101). With this simplistic definition, Gismondo sustains that love and desire are incompatible. Love is always good and cannot be the cause of grief.

Gismondo's love is only on the surface. Bembo makes this clear in the episode of the doves and the eagle. In the midst of their conversation, an eagle descends on a pair of cooing doves and snatches one away, whereupon the young ladies and men remain shocked and grieved. Gismondo, however, is unperturbed:

> If our dove was carried away by her abductor just as lovely Ganymede once was, her companion may find it less disheartening to have lost her, and we may wrongly blame the proud eagle . . . But inasmuch as to grieve further about these things which we cannot amend is surely a waste of energy, let us forget our grief along with Perottino's and enter now upon love's beneficence.

This cool attitude elicits Lisa's reply:

> This is a strange time, Gismondo, for you to lay your original reflections aside, particularly now that this event has left us all in doubt. For if we feel grief because we have seen that poor little creature in the talons of her enemy, and love because we have been attracted by her comeliness, it clearly follows that we can love and grieve at the same time; and here you might have to face the criticism uttered daily, that words are very far, in general, from the fact (pp. 108–09).

Gismondo evades reality; furthermore, unlike the unfortunate Perottino, he has never experienced love, but instead is in love with love.

Towards the end of his dialogue, Gismondo becomes effusive in his praise of love, placing special emphasis on its ennobling power. Love releases hidden virtues by sending a 'genial warmth through every vein,' lading 'the soul with sweetness,' firing 'our spirits' and changing 'us out of gross, material creatures into wise and civil men.' There may be a serious, authorial tone behind these words, as love, especially through the impulse of Neoplatonism, was indeed thought to awaken moral and intellectual powers. Yet the extensive enumeration of the accomplishments to which the lover can aspire seems to reveal a tongue-in-cheek parody. After leaving behind his 'rusticity,' the lover gives himself to arms, practises generosity and courtesy, serves a prince, turns to literary studies, reading history, philosophy, and stealing 'into the meadowland of poetry . . . weaves his lady

29

garlands of sweet flowers.' Finally, adorned with all his accomplishments, the perfect lover displays himself like a gaudy peacock:
'clothed in their mingled glory as in a rainbow of a thousand hues, he
shows his splendor to the world' (pp. 136–7). Here we have an
indication of a realistic perspective. While Bembo apparently
recognizes love's ennobling power, he also leaves us with a critical
impression of the lofty aspirations excited by courtly love.

In the assessment of Bembo's treatise, it is important to note the
irony concluding Gismondo's dialogue. Responding to Madame
Berenice's remark that she is looking forward to Lavinello's talk
because he is more temperate in his speech, Gismondo states: 'Have I
told anything which does not in reality occur? nay, rather told much
less. I can only suggest that if you wish to please her, Lavinello, you
should discuss what never does occur' (pp. 143–4). The first part of
his response is definitely ironical. It seems that much of what he said
does not, in reality, occur. If it does, it is not as exaggerated as he
would have us believe. Here we have an irony of character, since we
judge things not to be as Gismondo says they are, nor do we judge
him to be what he thinks he is. His final words, 'what never does
occur,' are also ironical; but the irony here consists in taking him at
his word. Taking place at the transition from his dialogue to
Lavinello's, this irony assumes structural and thematic importance.
The reader must bear in mind Gismondo's final words while judging
Lavinello's. Awareness of this final irony is important for an
understanding of Gli Asolani.

Lavinello tells his audience that love is both good and evil. This is
because love and desire are one and the same. Agreeing with
Gismondo that the natural desires are always good, Lavinello adds
that the will can be deceived; consequently, these desires can be either
good or bad according to the target set before them (pp. 144–5).
According to the target, love can be good and instil in the lover an
awakening of talents and a growing sense of worth, or it can cause the
lover to experience the calamities of a Perottino (p. 156). How to
avoid, then, the evils of love is the purpose of Lavinello's discourse and
the author's main concern. For Lavinello human love is the
aspiration of every lover; it is a virtuous love that consists of a 'desire
for beauty of mind no less than body' (p. 157). Such a love can only be
enjoyed through the spiritual senses of sight and hearing, which are
the windows of the soul, and through thought and memory when
separated from the beloved.

Sonnet 490 expresses the singular experience of human love, which sustains the poet during his absence from Lisi, his beloved. The quatrains present structural and ideological parallelisms. Each begins with a paradoxical statement of one and a half lines; the remaining lines resolve their respective paradoxes. These resolutions, in turn, complement each other. The initial quatrain posits two related paradoxes; separated from his lady, the poet is not absent from her, and in solitude he is not alone:

> Puedo estar apartado, mas no ausente;
> y en soledad, no solo; . . .

The reason for this is that his heart and passion are always with Lisi:[13]

> pues delante
> asiste el corazón, que arde constante
> en la pasión, que siempre está presente.

[I can be separated, but not be absent; and in solitude I am not alone, since by my side stands the assistance of my heart, burning faithfully in its passion, which is always present.]

The solitude–presence paradox continues in the second quatrain, where in solitude among the multitude he can accompany himself;

> El que sabe estar solo entre la gente,
> se sabe solo acompañar: . . .

The resolution of this paradox correlates with the prior resolution, and amplifies the condition enabling him to escape solitude. Because he is a *lover*, the memory of the beloved's beauty can evoke her image in his imagination:

> que, amante,
> la membranza de aquel bello semblante
> a la imaginación se le consiente.

[He who knows how to be alone in a multitude, can keep company with his solitude; because, as a lover, the remembrance of that fair countenance is granted to his imagination.]

In these quatrains there are twenty-four alliterated sibilants, which phonically transmit the sensation that the poet is whispering to himself, thereby sonorously reinforcing the idea that in solitude he is being accompanied by an invisible presence. The quatrains, structurally and ideologically, form a harmonious unity. The 'soledad–no solo' paradox is developed through repetition and amplification, and is reinforced with important elements of presence: heart, passion, memory and imagination. The ideas inherent in these elements and their emotional overtones are emphasized by the double enjamb-ments. All these elements either are placed at the beginning of their respective lines, or are highlighted by the prosodic stresses, or both. The contrast between the adjective *solo*, which resonates throughout the quatrains, and the forces of presence is magistrally presented.

Distance does not diminish love; indeed, Nobili states that it can excite love even more, causing greater felicity than the beloved's presence: '[distance] has been reputed to be rather a whetstone to ignite Love, than water to extinguish it; furthermore, it has been judged a cause of greater happiness to the lover than presence.'[14] The sonnet reaches its climax in the following tercet, where the poet expresses the experience of human love:

> Yo vi hermosura y penetré la alteza
> de virtud soberana en mortal velo:
> adoro l'alma, admiro la belleza.

[I saw beauty and penetrated the heights of sovereign virtue behind the mortal veil: I adore her soul and admire her beauty.]

These triple bipartite lines – along with what might be termed the chiasmus of near-synonyms of lines nine and ten (hermosura = velo, alteza = virtud), with the grammatical chiasmus of line ten (noun + adjective, adjective + noun) and the assonance of line eleven – create an admirably balanced structure reinforcing the poet's sensation of bliss and tranquility.

The sonnet, in effect, presents an argument. Given the experience the poet is having, in solitude but joyously accompanied by an invisible presence, he maintains that this is possible only because he has transcended Lisi's physical beauty, perceiving her spiritual splendor. Because of his present blissful state, he can therefore confirm that he is a pure lover. This recognition permits only one course of action. The attainment of human love brings with it a feeling of humility; consequently, he cannot presume to any merit. The beloved is beyond him; as she is so worthy and splendid, it would be sheer arrogance to expect her praise. Nor does he expect sexual satisfaction, base and disgraceful; indeed, he has dominated his desire. He presumes less for Lisi than for heaven itself.

> Ni yo pretendo premio, ni consuelo;
> que uno fuera soberbia, otro vileza:
> menos me atrevo a Lisi, pues, que al cielo.

[Neither reward nor relief do I seek; one would be pride, the other baseness: I dare less to reach Lisi, then, than heaven. (BB)]

The final line reveals his lady and underlines his complete adoration and humility. He, like every Christian, can aim at gaining heaven, but he cannot hope for Lisi. Divine love has a self-seeking aspect; his human love does not.[15]

After his exposition of human love, Lavinello introduces the hermit, who says that the most important consideration in loving is the welfare of the soul. The hermit corrects Lavinello's definition of love: 'For virtuous love is not merely desire of beauty . . . but desire of true beauty, which is not that human and mortal kind which fades, but immortal and divine' (p. 182). With this he begins his discourse on Neoplatonic love. The true way of love, he tells Lavinello, has no place for human love:

Know . . . that your love is not virtuous. Granted that it is not evil like those which are mingled with bestial desires, still it falls short of virtue because it does not draw you toward an immortal object but holds you midway between the extremes of desire where it is not safe to remain, for on a slope it is easier to slide into the depths than to clamber to the summit. And is not one who trusts to the pleasures of some sense, although he does not intend to fall into evil ways, likely to be ensnared? (pp. 186–7).

Although Lavinello is the ideal courtly lover, his love is not virtuous because it does not draw him towards an immortal object. Indeed, human love is a precarious state; inevitably, it will succumb to bestial appetite.

I cannot see . . . how all these mortal charms with which sight, hearing, and other senses nourish the mind, allowing them to enter and re-enter it a thousand times by means of thought, I cannot see how they avail when they little by little overmaster us with pleasure so that we think of nothing else, and, having lowered our eyes to worthless things, remain no longer true to ourselves, but change at last from men to beasts (p. 180).

True love must be purely intellectual. It consists in the contemplation of the beauty of nature, of the heavens, proceeding to the contemplation of universal beauty, and finally to the contemplation of the Final Cause:

Your delight and wonder will be even greater, Lavinello, if you can pass from these heavens which you see to those which are unseen and contemplate the things which are actually there, ascending from one to another until you raise your desire to that beauty which surpasses them and every other beauty. For those who are used to gazing with the eyes of the soul no less than of the body have no doubt that beyond this sensible, material world of which I have spoken . . . there lies another world which is neither material nor evident to sense, but completely separate from this and pure; a world which turns around this one and is both sought and found by it, wholly divided from it and wholly abiding in each part of it; a world divine, intelligent, and full of light, itself as much beyond itself in size and virtue as it draws nearer to its Final Cause (p. 189).

By loving God, man achieves the release of the soul, and is freed from the anguish caused by his subjection to a love for woman:

For every good accompanies this heavenly desire, and every ill is far from it. There none encounter rivalries, suspicions, or jealousies, since, however many love Him, many more may love Him also and enjoy their love as thoroughly as one alone could do; that infinite Godhead can satisfy us all and yet remain eternally the same . . . Neither anger nor scorn nor repentance nor change nor joy deceptive nor vain hope nor grief nor fear is found there. There neither chance nor fortune can prevail. There all is full of certainty, content and happiness (p. 192).

The evils of love for a woman can be avoided by directing all of one's love to God. Is this possible for a young man? The hermit thinks not: 'But what can I say to you, Lavinello? You are young, and in youth . . . such thoughts do not take root; or if they do, they for the most part grow poorly, as if they had been planted in the shade' (p. 191). What the hermit proposes as the true way of love is unrealistic for a young man; certainly, Lavinello is bearing out the truth of Gismondo's closing statement: he is discussing 'what never does occur.' Even with the wisdom and slackened passion of age, Neoplatonic love is hardly possible: 'To me indeed it seems a thousand years before I can unloose the wrapping of my flesh, and flying from this prison or deceitful inn, return to the place from which I came,' confesses the hermit (p. 194).

If an exclusively Neoplatonic or divine love is impossible for a young man, what can be said of human love? It is certainly feasible, since Lavinello has attained it, but it is short-lived; the lover will invariably succumb to the delights of the flesh. Reiterating Gismondo's words, what 'never does occur'? It would seem to be the complete liberation from grief, from the conflict between the soul and the flesh. The hermit tells Lavinello, 'It may be said therefore that old age is the health and youth the illness of ourselves' (p. 182). Grief is an illness which the lover must tolerate.

Jones's contention that Bembo is attacking the courtly tradition is untenable. If courtly love is solely sensual, what possible application can it have for the moral and spiritual improvement of the courtier? It is a school of exemplary amorous conduct, an ennobling process rightly regarded by Bembo. Yet courtly love cannot divorce itself

34

entirely from the school of hard reality. Bembo is also aware of this. Beneath the courtly and sophisticated atmosphere of *Gli Asolani*, there is a realistic contact with life. Huizinga notes that 'the courtly notions of love were never corrected by contact with real life. They could offer a literary amusement or charming game, but not more. The ideal of love . . . could not be lived up to, except in a fashion inherently false. Cruel reality constantly gave the lie to it' (p. 127). Bembo is aware of this schism between life and the ideal. He does not wholly condemn Perottino, for whom an abstract love was of no avail against the reality of the flesh; on the other hand, he ridicules Gismondo's avoidance of reality in his pursuit of the love sublime. He sees in the hermit's Neoplatonism a means of overcoming corporal grief and achieving the transcendence of the soul, but realizes that it is unrealistic for a young man to follow his example. Lavinello, then, remains as the hero; nonetheless, his human love is a precarious state.

Although Bembo is powerless to resolve the problem of sensual passion, *Gli Asolani* does voice a reaction against dolorous love. However, it would be a mistake to identify this reaction with an attack on the courtly ideal. Instead, Bembo is concerned with the problems entailed in this aspiration: what can be done to alleviate its grief? Of the three young lovers, Lavinello is the most reasonable. So that the lover may shun evil and pursue the good, he reasons that he should love the mind, the soul, as well as the body. The hermit, on the contrary, sustains that Lavinello's human love is unreasonable: 'how can any desire be virtuous which rests on sensuous pleasures as it were on water, pleasures degrading those who have them, tormenting those who lack them, and all as fugitive as the brief moment?' (p. 187). Yet it is equally unrealistic to believe that the Neoplatonic contemplation of nature and the heavens can entice the young lover away from his beloved. Neither is it conceivable that the beloved herself can serve as a firm platform for the Platonic ascent, since the lover would be more inclined to contemplate the flesh.

Ultimately, there is no resolution. Given the alternatives confronting the young lover, Lavinello's human love appeals the most to reason. If youth, as the hermit indicates, is an illness, then it behooves the young lover to avail himself as best he may of reason to help mitigate the flesh's grief. There is no solution, except with age.

Baldesar Castiglione is an exponent of that Neoplatonism which has as its inception the contemplation of the beloved's beauty. His *Il libro del cortegiano* was more popular outside Italy than Bembo's *Gli*

Asolani, and it was translated into Spanish by Juan Boscán in 1534. Together with Leone Ebreo's *Dialoghi d'amore* (León Hebreo, *The Dialogues [Philosophy] of Love*) – translated into Spanish in 1586 by the Inca Garcilaso de la Vega but well known before then – it initiated a vogue for Neoplatonic love, but this had limited popularity. It is even more idealistic than human love, and runs counter to the Spanish propensity for realism. *Il cortegiano* did more to advance the appeal of the perfect courtier and the courtly ideal than to foment Neoplatonic love.

Il cortegiano reaffirms the courtly ideal, seeing in human love the source of all virtue. But there are indications that the courtly ideal is looked upon with nostalgic reverence, as having existed in a golden age. Such a golden ideal is demonstrated in the third book, where Cesare Gonzaga invites the company's admiration of a remarkable deed:

What will you say of another, who for six months lay beside her dear lover nearly every night; nonetheless, in a garden full of sweetest fruits and incited by her own most ardent desires and by the entreaties and tears of one dearer to her than her life, she refrained from tasting them; and, although she was taken up and held close in those beloved arms, she never gave in, but kept the flower of her chastity immaculate (p. 247).

Such temperance is looked upon with awe by the company, for this sort of asceticism appealed greatly to the idealistic mentality of the Renaissance. This appeal is a major reason for the pursuit of the courtly ideal in this period. The virtue of temperance does not take away the body's passions; and, while it is an aid to the virtue of chastity, it causes torment. Thus, in the fourth book the Duchess requests that Bembo teach 'the Courtier a love so happy that it brings with it neither blame nor displeasure' (p. 335).

The Neoplatonism of *Il cortegiano*, in the intellectual process and ultimate goal, is the same as that related by Bembo's hermit; there is one important difference, however. Here Castiglione introduces Bembo as a character explaining a Platonic ascent which begins with the contemplation of the beloved's beauty. Part of this process is illustrated in sonnet 484, which González de Salas entitles, 'Continúa la significación de su amor con la hermosura, reduciéndole a doctrina platónica' ('He continues his definition of love for the beauty which causes it, reducing it to Platonic doctrine'):

Lisis, por duplicado ardiente Sirio
miras con guerra y muerte l'alma mía;

y en uno y otro sol abres el día,
influyendo en la luz dulce martirio.
Doctas sirenas en veneno tirio
con tus labios pronuncian melodía;
y en incendios de nieve hermosa y fría,
adora primaveras mi delirio.
    Amo y no espero, porque adoro amando;
ni mancha al amor puro mi deseo,
que cortés vive y muere idolatrando.
    Lo que conozco y no lo que poseo
sigo, sin presumir méritos, cuando
prefiero a lo que miro lo que creo.[16]

[Lisis, through a duplicated and ardent Sirius you look on my soul, causing
strife and death; and with both of these suns you brighten the day, imparting
through the light a sweet martyrdom. Learned sirens in poisonous Tyrian
[color] voice melodies with your lips, and in fires of beautiful and cold snow
my delirium worships Springtimes. I love and I do not hope, because my love
adores; pure love is not tarnished by my desire which lives in courtesy and
dies in idolatry. What I know and not what I possess I follow, without
presuming merits, when I prefer to what I see what I believe. (BB)]

The sonnet begins with a light conceit. The beloved's eyes are as
ardent as Sirius, the star of Canis major. Popular belief endowed this
star with power, and sacrifices were made to ward off its influence.
Being the brightest star in the northern hemisphere, Sirius is also
another name for the sun (Sainz de Robles, p. 683). The poet
incorporates these meanings, reinforcing them with courtly topics.

Enamoration, or the first step in the Neoplatonic process, begins
with the 'optics of love,' the visual and sensual attraction to the
beloved, *vulgar eros*. The eyes are the windows of the soul and also
Cupid's abode; therefore, when the beloved sees her lover's soul, or
her image via the optical spirits makes its way to his soul (and/or
heart), Cupid shoots his arrows, causing strife and death. The poet is
love-slain. Her eyes are suns whose rays cause the lover to surrender in
sweet martyrdom. Thus, the beloved's eyes are suns in that they bring
light, but like Sirius they have an influence over the poet, making him
fall in love. An important corollary is the awakening of desire,
traditionally associated with the heat of the dog-days.

In the second quatrain the beloved affirms her conquest through
the auditory sense, dramatized by a second conceit. The sirens' poison
crimson refers to the beloved's lips; the sirens are the words of her
melodious voice. They are wise because, as Homer says, they promise
knowledge to anyone who comes to them; thus, the beloved's

melodious voice enchants the poet, luring him to an amorous death. The pattern of influence initiated by the star and sun metaphors is continued in the siren metaphor. The beloved's voice causes the lover, inflamed by the intense summer heat, to become delirious and see in her fiery and snowy complexion the expectations of spring; that is, the beloved is simultaneously winter and spring. As spring she gives the expectation of love's fruition, but her coldness prevents its maturation; therefore, the lover can only adore and keep desiring.

At this stage where 'those lively spirits... continue to add fresh fuel to the fire,' Bembo says the lover 'ought to... arouse his reason, and therewith arm the fortress of his heart, and so shut out sense and appetite' (Castiglione, p. 347). Applying reason, the poet affirms a love that seeks no physical reciprocation, making a distinction between *amar*, virtuous love, and *querer*, physical love. The lover idolizes the beloved, and, although conscious of his desire, he is able to restrain it. Here he has arrived at the courtly ideal of human love. Indulging only the spiritual senses of sight and hearing, he loves in her, 'the beauty of her mind no less than that of the body' (p. 348). Yet it is dangerous to dwell here, as the body's beauty can pervert judgment. Furthermore, if the flame has not been completely extinguished, the 'Courtier ... must firmly resolve to avoid all ugliness of vulgar love, and must enter into the divine path of love, with reason as his guide' (p. 347). The courtly ideal thus becomes but a way station in the Platonic ascent.

In the final tercet the poet announces his intention of ascending the Platonic scale of love. From the contemplation of the beloved's particular beauty, he will seek that beauty which he knows to be superior. With 'lo que poseo,' he does not refer to the physical possession of the beloved's beauty; rather, as noted before, solely to that possession granted him through sight and contemplation. Yearning to go beyond this level of possession, the poet prefers not what he sees, but what the intellect envisions. The distinction between 'mirar' and 'creer' is similar to the one made between 'ver' and 'entender' in sonnet 457, which is likewise Neoplatonic:

> no fuera lo que vi causa bastante,
> si no se le añadiera lo que entiendo.
> Llamáronme los ojos las facciones;
> prendiéronlos eternas jerarquías
> de virtudes y heroicas perfecciones.

[What I saw would not be cause enough, if what I understand were not added to it. My eyes were summoned by her features; they were captured by eternal constellations of virtues and noble perfections.]

Through the soul's eye, the mind ('l'occhio dell'Anima,' Nobili), the poet perceives that the beloved's particular beauty is only a reflection of a superior beauty. He abstracts her particular beauty, forming an idea of it, and proceeds to the contemplation of the universal beauty which adorns all bodies (Castiglione, p. 352). By this cognitive effort he gains knowledge of that eternal subsisting thing which lies beyond the ephemeral and visible. Only this intelligible thing is in the category of being.[17] One goal of Neoplatonic love, then, is to love an archetype existing in a universe of Ideas which constitute reality. By endeavoring not to be lured by the physical beauty of his 'sirena,' the poet aspires to knowledge through it. In this sense is her song's promise of wisdom to be achieved.

Otis Green takes exception to the Platonic doctrine of this sonnet:

Here the courtly elements all but destroy the 'doctina platónica': 'guerra–muerte, dulce martirio, veneno, incendios de nieve, delirio.' There is the same distinction between 'amar' and 'querer' . . . seen in other sonnets; the same idolatry of the 'religion of love'; the same courtly humility, the 'chaste éloignement' of making no demand on the basis of 'méritos' (*CLQ*, p. 31).

By claiming that the courtly elements enervate the Platonic aspiration, Green maintains that Quevedo is really a courtly lover. An attention to these elements without consideration of their context and structure can be misleading. There is an amorous and intellectual gradation in the sonnet. There is first the attraction of the senses, then the resolve to maintain the love pure and courtly, while acknowledging as well the presence of desire which causes suffering. Rather than a suffering ideal, it is better to aspire to an ideal eliminating suffering. As such the sonnet demonstrates a reaction against courtly love. Furthermore, it is an expression of what the poet must have wanted to believe was the noblest way to love. Virtuous love was highly regarded in Quevedo's time, no doubt more so in literature than in life. This belief was a constant source of agony, inciting a struggle between what he believed to be morally right and what he felt and experienced. It is this existential tension that is so forcefully expressed in much of his love poetry.

39

In the cognitive process of Neoplatonic love, the idea of universal beauty arouses the soul, causing it to remember its origin and filling it with a yearning to transcend the body. This yearning is expressed in the conclusion of sonnet 457:

> No verán de mi amor el fin los días:
> la eternidad ofrece sus blasones
> a la pureza de las ansias mías.

[Time will not see the end of my love: eternity offers to emblazon the purity of my yearnings. (BB)]

This transcendence is expressed in sonnet 458, where the poet alludes to Neoplatonic theory rather than presenting the process itself. González de Salas gives the sonnet this epigraph: 'Dice que su amor no tiene parte alguna terrestre. Seméjale con la causa astronómica de eclipsarse la luna y no otros planetas' ('He says that his love has no terrestrial parts. He likens it to the astronomical phenomenon whereby the moon is eclipsed and other planets are not'):

> Por ser mayor el cerco de oro ardiente
> del sol que el globo opaco de la tierra,
> y menor que éste el que a la luna cierra
> las tres caras que muestra diferente,
>   ya la vemos menguante, ya creciente,
> ya en la sombra el eclipse nos la entierra;
> mas a los seis planetas no hace guerra,
> ni estrella fija sus injurias siente.
>   La llama de mi amor, que está clavada
> en el alto cenit del firmamento,
> ni mengua en sombras ni se ve eclipsada.
>   Las manchas de la tierra no las siento:
> que no alcanza su noche a la sagrada
> región donde mi fe tiene su asiento.

[Because greater is the circle of burning gold of the sun than the opaque sphere of the earth, and smaller still the one which encloses the moon's three faces revealed [in] distinct [phases], at times we see it waning, then waxing, or the eclipse buries it from us in shadows; but against the six planets it [the eclipse] does not war, nor can a fixed star feel its insult. The flame of my love, which is fixed in the high zenith of the firmament, does not wane in shadows, nor can it be eclipsed. The blemishes of the earth I do not feel, for its night does not reach the sacred region where my faith has its seat. (BB)]

Unlike that in sonnets 484 and 457, here the cause is the experience, not the aspiration to it.

The sonnet's structure is based on a metaphor, the quatrains presenting the vehicle, and the tercets the tenor. In the former the

THE CONCEPTION OF AN IDEAL

poet explains the cause of eclipses. The sun is larger than the earth, and smaller still is the moon. Because of the intersection of the earth between the sun and moon, the latter always changes. It waxes and wanes, and occasionally plunges into the darkness of an eclipse; however, the eclipse cannot reach the six planets and the fixed stars. Here the poet expresses the vehicle of the comparison and alludes to a Neoplatonic conception of the universe. This universe consists of four hierarchies of gradually decreasing perfection: (1) the Cosmic Mind, *mens mundana*, a purely intelligible and supercelestial realm containing the ideas and intelligences, angels, which are the prototypes of whatever exists in the lower zones; (2) the Cosmic Soul, *anima mundana*, a realm of pure causes identical with the celestial or translunary world divided into the familiar nine heavenly spheres: the empyrean, the sphere of the fixed stars and the seven spheres of the planets; (3) the realm of Nature, the sublunary or terrestrial world connected to the celestial world through the medium called *spiritus mundanus*; and (4) the realm of Matter, which is formless and lifeless. This universe is a divine influence emanating from God which penetrates the heavens, descends through the elements and comes to an end in matter. The whole system is bound up by a current of supernatural energy forming a *circuitus spiritualis*. In Neoplatonism love is the motive power by which God causes Himself to effuse His essence into the world, and which, inversely, causes His creatures to seek a reunion with Him. Love is identical with the *circuitus spiritualis* from God to the world and from the world to God (Panofsky, pp. 132, 141).

In the tenor the poet's love is a flame fixed in the zenith of the firmament, where it neither wanes nor is eclipsed. As a splendid and immutable star, one of the *stellae fixae*, it is untouched by the stains of the earth. The earth's night cannot reach the sacred region of his faith. Such an experience coincides, to some extent, with Bembo's description of what happens to the soul when it perceives its own angelic substance. At this level of love the soul becomes blind to earthly things and acquires a perception of heavenly things. Then rising to its noblest part, the intellect, 'no longer darkened by the obscure night . . . it beholds divine beauty' (Castiglione, pp. 353–4). The sonnet's immediate source is found in Hebreo's *Dialogues*, where Sophia asks Philo if 'there is any counterpart of the moon's eclipse amongst the activities of the soul'; Philo responds that 'The same occurs in the soul when corporeal and terrestrial things come between

41

it and the intellect [sun], whereby it loses all the light which it received from the intellect, not only in its superior, but also in its inferior and practical corporeal part' (Hebreo, p. 224). The poet has thus raised his love to the intellectual level of the soul, becoming consubstantial with it[18] and transcending body and earth. Now in the eighth heaven of the Cosmic Soul, his love, unlike the moon below, will remain constant.

The sonnet develops a sustained, organic metaphor rather than an extended conceit, as E. Navarro de Kelley maintains (pp. 109–10). In it we do not experience that feeling of surprise and rational admiration caused by the joining of disparate elements, nor do we encounter what Baltasar Gracián, a seventeenth-century Spanish theoretician of wit, considers indispensable for a conceit: 'some very subtle artifice which is the . . . truly essential constituent of the conceit . . . an ingenious correlation,'[19] which we found to some extent in sonnet 484.

In sonnet 458 the poet has overcome the senses, achieving an intellectual love. In the expression of this experience, we perceive no underlying element of tension, the usual agent of the poet's conceits. Instead, he desires an uncomplicated and effective expression of the rapture of Neoplatonic love, which the astronomical metaphor achieves. The lack of a 'dynamic' structure is a sign of the soul's serenity, a stasis in the heavens.

'In the highest stage of perfection' beauty guides the soul 'from the particular intellect to the universal intellect,' and, aflame with 'divine love,' the soul ascends to the summit of 'pure divine beauty,' *heavenly eros* (Castiglione, p. 354). In the Neoplatonic scheme this is the theoretical end of the courtier's sensual attraction to a woman, *vulgar eros*. Plato never considered woman as a means to this ascent; for him she was intellectually inferior. Yet the pressure of four centuries of courtly love made it inevitable that Renaissance Neoplatonists should include in the process the sensual attraction to women, and to make the ideal of human love a slightly less than intermediate level in the Platonic ascent. The good lover contemplates the ideal spiritual beauty of the beloved, and overcomes desire and grief. Rightfully, he should go on to seek God, but this rarely, if ever, happens. The highest summit he will attain is the archetype of beauty and, perhaps, some sense of fusion with the Cosmic Soul. However, this ethereal region is too rarefied for a lover. Nobili says that Petrarch may have enjoyed a brief flight to the realm of universal and eternal beauty, but he usually hovered near the particular beauty of Laura.[20] To pursue God one should heed the advice of Lavinello's hermit and start from a different source. A lady's physical beauty is a shaky platform for the celestial ascent.

Bembo, the interlocutor, is much more optimistic than Bembo, the author. In *Il cortegiano* human love is not only virtuous but also can be a means to divine love. Although this Neoplatonic love was appealing, in general, it was too rigorous and idealistic for the Spanish mentality. Instead, energy was concentrated on achieving the less noble ideal of human love; and as the courtly code was preferred, the concept of dolorous love continued. While they were being inspired by the courtly model of *Il cortegiano*, the poets were also following Petrarch.

The evasion of reality in *Il cortegiano* is noted in its rarefied and courtly setting. Here a company of aristocrats discusses what a perfect courtier should be like; he is an archetype, the summation of indispensable virtues. Although he is looked upon with nostalgic reverence, he is not given up as an unrecoverable dream but regarded as a model worthy of imitation. Thus considered, *Il cortegiano* is an example of applied idealism. This ideal does not square with life, but in the Renaissance no convinced humanist would believe that life could not be better. This illusion would come to an end, as reality would gradually corrode the courtly ideal.

Gli Asolani and *Il cortegiano* are less philosophical treatises than aesthetic responses to philosophical inquiry regarding love and virtuous conduct. More philosophical is Flaminio Nobili's *Il trattato dell'amore humano*, a love treatise closely read by Quevedo. Nobili differs from Petrarch, Bembo and Quevedo in that he has barely experienced love. This does not disqualify him from speaking of it, for love is known least by those who experience it most. If pleasure is derived from it, it is judged to be better than it is; and if it provokes suffering, it is judged to be much worse. Passion twists the eyes and distorts reality.[21] Nobili, therefore, will rely on the authority of Petrarch and the philosophers, and on his personal observations.

Love, as Nobili has learned, is an inclination and attraction of the soul to beauty. The latter is defined as the harmonious composition and proportion of the bodily parts, together with appealing color and grace, which is a certain light that shines from the soul and glows in the face and most of all in the eyes.[22] With this definition, it follows that beauty can be possessed only by the cognitive faculty, aided by

43

the spiritual senses of sight and hearing serving as windows through which the mind's eye strains to perceive a glimmer of the beloved's soul.[23] Nobili's first definition of love, then, is the desire for beauty. For an example of this type of lover, he refers the reader to Bembo's Lavinello.[24]

Nonetheless, Nobili has never met a Lavinello who could content himself with this type of love: 'I have certainly never happened to meet any Lavinello who was content to enjoy beauty in that way in which it is properly enjoyed . . . by seeing, by hearing, by thinking.' Rather, he has seen that when one wants to enjoy beauty, he desires physical union with the beloved, desiring to 'satisfy himself completely.' Given the manner in which beauty is to be properly enjoyed, all that is required is an appropriate distance between the lover's eyes and the beloved; however, if it is spiritual beauty that one desires to enjoy, this is impossible in this world, since we cannot overcome the barrier of our material and gross bodies. This type of beauty can only be enjoyed in the Absolute, in the Fountain of Divine Beauty.[25]

Since no Lavinellos exist, and man's natural inclination is to physical union with the beloved, Nobili proceeds to a practical definition of love. Nobili finds in Plato that love is not so much desire of beauty as desire of immortality through generation: 'Plato reasonably denied Love to be desire in beauty, not because in Love one does not desire to see the beautiful, which one ardently desires, but because this was not the principal end of amorous desire; rather, one seeks to achieve immortality through the birth of one's children.'[26] Such a definition implies that love should be reciprocated, leading Nobili to the third definition of love. Aristotle strikes him as being very close to the truth when he maintains that the goal of love is to be loved in return: 'Aristotle is wont to penetrate more deeply than others; so it seems to me that in this he put his finger on the truth, concluding through firm reason that reciprocal love is the desired end of love'; consequently, the proof of a woman's love calls for the surrender of her body: 'And let us conclude, that Woman has almost no other tribute to assure you of her love, the certainty of which is ardently desired by her, except to make you the gift of her person.'[27] The end of love, however, ought not to be the union of bodies; but this union is an unavoidable necessity because, as Aristotle claims, by it the souls of the lovers come closer together: 'It is likewise said by Aristotle that it was customary to say that Love should be neither

44

through the union of bodies nor without it, almost inferring that the principal end should be the union of souls; but, since souls are enclosed in bodies, it seems that the more the bodies draw close to each other, the more the souls unite.'[28]

Within the confines of human love, the only way in which physical union can be permitted is with the kiss. This accords with the courtly tradition, and is a concession granted by Bembo in *Il cortegiano*. Thus Nobili states: 'The kiss is granted, which in final consideration is indeed the union of bodies, common also to all animals, but only when this union does not repudiate human love (meaning that Love which is governed by reason and honesty), which is not in violation of any law, and which does not exceed the limits of temperance.'[29] The lover will then be content, for his love will have been reciprocated and the laws of human love will not have been violated (see p. 2). But will this theory square with reality; will the lover really be content to love only humanly? No, 'he will curse fortune more than once if it grants another the possession of her body.' Nobili cannot in truth avoid the conflict between the reality of the body's demands and the sublime aspirations of human love. Taking into consideration the three definitions of love in accordance with the 'rule of correct and good reasoning,' Nobili concludes that man can only love in two ways: either to have 'his beloved as his wife' or 'to gratify his soul and his sight' (see p.19).

At this point Nobili turns to Neoplatonic love. The Neoplatonism he relates derives from *Il cortegiano*, which he illustrates through Petrarch. He notes that the poet can sustain only briefly Neoplatonic contemplation, as he cannot resist the beloved's particular beauty. He concludes that a woman's beauty is not a stable ladder to divine love: 'I do not know how necessary a ladder to Divine Love is feminine beauty; therefore, considering the miraculous yet ordered effects of Nature, the stable movements of Heaven, the force of light, the perfection of the universe, these seem to me a much surer road to lead us to the knowledge of the highest Beauty than losing oneself, transfixed in a face.'[30] He finds support for his conclusion in the recollection that Bembo's hermit never included a woman among the beauties that can lead to the source of true happiness.[31] Human love is incompatible with divine love. The goal of the latter is the satisfaction of the soul's intellective function, which is achieved in the contemplation of divine beauty. Neither the beloved's physical nor her spiritual beauty can satisfy this function.[32] Nobili does not attempt to rationalize the relations between divine love and human love. They move in different spheres.

If divine love is not the goal of human love, what is? This is the question that perplexes Nobili:

It is reasonable, therefore, for one to be uncertain about what is the ultimate purpose of Human Love: to enjoy beauty, or to procreate through beauty, or to be rewarded with equal Love. And to begin to solve this puzzle, I myself cannot hold that it should be the mere fleeting pleasure and beauty enclosed within the so very narrow limits of a woman; for I do not see how Nature could be excused if, for such a frivolous purpose, it had produced in us so noble an emotion as Love is seen to be.[33]

In this renewed inquiry Nobili rejects the first definition, that love is the enjoyment of beauty. There is no Lavinello to support this: ' It has never yet happened to me, as I have attested other times, to find any Lavinello who was satisfied by Beauty alone. Although confessing that the Beauty of the beloved Woman pleases the Lover marvelously through the order of Nature, which has chosen to employ this pleasure for another end, we will not concede that enjoying beauty is the most true and principal end of our love.'[34]

Nobili returns to the authority of Plato and Aristotle, since it remains to determine what is the end of love: 'The enjoyment of Beauty having been excluded, there remains to judge between Plato, who designated procreation in the beautiful as Love's end, and Aristotle, who esteemed mutual Love to be supremely desired.'[35] Nobili notes that the best authors say that the lover gives himself to the beloved and dies unto himself; thus, by placing in her all his thoughts and desires, his soul seems to become her soul, so that 'the soul is where it operates,' residing more where it loves than where it lives.[36] For this reason the lover is justified in desiring reciprocated love. Judgment is determined in the following manner: 'So, in the natural sense, procreation is the principal end, as Plato affirmed, but almost by accident; that is, because of that alienation of the soul requited love becomes the principal end, as Aristotle believed.'[37]

With the support of these philosophers, Nobili arrives at the definition of human love: ' a noble inclination of the appetite and of our will, excited by known beauty, and resolving itself in the desire to procreate in beauty or to attain the favor of the beloved Woman.' This definition is not final until one adds: 'But if we should take the word "human" in the sense of conforming to proper reason, then it

46

would be suitable to add to the definition that it is an honest desire, that is, according to the spirit of the laws, and in no way in violation of them.'[38]

Experience, reason and the philosophers lead Nobili to recognize that physical union with the beloved is the end of love. By it the lover recovers his soul, and only in this way can the beloved satisfy her lover's desire to be loved. His amendment to the above definition should not be construed as a refutation of it; rather, Nobili now has to give a new meaning to human love. It is no longer a chaste love content with only the spiritual and physical contemplation of the beloved, since this is not possible, but a love that condones physical love tempered by reason; that is, it should not become excessive, degenerating into ordinary appetite, nor should it violate the laws of society. Here Nobili implies, as further reading bears out, that the lover should not be an adulterer, a cheat or a violator of women. Nobili's acceptance of reality does away with the unrealistic configuration of the courtly convention, but this does not mean that the lover ceases to be courteous. He is still a gentleman, responding to the noble impulse of love and treating the beloved with courtesy. Theirs is a refined and tempered love, both physical and spiritual.[39]

'I do not see how Nature could be excused if, for such a frivolous purpose, it had produced in us so noble an emotion as Love is seen to be.' With this question Nobili reveals a personal, but universal preoccupation. He never finds the answer to the question, and throughout the treatise he skirts the issue. As in most other Renaissance love treatises, there are contradictions in Nobili's treatise concerning the nature and purpose of love;[40] furthermore, in his inquiry there is an underlying frustration. He recognizes man's desire for perfection and transcendence; yet, from what he has read and seen, he does not feel that a woman's love can satisfy this desire. With this question that Nobili puts to himself, we arrive at the twilight of the courtly ideal. Ironically, the same question was probably asked in the dawn of courtly love. This noble yearning that Nobili perceives is Eros, he by whom 'all is bound together' (Plato, *Symposium*). Eros is the drive for wholeness and perfection, a yearning for the ultimate formation of ourselves (May, p. 74).

When we scrutinize courtly love, we find that it is not only important for its celebration of woman or because it determined a literary genre with far-reaching consequences, but that it is also important for its expression of Eros. The first lyric tradition of the

47

post-Classical era is inspired by the yearning for transcendence. In the dawn of courtly love Nobili's question, that impulse he felt, was regarded with optimism. Man did not look to heaven in his search for perfection; he sought it in this world, in the spiritual and rational love for a woman. He regarded her with the utmost courtesy and became a courtly lover. However, because he believed that sexual passion was wicked, human love became an ideal divorced from the real demands of the body. The same sexual passion he condemned was paradoxically used as an ascetic flagellation of the flesh. Suffering proved his worth and, to his mind, was a virtuous aid to perfection. Confused as it may have been, courtly love expressed a fundamental reality, the yearning for transcendence that is Eros. From the beginning courtly love rested on a tension that would eventually undermine it; but in the meantime it gave rise to a literary genre that was to change the sensibility and thinking of ages to come.

In the late sixteenth century reality and reason were putting an end to courtly love. The medieval conditions which had helped sustain it had long passed away, but, ultimately, external circumstances had little to do with its defeat. The reality that defeated it was the very limitations it sought to transcend. At this point Nobili's question heralds the demise of the courtly ideal. It is no longer regarded with optimism but underlined with frustration. The opening words of his treatise reveal the nature of the conflict: 'The human affections are difficult to understand because of the duality of our Nature.'[41] Courtly love is a magnificent failure. Even when it is modified by Nobili to include physical union, the attainment of Eros is still frustrated.[42] Physical union is brief, and complete spiritual union is not possible. This unavoidable reality finally undermines a sublime aspiration.

The courtly ideal of human love continued unchanged from the time of the troubadours to the Baroque. As Green has pointed out, 'Even when modified at the Renaissance by Ficino's philosophy, as transformed by Bembo, Castiglione, and León Hebreo, it knows grief and jealousy' (1968, I, p. 75). The desire to overcome these afflictions resulted in a search beyond the woman for perfection. It resulted in the attempt by humanists to reconcile a new, 'Neoplatonic,' conception of love between man and woman, and traditional Christian concepts and moral teaching. Without ·the impulse of courtly love, Neoplatonism would have had different manifestations. By attempting to make human love a means of ascension to divine love, the

Neoplatonist concomitantly sought to overcome sensual grief and to moralize courtly love. Eros was Christianized, becoming the power that drives man towards God.[43] The courtly lover, however, would have little to do with this new scheme; he tacitly accepted it, but the true object of his love and perfection remained a lady. Bembo and Nobili recognized the futility of reconciling human love with divine love. The ascent to God had to take a different direction. One had to contemplate the stars, as did Fray Luis de León, or take an inventive route, like Francisco de Aldana, who searched for Him in the shimmering iridescence of a seashell.[44] For a very few Neoplatonism was not necessary; Eros drove them to experience direct union with God. The yearning for transcendence, first manifested in courtly love, had passed on to the mystics.

Courtly love had run its course by the seventeenth century. The exhausted idiom and commonplaces were not capable of expressing the ideology and emotions that had originally informed them. Now in an age of reality Quevedo, from outside the genre, could call courtly poets 'hortelanos de facciones' ('portrait gardeners').[45] The convention continued formally, often incorporated into the *comedia* where it served as the background of honor plays and cloak-and-dagger intrigues. As a serious lyric only a few poets could resuscitate it, notably by moving love poetry into other areas of experience, thereby achieving thematic and tonal variety (Terry, *Anthology*, II, p. xxv). As a poetry of the analysis and expression of thought and feelings, it became an excellent vehicle for the expression of metaphysical preoccupations and Baroque *desengaño*. It is in this context that we can fully appreciate Quevedo's love poetry. Mired in a chaotic and pessimistic era, yet intensely preoccupied by the welfare of the spirit, he pursues the courtly ideal. Simultaneously, he has a critical and realistic awareness of the courtly tradition.

3

Quevedo and courtly love

There are few sonnets which portray Quevedo as a conventional courtly lover. It is rare to find an expression of his total satisfaction with the spiritual reward of human love, as in sonnet 490, 'Puedo estar apartado, mas no ausente.' There are sonnets which appear to express this experience, but these either take on a Neoplatonic configuration or go beyond the convention, employing love as a defense against solitude and the imminence of death's oblivion. Quevedo's aspiration to the courtly ideal is strained by his sensual desire. We shall now examine a group of sonnets which will demonstrate the poet's reaction to the courtly ethos, culminating with his frustration with this tormenting ideal.

QUEVEDO AND PETRARCH

The opinion that Quevedo was an uncritical imitator of Petrarch may have been influenced by the poet's first editor, J. González de Salas, who states in his introduction to the 'Erato' section of *El Parnaso Español*, 1648: 'I confess that, taking note of the amorous discourse which can be inferred from the text of this section, which I reduced to its present form, I became convinced that our poet greatly desired that his love resemble Petrarch's. We are to see many parallels in these two similar experiences, which both expressed in their poetry.'[1] Keeping in mind that Petrarch's influence had been diffused into 'Petrarchism,' recent studies have demonstrated that the direct influence of Petrarch on Quevedo is minimal; what is discernible in the latter are the inevitable vestiges of Petrarchism and the slight influence of poets closer to his spirit and generation.[2] Perhaps an illustration of the differences between the two poets can be best provided by comparing two sonnets which appear to have the most similarities. Quevedo's sonnet 359 is an imitation of Petrarch's *Rime* 226 (Fucilla, p. 196):

Más solitario pájaro ¿en cuál techo
se vio jamás, ni fiera en monte o prado?
Desierto estoy de mí, que me ha dejado
mi alma propia en lágrimas deshecho.
Lloraré siempre mi mayor provecho;
penas serán y hiel cualquier bocado;
la noche afán, y la quietud cuidado,
y duro campo de batalla el lecho.
El sueño, que es imagen de la muerte,
en mí a la muerte vence en aspereza,
pues que me estorba el sumo bien de verte.
Que es tanto tu donaire y tu belleza,
que, pues Naturaleza pudo hacerte,
milagro puede hacer Naturaleza.

[On what roof was a more solitary bird ever seen, or beast in wood or field?
Deserted am I by my self, since my own soul has left me in tears, broken and
distressed. I shall ever weep my greatest good; grief and gall will any morsel
be, nights [will be] torments, my rest [will be love's] anxieties, and my
bed a harsh battlefield. Sleep, which is an image of death, for me is greater
asperity than death, since it denies me the supreme good of seeing you. For
such is your charm and your beauty, that, since Nature was able to create
you, Nature can perform miracles. (BB)]

The model is:

Passer mai solitario in alcun tetto
non fu quant' io, né fera in alcun bosco,
ch' i' non veggio 'l bel viso et non conosco
altro sol, né quest' occhi ann'altro obietto.
Lagrimar sempre è 'l mio sommo diletto,
il rider doglia, il cibo assenzio et tosco,
la notte affanno e 'l ciel seren m'è fosco,
et duro campo di battaglia el letto.
Il sonno è veramente, qual uom dice,
parente de la morte e 'l cor sottragge
a quel dolce penser che 'n vita il tene.
Solo al mondo paese almo felice,
verdi rive fiorite, ombrose piagge:
voi possedete et io piango il mio bene.

[No sparrow was ever so alone on any roof as I am, nor any beast in any
wood, for I do not see her lovely face, and I know no other sun, nor do these
eyes have any other object. To weep always is my highest delight, laughing is
pain, food is gall and poison, night is labor, and a clear sky is dark to me, and
my bed is a harsh battlefield. Sleep is truly, as they say, akin to death, and
relieves the heart of the sweet care that keeps it in life. Sole in the world, rich
happy country, green flowering banks, shady meadows: you possess and I
yearn for my treasure. (Durling, p. 382)]

51

Quevedo transcribes almost literally Petrarch's first two lines expressing the speaker's solitude. A difference is noted in the next lines in which Petrarch's speaker identifies himself as a lover, alone but devoted to his beloved; he would prefer to remain in metaphorical darkness rather than seek the rays of another woman's resplendent face. Quevedo intensifies this spiritual gloom. As he makes no reference to a beloved, our immediate response is to an existentially tormented speaker; that is, we first see the speaker in a non-amorous context, who, because he does not express the first cause of his self-alienation, draws our attention to a life tormented by solitude. Indeed, the first cause of his torment is not verbalized until line eleven; however, the context of the imitation and the amorous allusions of the second quatrain identify the speaker as a solitary lover, but not until we have first perceived him as a tormented individual abandoned by his soul. In the amorous context we note the Platonic idea that the soul belongs more to the beloved than to him to whom it gives life; this became a commonplace in the Renaissance phenomenology of enamoration. As we recall, it was repeated by Nobili: 'The soul is where it operates . . . the soul resides more where it loves than where it lives.' Quevedo intensifies the topic by making explicit an important distinction; the speaker states 'I am deserted by my self.' In making evident the equation of self and soul, the poet forcibly expresses the experience of psychological and spiritual desolation. This development of the idea of death-in-life points his sonnet in a different direction from Petrarch's. By stressing self-alienation through the loss of the soul, Quevedo transcends the idea that fidelity is a determination of the will. The lover has no choice but to remain constant to his soul's captor; his very being depends on her.

In the second quatrain Petrarch's lover states that lamentation is his greatest delight. This is the perfect courtly lover who has no other consolation than the tears he sheds over his lady. His life is a voluntary *vivir contento*, a contented living, in his grief. Quevedo's lover does not express such an idea. Weeping is not for him a 'mayor provecho'; rather, he grieves over the loss of his greatest good: both his soul and his lady. For both lovers solitude makes daily existence a bitter one, and night brings torment. Without the splendor of her face, the clear sky becomes gloomy for Petrarch's; for Quevedo's rest and the calm of night bring 'cuidado,' the anxiety of love. In double homage to Petrarch and Garcilaso de la Vega (Soneto XVII), he retains the insuperable line, 'y duro campo de batalla el lecho.' Sustained only by the memory of his lady, the bed becomes a battlefield for Petrarch's lover because he struggles against sleep, which is akin to death and steals the heart's sweet care. Falling asleep deprives the heart of its sustenance. In this tercet we again note a sign of volition. The lover resists sleep so as to think about his lady, thereby demonstrating his courtly dedication. Quevedo elaborates this tercet: sleep is death's image. Although this comparison is more forceful, it is not original; *somnium imago mortis* was a Renaissance commonplace.

The originality is perceived in the next lines. Lying in bed, the speaker says that sleep is harsher than death because it obstructs the vision of his supreme good. With this conceit Quevedo replaces Petrarch's *thoughts* of the beloved with the *vision* of her, and expresses the lover's paradox. God is man's *summum bonum*, and death enables man to see Him face to face; for the lover the *summum bonum* is his lady. To see her now is a vision of the supreme good, but one can enjoy this vision only if one is dead; the lover, therefore, must be dead, which he is indeed, since he is metaphorically love-slain, 'a la muerte.' The quatrains relate the loss of his soul and self, and the wasting effects of love's absence. If sleep is a step beyond death, then being awake is the same as being dead, 'y vi que con la vida estaba muerto' ('and I found that with life I was dead,' 337). The paradox, then, is that he sees his *summum bonum* while awake but dead.[3] The rhyme underlines this idea: 'muerte–verte.'

It seems that Quevedo knew that Petrarch had based part of his sonnet on Psalm 102: 4, 7, 9.[4] The *summum bonum* conceit, while apparently elaborated from the Tuscan's 'sommo diletto,' seems to be more closely connected with verse 2 of the Psalm; furthermore, Quevedo's sonnet gives more emphasis to the Psalm's lament of death's proximity:

1 Yahweh, hear my prayer,
  let my cry for help reach you;
2 do not hide your face from me
  when I am in trouble . . .
3 For my days are vanishing like smoke,
  my bones smoldering like logs,
4 my heart shriveling like scorched grass
  and my appetite has gone;
5 whenever I heave a sigh,
  my bones stick through my skin . . .
7 I stay awake, lamenting
  like a lone bird on the roof . . .

9   Ashes are the bread I eat,
what I drink I lace with tears
10 under your furious anger,
since you only picked me up to throw me down;
11 my days dwindle away like a shadow . . .

(The Jerusalem Bible)

In an hour of distress, the beloved does not 'hide her face'; the lover sees his *summum bonum*. He is no longer deserted by his soul–beloved, but is experiencing the glory of their presence. If the beloved can cause the lover's death by her absence or her scorn, her presence can give life to the dead. She resurrects Quevedo's lover, and this is a miracle. The conceit is what Baltasar Gracián would call an 'ingenious transposition,'[5] taking the *summum bonum* from the context of the beatific vision of God, and transposing it to the life-giving vision of the lover's lady.

The beloved's miraculous nature, pointed to by the conceit, is made explicit in the final tercet. Since the lover has already experienced a miracle, Quevedo's conclusion departs from Petrarch's. The latter's speaker continues in a melancholy vein, unable to see his lady. If she were with him, she could effect a *locus amoenus*; figuratively, this is the miracle she could work. Quevedo's lover has already experienced his lady's miracle; consequently, his conclusion exclaims astonishment. Nature, by definition, cannot produce miracles; but because he is seeing his *summum bonum* while awake, and because of the miraculous restorative powers of this vision, his lady proves the contrary. Since Nature made her, she is living proof that Nature can work miracles.

Whereas Petrarch's lover struggles against sleep to keep from 'dying,' in Quevedo's sonnet there is the impression that his lover's thoughts and vision of the beloved do not let him sleep. Garcilaso had made this explicit ('Del sueño, si hay alguno' – 'Of sleep, if there is any'). In lines 9–10 we have interpreted the expression 'vence en aspereza' to mean that sleep is harsher than death. However, 'aspereza' also has the meaning of difficulty;[6] thus the tercet can be read to mean that sleep has difficulty overcoming a man already dead and enjoying the vision of his *summum bonum*. In this sense we wonder if the conceit does not convey a feeling of desire. Passion is invariably implied in 'cuidado,' and is made more perceptible by the antithesis with 'quietud,' and contrasts with Petrarch's 'dolce penser.' Silence does not bring peace of mind, especially in bed where the mind is

54

stirred by thoughts of desire. Taking this perspective, we can ask if it is not desire that causes the lover's bed to be a battlefield, and if it is not his vision of the beloved that causes, not only death, but an erotic death that paradoxically regenerates him? It would not be un-expected of Quevedo not only to transpose and invert the theological idea of the *summum bonum*, but also to invest it with erotic overtones.

We need not insist on this perception of erotic desire in order to appreciate the difference between Quevedo's sonnet and Petrarch's. The intention of the latter's is a demonstration of the lover's solitude; Quevedo's is this and more. In the first place, with the expression of 'Desierto estoy de mí' Quevedo gives more emphasis to the feeling of alienation, a feeling of a solitude that causes diminution to 'utter nothingness' (Hoover, p. 104). Concomitant with this anguish, there is an air of levity. We get the feeling that Quevedo is playing with a source and playing with a convention. Warnke has called attention to the ludic element in Baroque love poetry. One way this is manifested is in a use of hyperbole that tends toward the sphere of play, and by which the poet can impose a double view; he can create an ironic distance, simultaneously voicing his personal passion and standing outside that passion as a half-amused observer (1972, pp. 98–104). At the same time that the poet expresses the anguish of solitude, voicing his personal passion of what it feels like to be isolated and love-slain, in the sense of physical and psychological enervation, by an absolutely aesthetic awareness of the topic (Warnke, 1972, p. 104) of the soulless lover, he distances himself from that very same passion. The topic is developed into the *sumo bien* conceit.

This conceit implies, again, emotional distance, as the poet takes aesthetic recreation in the elaboration of another topic, pushing the '"religion of love" over the brink into the exaggeration and absurdity it always borders on.'[7] Yet he does not compromise the seriousness of his statements; he goes beyond the topic and the jaded phoenix symbol of the lover's regeneration. In sonnet 450 Quevedo says that with him the phoenix comes true, 'Hago verdad la fénix.' Through this aesthetic recreation, he re-creates, rediscovers, the emotion that originally infused Petrarch's symbols and hyperboles.

Quevedo's imitation demonstrates respect for Petrarch and, on the surface, reveals aesthetic continuity. Upon scrutiny, however, the latter is perceived as aesthetic distance. The convention is not capable of expressing his experience, but must be invigorated with wit. A good deal of the sonnet's effect depends on the reader's awareness of the tension between Petrarchan hyperbole and Quevedo's simultaneous burlesque and rehabilitation of it.[8]

Another difference between the sonnets is the voice. Petrarch's lover speaks in a single register; it is the plaintive, melancholy voice of the absent lover. The voice of Baroque love poetry is complex, having different registers and often ranging from one extreme to the other. Further complexity is achieved in Quevedo's sonnet by, first, having his protagonist give the impression of bemoaning life itself, speaking in an anguished, desolate voice unrelated to amorous afflictions. Emotional shading is accomplished by the subsequent identity of the speaker, who continues the lament but who ends up voicing astonishment and a subtle feeling of rapture. There is a definite tonal change in the conclusion that is difficult to explain if we do not grasp the conceit of line eleven, and in which the speaker addresses the beloved for the first time. Existentially, it might be said that an important difference between Quevedo's love poetry and Renaissance Petrarchism is this voicing of emotion. At either end of the emotional spectrum, Quevedo's voice is often more intense.

For Quevedo's lover, weeping is not a 'sommo diletto,' as it is for Petrarch's model courtly lover. And although the former is resigned to weep over his 'mayor provecho,' he does not willingly 'fight sleep' so as to indulge amorous contemplations which result in a 'sweet martyrdom.' Grief is caused by his inability to avoid thinking about his soul and his lady. Conversely, this intensity of thought incites her vision and brings the lover joy. Not only is his lady Nature's miracle, but she can contrive miracles of her own. She takes his soul, causes him to lead an empty and bitter existence, pervades his mind and heart, and causes him restless nights; yet her miraculous vision gives him back his soul, briefly bringing him new life and pleasure. As the Psalm says, like Yahweh, she has the power to pick him up and throw him down – repeatedly.

Regarding Petrarch's sonnet, Nobili remarks: 'thinking and imagining are, as Aristotle said, a way of feeling, no matter how much weaker, and are as important to the Lover as seeing and hearing; so that often he laments the sleep which takes away from the heart that sweet care which keeps him alive.'[9] Like others before him, Quevedo probably had an aesthetic urge to imitate this famous sonnet; yet, in all likelihood, Nobili's comments spurred the imitation with another motive. Petrarch fights sleep because he wants to feel the presence of his lady. The suggestion of feeling is intensified by Quevedo to demonstrate that, for him, thought and imagination are not a 'weaker' way of feeling. Quevedo says that 'Soledad es absencia o privación de las cosas por elección o fuerza' ('Solitude is the absence or deprivation of things through choice or force,' 'Sentencia 490'). Through the intensity of his thought and imagination, he briefly abolishes his solitude in the reunion with his soul and lady. Indeed, not only does he feel his beloved's presence, he is brought back to life.

Considering again González de Salas's comments, rather than just an imitation or a strong similarity, we can take him to mean that Quevedo may have aspired to a love as noble as Petrarch's; but also, and perhaps more importantly, that he set forth to write love poetry which would rival the stature and fame of the Tuscan's.

THE BURDEN OF COURTLY LOVE

A popular motif of the love literature of the Spanish Golden Age was the legend of Hero and Leander. Every night Hero, a priestess of the goddess Venus, would light a torch in her tower on Lesbos. Guided by the flame, Leander would swim the Hellespont and enjoy her love. One night Notus, the south wind, caused a storm; the torch was blown out and Leander drowned. At dawn, when she saw his body washed up on the shore, Hero threw herself from the tower. In sonnet 311 Quevedo employs this legend to dramatize the courtly lover's dilemma:

> Flota de cuantos rayos y centellas
> en puntas de oro, el ciego Amor derrama,
> nada Leandro; y cuanto el Ponto brama
> con olas, tanto gime por vencellas.
> Maligna luz multiplicó en estrellas
> y grande incendio sigue pobre llama:
> en la cuna de Venus, quien bien ama,
> no debió recelarse de perdellas.
> Vela y remeros es, nave sedienta;
> mas no le aprovechó, pues, desatado,
> Noto los campos líquidos violenta.
> Ni volver puede, ni pasar a nado;
> si llora, crece el mar y la tormenta:
> que hasta poder llorar le fue vedado.

[In a fleet of many lightning-flashes and sparks, which blind Love pours as darts of gold, swims Leander, and as loud as the Hellespont roars with its waves, so he groans to overcome them. A malignant light was multiplied in stars, a raging fire follows a feeble flame: in Venus's cradle, he who loves well should not fear their loss. A sail and oarsman, a thirsty ship he is; but to no avail, since, unleashed, Notus does violence to the liquid fields. He cannot turn back nor swim across; if he weeps, the sea and storm increase: for even tears were denied him. (BB)]

As Leander has to swim the stormy Hellespont to reach Hero, the sonnet also incorporates the popular topic of the sea of love, as in sonnet 449, 'Leandro, en mar de fuego proceloso' ('Leander, on a stormy sea of fire').

In this portrayal of the lover's ordeal, blind Love commands a fleet of ships, cannonading the sea with flashing darts. Leander has to swim through this barrage of lightning, struggling against the powerful waves. The rhythm of this quatrain suggests the violence of a tempestuous sea. Across the Hellespont stands Hero with a torch. On the narrative level 'maligna' is used in the Latin sense of 'meagre'; thus Hero's torch is a small beacon, an impoverished flame, flickering among the brilliant stars and flashes of lightning. On the allegorical level the torch is malignant because it leads Leander to his destruction. The inner fire of his passion pursues Hero's torch, which serves like the stars to the navigator. The lightning disorients him, however, and he loses his way; yet whoever swims in Venus's cradle, the sea of love, and is a pure lover, 'quien bien ama,' should not fear the stars' loss. He will be guided by the light burning pure in his heart.

The witty imagery of the initial tercet amplifies Leander's intense passion. The conceit of line nine frames Leander, because he travels over water, as a 'nave de vela,' a sailing ship; and, since he swims, he is also an oarsman.[10] Externally, this fits the narrative level. However, part of the conceit is the suggested saying 'a velo y remo,' with sails and oars for greater speed. The saying reinforces the conceit in the sense that we now picture Leander making haste to reach Hero. Furthermore, 'vela' also means candle, a metaphor for his passion which the waters cannot extinguish. The conceit reveals a second correlation between a ship and Leander: in a storm they both seek a port, and Leander's port is his beloved. The catachresis 'nave sedienta,' part of the conceit, emphasizes this idea: as a ship speeds for a safe port, Leander thirsts for Hero's embrace. The adjective advances the central idea that Leander is impelled by desire. The correlation does not end here, as Leander and the ship also converge on the plane of the shipwrecked lover. On the sea of love he is a 'náufrago de amor.'

This conceit, like the one in sonnet 359 and like most of Quevedo's, is organic in the manner described by Arthur Terry: 'that which has an organic function in the context, illuminating a particular theme or idea which is important, either for the poem as a whole, or for a substantial part of it.'[11] The Leander–ship conceit has an organic function in the allegory of the courtly lover's plight. Being a metaphor, it also demonstrates the Renaissance theory that a metaphor, besides making for intellectual richness, provides dignified ornamentation, adding variety or *copia* (Tuve, chap. 6). Thus the conceit is both organic and relevant ornamentation. As it artistically delights, it illuminates the central idea of desire, the cause of Leander's perdition.

Leander's effort to reach Hero is futile. The wind creates a violent squall, making it impossible to swim to Hero or return. He drifts at the mercy of the sea; if he cries the tears make the sea rise and the storm worse. He does not drown, as in the legend, nor can he drown in his own tears; rather, his fate is to endure incessant grief. The final tercet underlines the allegorical dimension of the sonnet. Unlike the pure lover, Leander represents the lover who seeks sexual consummation, but who is denied this final satisfaction by the rules of the courtly convention. The sonnet itself does not make this identification, but the imagery *per se* suggests this situation. Remove 'Leandro' and 'el Ponto' and what else could the sonnet mean? Quevedo's lover is sensuously attracted to the beloved and yearns to satisfy his desire, yet the rules of the convention forbid this final satisfaction. The lover, therefore, is caught in a frustrating situation. He is adrift on a sea of passion, stormed by thoughts of carnal desire. Even his tears are of no consolation, as they only provoke his torment. To love like this is to be damned to a hell-in-life.

The courtly lover frequently complains of the loss of his will and reason, which results from the beloved's captivation of his soul. With memory, these are the three faculties of the soul according to Scholastic psychology. The lover retains his memory but it is possessed by the anguished recollection of his lost freedom and the power of the beloved's beauty. Without his will and reason, he becomes love's slave. León Hebreo states that in such a situation freedom is impossible, as the lover cannot even will to be free:

He who finds himself in such condition – do you not think he would free himself, if he could? But he cannot, because he is not at liberty to free, or seek to free, himself. How then can he be governed by reason, who is not at liberty? For all corporal bondage leaves free at least the will, but the bondage of love first fetters the lover's will, then subjects his whole person to the will [thus bound] (p. 61).

59

This loss of will and reason is expressed in sonnet 442:

¿Qué importa blasonar del albedrío,
alma, de eterna y libre, tan preciada,
si va en prisión de un ceño, y, conquistada,
padece en un cabello señorío?
    Nació monarca del imperio mío
la mente, en noble libertad criada;
hoy en esclavitud yace, amarrada
al semblante severo de un desvío.

[What does it matter to boast of free will, [and of my] soul, so prized as immortal and free, if it is imprisoned by a frown and, vanquished, it suffers serfdom to a lock of hair? Born monarch of my own domain, my mind was raised in noble liberty; today in slavery it lies, bound to the austere countenance of your displeasure.]

The reason for this loss is the captivating power of the beloved's beauty:

Una risa, unos ojos, unas manos
todo mi corazón y mis sentidos
saquearon, hermosos y tiranos.

[A laugh, eyes and hands, beautiful and tyrannical, have plundered my whole heart and senses. (BB)]

This force is described by Quevedo in *La cuna y la sepultura*: 'si miras en sí qué es la hermosura, que te aparta de toda paz y de todo bien, verás que es un cautiverio de tus sentidos, donde tu memoria, entendimiento y voluntad padecen servidumbre' ('If you look closely to see what beauty is, which separates you from all peace and well-being, you shall discover it is the enslavement of your senses, wherein your memory, understanding and will all suffer in bondage,' *Prosa*, 1958, p. 1197).

The loss of reason can provoke insanity, as the poet complains in sonnet 360. This complaint involves a transgression of the rule of silence, a rule he adhered to in sonnet 451, and to which he professes allegiance: 'Las entrañas abrasadas de amores hacen enmudecer las lenguas, y el que pasa en amores su vida ha de tener la boca cosida' ('When the vitals of our being burn in the flames of love, the tongue is silenced, and he who spends his life loving needs must have his mouth sewn shut,' 'Sentencia 1115'). Nonetheless, there are exceptions where he voices his grief, such as the famous sonnet 485, where the wound of passion becomes too intense to conceal: 'dilato en largas voces negro llanto' ('I draw out in long cries my black tears').

Another exception is 360, where the tension between human love and desire drives the lover crazy, causing him to lament loudly the loss of his reason and freedom:

> Dejad que a voces diga el bien que pierdo,
> si con mi llanto a lástima os provoco;
> y permitidme hacer cosas de loco:
> que parezco muy mal amante y cuerdo.
>   La red que rompo y la prisión que muerdo
> y el tirano rigor que adoro y toco,
> para mostrar mi pena son muy poco,
> si por mi mal de lo que fui me acuerdo.
>   Óiganme todos: consentid siquiera
> que harto de esperar y de quejarme,
> pues sin premio viví, sin juicio muera.
>   De gritar solamente quiero hartarme.
> Sepa de mí, a lo menos, esta fiera
> que he podido morir, y no mudarme.

[Let me shout aloud the good I lose, if with my tears I can move you [readers] to compassion; and allow me to behave like a madman, since it becomes me ill to be a lover and sane. The net I tear and the fetters I gnaw and the tyrannical cruelty I adore and experience, are insufficient to reveal my suffering, if to my hurt, I remember what I was. Hear me all; allow me at least, now that I am glutted with waiting, [hoping] and complaining, since I lived without reward, to die bereft of reason. Let me glut myself with shouting. Let her know, at least, this beast, that I have been able to die but have not changed [in my condition]. (BB)]

This sonnet explicitly addresses the readers, because it is about making his passion public. The lover requests our indulgence to make a spectacle of himself. To demonstrate he is not a bad lover, he must be allowed to act as a madman. The paradox is that one cannot be a good lover and be sane, as there is a contradiction between 'amante'. and 'cuerdo.' As a madman and true lover he will loudly lament the loss of his reason, 'el bien que pierdo.'

The second quatrain clarifies the cause of his insanity. When he remembers his lost liberty, the violent remonstrations against his jailer are not enough to express the intensity of his grief. This grief is compounded by the inability to resolve a spiritual and physical contradiction. The poet is a prisoner of Love, who commands that he adore the beloved and respect her virtue; but this is a cruel experience. The verb *tocar*, meaning here 'to experience,' also suggests his physical attraction to her, which he must contain. In a concrete manner, both verbs give an imposing presence to the lady's virtue standing over the deranged lover. The conflict between the spiritual and the physical has devastating psychological effects. The concrete imagery of the fifth line figures forth the poet's frustration. It is useless to tear the net and gnaw on the fetters that bind him, for he is still enslaved by the beloved's unyielding chastity.

Because the lover is exhausted from hoping and complaining, since he has lived without the guerdon of his love, he appeals that he be allowed to die without his senses. In other words, it is senseless to love and not expect sexual satisfaction. With the vulgar word 'harto,' the poet effectively expresses his torment. In contrast with its restrained use in sonnet 335 ('hartura'), here it adds impact to the pell-mell force generated by the imperatives and the poet's psychological anguish. This indecorous diction is compatible with the tone of desperation. D. Alonso has called attention to the 'ripping' effect ('desgarrón') generated by Quevedo's insertion of extra-poetical diction, calling such a style 'highly Quevedesque.'[12] Glutted with hoping, waiting and complaining, the poet despairs putting up with a situation which is driving him mad. The only alternative is a senseless death.

In the concluding tercet the poet adds a nuance of irony to 'hartar.' It is often a euphemism for sexual fulfillment,[13] but, since he cannot satisfy his desire, his only alternative is to get his fill of shouting. This line is closed with a full stop, and the pell-mell impetus and shouting come to a halt.[14] What happens between this line and the next one approaches modern poetry. In a moment of silence the poet experiences emotional and psychological death. All the appeals to be allowed to vent his frustration by shouting and acting as a deranged lover are not as expressive as this momentary silence. With it the complexion of the poem changes. In the final lines the poet wants to communicate that sudden experience, that sudden realization, to his lady, and here he transfers the epithet. Although he is condemned to act as a caged and deranged animal, his lady, because of her cruelty, is also a beast. But despite her inhuman nature, the lover remains constant. Nothing has changed their situation; he is still besieged by the conflict between adoration and desire. Furthermore, the whole situation is hopeless because it cannot be resolved. It is a type of insanity of which the poet is paradoxically a willing victim. This sentiment is revealed in another sonnet, 353, dealing with the same cause:

Si no es amor mi gran desasosiego,
de conocer lo que me acaba dudo:
que no hay de sí quien viva más rendido.

[If my great restlessness is not love, I doubt I can know what causes my death: for there is no one who lives more subjected to himself. (BB)]

The realization that there is no escape from this oppressive situation is a devastating dilemma and a cause of spiritual annihilation.

In this sonnet the burden of courtly love is becoming unbearable. The poet says it is senseless not to expect sexual gratification, but he implies it is even more senseless to love and know that it will not be forthcoming. It would not be wrong to say that the courtly lover is a neurotic, for this is what he certainly seems to be. Yet for Quevedo he is more than this: he is a madman. Such an assertion demonstrates the wracking torment he is experiencing in his psyche. He has inherited an ideal and a genre. He is trying to live up to them, but it is driving him mad.

The prison of love is one of the standard metaphors of courtly lyrics. As noted in the previous sonnet, Quevedo employs it to express the lover's loss of reason and his violation of the rule of silence. In sonnet 474 it is employed to express an overwhelming sense of desolation, a confinement to the vault of the living dead:[15]

> ¿Qué buscas, porfiado pensamiento,
> ministro sin piedad de mi locura,
> invisible martirio, sombra oscura,
> fatal persecución del sufrimiento?
> Si del largo camino estás sediento,
> mi vista bebe, su corriente apura;
> si te promete albricias la hermosura
> de Lisi, por mi fin, vuelve contento.
> Yo muero, Lisi, preso y desterrado;
> pero si fue mi muerte la partida,
> de puro muerto estoy de mí olvidado.
> Aquí para morir me falta vida,
> allá para vivir sobró cuidado;
> fantasma soy en penas detenida.

[What do you seek, obdurate thought, merciless minister of my madness, invisible martyrdom, dark shadow, lethal persecutor of my suffering? If for the long journey you thirst, drink my sight, drain its flow; if Lisi's beauty promises you a reward for news of my death, return contented. I die, Lisi, in prison and exiled; but if my death was the departure, as totally dead, I am forgotten [even] by my own self. Here to die I lack life itself, there I had too many cares to live: I am a phantom bound [in limbo] to my suffering. (BB)]

The sonnet begins with an address to the poet's obstinate thought, taking literally the idea of his thought being with the beloved. Like a jailer, it has returned to the poet's cell to ascertain his condition. What does his thought – the merciless minister of his madness, his invisible martyrdom, dark shadow and fatal persecution of his suffering – seek? The poet's thought is not to blame for his suffering. It is likewise held in bondage by the beloved and must administer her cruel demands. If it seeks release from bondage, it may prefer to end the short trip of life, 'Vivir es caminar breve jornada' ('To live is to travel a short journey,' 11), and embark on the long road of death. Thus his thought should drink his sight and drain dry its current; in other words, he tells his thought to end the flow of life, metonymically expressed by sight, and shut his eyes. On the other hand, if Lisi's beauty promises a reward for news of the poet's moribund condition, 'por mi fin,' then it should return contented to her. Love is the cause of his perdition, but Lisi's beauty is such that he cannot be blamed for surrendering himself to her: 'Quien a bebedizos de prendas raras entrega el alma, alguna disculpa tiene, el albedrío' ('Whoever surrenders his soul to poisonous philtres of rare love has an excuse, his will,' 'Sentencia 1068').

Hoping for Lisi's compassion, he addresses her directly, telling her that he is dying, grieving, in prison and in exile.[16] His departure for prison was an emotional blow, a death caused by the thought of his imminent solitude and his separation from Lisi. In prison he is cut off from the world of the living; now he is dead, 'puro muerto,' because he is forgotten by society and Lisi, and, most devastatingly, abandoned even by his own reason. There is also the strong implication that he cannot die completely, since he he is forgotten by death itself. He languishes in prison, deprived of the love that could make his existence, and taunted by his persistent thought of unrequited love. The paradoxes in the conclusion express his dolorous plight. In prison he cannot die because he does not have enough life; near Lisi he could not live because he felt too much passion for her; consequently, he is a phantom imprisoned by his afflictions, unable to live or die. The expression 'fantasma en penas' calls to mind 'alma en pena,' meaning a solitary, anguished individual, and also a soul suffering in purgatory.[17] Thus the poet is lonely and tormented, caught like a soul between heaven and hell; but, whereas a soul will eventually be released from purgatory, there is no hope that he will attain the splendor of Lisi. There is no relief from his tormenting passion for her.

RELIEF THROUGH SAFETY VALVES

Love's affliction cannot be endured without resorting to a safety valve for the release of tension (Forster, pp. 84–121). One traditional safety valve is the dream, in which the lover takes pleasure in the fictional sexual intercourse with his lady. Such an experience is not considered a breach of courtesy because dreams are beyond his control. By means of the dream the lover is given nocturnal relief from his daily affliction. There is another situation that, while not normally considered a safety valve, can permit a degree of relief for the lover. Such are poems praising the beloved's beauty and her accomplishments, describing her picture, describing her holding a flower or at her toilet combing her hair. Such 'occasional' descriptions fall under the category of 'external Petrarchan conceits.'[18] They can offer relief in the sense that the poet distracts himself from his affliction, concentrating his energy instead on the depiction of delightful circumstances. A major characteristic of this poetry is the elaboration often given to the re-creation of experience, the latter sometimes taking place only in the poet's imagination. For this reason the term *précieux* is sometimes applied to this poetry (de Mourgues, 1953). It is noticeably artificial, the implication being that it is not to be taken seriously. Quevedo has written poetry utilizing these 'external conceits,' and, as we recall, a few critics seem to have regarded them as evidence for a lack of sincerity. We shall now examine two so-called *précieux* sonnets, and we shall find that the conceits are more than external. By the seventeenth century these conceits had long been commonplaces; however, Quevedo employs them in a most dynamic manner.

Sonnet 339, 'A Flori, que tenía unos claveles entre el cabello rubio' ('To Flori, who wore carnations in her blonde hair'), is an 'occasional' piece ostensibly praising the beloved's beauty and superiority.

> Al oro de tu frente unos claveles
> veo matizar, cruentos, con heridas;
> ellos mueren de amor, y a nuestras vidas
> sus amenazas les avisan fieles.
> Rúbricas son piadosas y crueles,
> joyas facinorosas y advertidas,
> pues publicando muertes florecidas,
> ensangrientan al sol rizos doseles.
> Mas con tus labios quedan vergonzosos

(que no compiten flores a rubíes)
y pálidos después, de temerosos.
Y cuando con relámpagos te ríes,
de púrpura, cobardes, si ambiciosos,
marchitan sus blasones carmesíes.

[The gold of your brow I see adorned [and splattered] with the wounds of blood-red carnations; they die of love, and their faithful threats forewarn our lives. They are red rubrics, merciful and cruel, criminal jewels and [warned] forebodings; as they publicize flowering deaths, they smear with blood the sun's canopy of curls. But beside your lips they stand ashamed (for flowers do not compete with rubies) and then they blanch from fear. And when with lighting-flashes you laugh, although ambitious for the purple, [as] cowards their scarlet blazons wither. (BB)]

In a more overt manner than in sonnet 303, the carnations point to unrequited love. In the exposition carnations adorn the beloved's hair. Their scarlet color gives the visual impression that they are bleeding to death, which, from a subjective perspective, is caused by the wounds of love. Their death is a warning of love's fatal effect. The second quatrain expands this idea.

The bleeding carnations are rubrics which paradoxically arouse compassion and are cruel. This conceit is amplified by a subsequent conceit: the carnations are criminal jewels that give warning, and, by publishing flowering deaths, they make evident a truth previously suggested in 'rúbricas.' Besides its etymological meaning of 'red,' *rúbrica* is the blood shed when attesting to a truth.[19] The bleeding carnations give visual evidence of the deadly effects of love. Such evidence is as obvious as the flourish of a signature, the common meaning of *rúbrica*. But the 'joyas' are also criminal, 'facinorosas' – one of the poet's favorite extra-poetical adjectives – in that they bloody the beloved's hair. She again is hyperbolized, this time as the sun with a canopy of golden curls. The beloved is a cosmic force; and, since a canopy is often used to enclose a religious or regal image, she is also glorified. The argument, then, is that the carnations, because of their redness which gives the appearance of bloody blotches, are dying from the wounds of love; but, in bleeding to death, they are guilty of a criminal act. They have stained the hair of a divinely beautiful person; consequently, the carnations are not worthy to adorn her hair. The rest of the sonnet proceeds with the argument of the carnations' inferiority: they wither away next to the lady's splendor.

When they compare themselves with the beloved's lips, the

carnations are overcome and blush with shame. Flowers cannot compete with rubies in the intensity of color or in value, and they pale from fright. Yet the red stone, however priceless, is cold compared to flowers which have more feelings. In the concluding tercet we have an admirable development of the image of morning's laughter, 'risa a la mañana,' of sonnet 303. The poet figures forth the beloved's disdain through a vivid, sensual impression of lightning. The carnations, if at first ambitious for the purple hue of her regal lips, are cowards whose scarlet blazons wither and turn pale before her laughter. 'Blasones carmesíes' is a key metaphor fusing the two principal arguments of the sonnet. First, it is an extension of the 'rúbricas–joyas' conceits, a scarlet sign heralding the message of death due to love. Second, from a connotation of blazons, we have vanity; hence, it was vain of the carnations to presume to compete with the lady's beautiful hair and lips. This vanity can be considered a criminal act.

Quevedo's sonnet deals with a trivial subject, expanding 'the conventional hyperboles that the lady's beauty "kills" all who see her, and that her lips are redder than carnations' (Price, p. 107). The reworked hyperboles, however, discover a note of irony and tension. The admonition to 'a nuestras vidas' refers to the poet and the reader, warning us of love's fatal effect; however, the warning is also addressed to Lisi along a conventional but disguised line. The brief life of a flower's beauty is a portent of vanishing youth. Like the carnations, Lisi's beauty will wither. Thus the sonnet alludes to the topic of *carpe diem*, inviting her to take advantage of her youthful beauty, and to return the poet's love. In her confident and derisive laughter, she does not appreciate this twist, and just accepts the compliment. Beside her incomparable beauty and nobility, like the presumptuous but insignificant carnations that die of love, 'mueren de amor,' the poet aspires to her beauty but is vastly inferior, and is dying of a bleeding heart. Here we note a tension between his love and the unattainable. Suffering is inexorable and a death-in-life. His lady is an executioner splashed in blood.

In sonnet 465, 'Retrato de Lisi que traía en una sortija' ('A portrait of Lisi which he carried in a ring'), we find what is probably the most scintillating description of the beloved recorded in Spanish lyrics:

> En breve cárcel traigo aprisionado,
> con toda su familia de oro ardiente,
> el cerco de la luz resplandeciente,

y grande imperio del Amor cerrado.
Traigo el campo que pacen estrellado
las fieras altas de la piel luciente;
y a escondidas del cielo y del Oriente,
día de luz y parto mejorado.
Traigo todas las Indias en mi mano,
perlas que, en un diamente, por rubíes,
pronuncian con desdén sonoro yelo,
  y razonan tal vez fuego tirano
relámpagos de risa carmesíes,
auroras, gala y presunción del cielo.

[In a compact prison I bear captive, with all its family of burning gold, the sphere of resplendent light, and the glowing realm of Love enclosed. I bear the starry field grazed by the lofty beasts of gleaming skin, and, concealed from the heavens and the east, a day of light and better birth. I bear all the Indies' wealth on my hand, pearls, which in a diamond, through rubies, pronounce with scorn sonorous ice, and proclaim at times tyrannical fire, scarlet lightning-flashes of laughter, auroras, regalia and presumption of paradise. (BB, JO)]

The sonnet is a mine of wit. The numerous conceits form a scintillating, sensual impression; yet they are organically linked, and lead to a universal experience which is the poem's cause.

The sonnet begins mysteriously. In a small, unidentified cell the poet has imprisoned the sun and its golden rays, and by extension the entire universe; consequently, he has also enclosed Love's empire.[20] Recognizing the hyperboles, we perceive that the poet is referring to Lisi. She is the sun with rays of golden hair, the universe in which Love reigns, and he has her imprisoned. The poet also has the starry field where the lofty beasts of the luminous skin graze. This is a figurative description of the constellations slowly moving in the heavens. Metaphorically, the poet is describing the beloved's sparkling eyes and shining face. In the rest of the octave, he informs us that, hidden from the sky at night and the east where the sun rises, he has a better day of light and birth. Since he has Lisi imprisoned, she can never leave him; therefore, she is better than any day or dawn because she is a light that never grows dark. The beloved is a celestial being, a cosmic phenomenon bringing perpetual light to the poet.

In line nine the poet tells us he has all the Indies, all the riches of the east, on his hand. The mystery becomes clear; he is describing a locket ring containing a portrait of Lisi. These rings had a case studded with jewels; thus the sonnet proceeds on two levels. On the narrative level the ring is described as gold and covered with jewels; hence it contains all the wealth of the Indies. On the metaphorical level the poet is describing Lisi. The ring also explains the use of the words 'cerco,' 'cerrado'; he has the empire of Love enclosed within a sphere. The ring, as a locket, is the beloved's 'breve cárcel,' and when he opens it to reveal her portrait, dawn breaks and the sun shines. He can do this even at night; thus he has hidden away, 'a escondidas,' a day of perpetual light. With the identification of the locket ring, the organic progression of the conceits is now made more obvious. For the poet Lisi represents all the riches of the Indies; therefore, the jewels are transferred to her. She is a diamond, splendid, pure and unyielding. Her beauty is the cause of the poet's love, but she insists on a chaste love, and is therefore hard. And because she makes the lover suffer a frustrated desire, she is also cold; consequently, from her pearly teeth and ruby lips come disdainful words of sonorous ice. 'Yelo' is a Petrarchan commonplace; 'sonoro yelo' is an inventive metaphor pointing to his emotional turmoil. Because of her adamantine nature, the beloved's words are like sonorous ice which emotionally injure the lover; they are hailstones. To hear the beloved's icy words of disdain, then, is to suffer an emotional hailstorm. The ingenuity resides in the configuration of dead metaphors around a dynamic conceit, 'sonoro yelo.'

In contrast to Lisi's icy words, there is another level of communi- cation. If her teeth pronounce, 'pronuncian,' a cold and numbing disdain, her lips relate, 'razonan,' a different impression. Lisi's ruby lips convulsed in laughter produce a sensation of marked sensuality which incites the lover's passion. On the one hand the lover is frozen by her cold disdain, and on the other he is inflamed by her scarlet lips. Through the organic development of the images and their juxtapo- sition, the poet has devised an original expression for the familiar paradox of the icy fire. Because the beloved's lips are convulsed in laughter, they are scarlet flashes of lightning startling the lover with resounding thunder. Here the poet creates a conceit more striking than 'sonoro yelo.' The proparoxytone 'relámpagos' conveys the zig- zag effect of lighting. The sonorous quality of this kinetic image is enhanced through the alliteration of the *r*s. The image also produces a tactile sensation, as the second and third prosodic stresses on the *i*s give a piercing effect to Lisi's laughter. The scarlet lightning of the beloved's laughter is an image that approaches an avant-garde synaesthesia.[21] This vivid sensual impression at once inflames the poet and dazzles him with such a display of auroras and regalia that she can presume to be as beautiful as all of heaven.

At this point we should take into consideration the ludic element of this sonnet, an element which, unjustly considered, most certainly has contributed to a defective, if not negative, appreciation of this type of poetry. This ludic element or dimension was noted in sonnet 359, was implied in the previous sonnet, and will be apparent in some of the sonnets yet to be studied. Its discussion is especially relevant here. The Petrarchan hyperboles, through an 'arbitrarily and absolutely aesthetic mode of existence' (Warnke, 1972, p. 104), provide the poet with material which he elaborates into a sort of 'super hyperbole.' Responding on this purely aesthetic plane, the poet 'plays' with a convention; looking on it as a half-amused observer, he achieves a distance from both his passion and the passion the hyperboles originally expressed. On the other hand this aesthetic recreation, in a sense, defamiliarizes the hyperboles; and through this re-creation he voices his passion, personalizing and releasing the emotion restrained by a weakened tradition. Again, the sonnet's total effect depends on the reader's response to the tension between these two points of view, on his awareness of the tension between the Petrarchan hyperboles and Quevedo's simultaneous burlesque and rehabilitation of them.

In this sonnet the distance between this double view becomes progressively narrower, and the views converge in the final conceit, which the imagery is patterned to illuminate. The expression 'presunción del cielo' is a conceit evolving from the ambivalent nature of Lisi's laughter. Her laughter is so beautiful that she is comparable to heaven, or rather she merits that heaven open up for her. But for the poet her laughter indicates heaven's reward; for him she is the hope of happiness and the satisfaction of his passion. However, the virtue of hope has two sins against it, which are despair and presumption. The latter is to hope for heaven when one in no way deserves it, and this 'sin' is relevant here. Sometimes Lisi's laughter is a sign of tyrannical love commanding subservience, and sometimes it offers the joy of heaven. Yet when he presumes her laughter as an invitation to love, he incurs the wrath of burning thunderbolts. The allusion is to the thunderbolts which Jove hurls down on his transgressors. This is the poet's dilemma. He is in love with a beautiful woman of whom he feels unworthy, consenting to be her servant. Nonetheless, he is sensually attracted to her beauty, and in the surge of passion he is stricken by the realization that his desire will not be fulfilled. Lisi's beauty is an unbearable splendor.

The sonnet's imagery requires an additional comment. Some

readers may read into the imagery the vivid representation of the sensuous qualities of experience, and for this reason alone perceive in Quevedo an expression of the modern sensibility. Such a consideration disregards the poet's position in the context of Renaissance poetics. While it is undeniable that the nature of his wit and his choice of diction demonstrate a transition from Renaissance poetics and the principle of decorum, in general he adheres to its concept of the function of imagery.

R. Tuve has cleared up many of the misconceptions modern readers are prone to have of Elizabethan and seventeenth-century poetry, and her observations can be extended to many of the literatures of these periods. One of these misconceptions is the critical commonplace that imagery was deliberately and richly sensuous. Actually, this type of imagery was not intended solely to convey an accurate representation of a sensuous experience, but is related to the poem's cause and accords with the principle of imitation (Tuve, p. 3). According to this principle, imagery is evaluated under three categories: (1) the images must be artificial, artful constructs which please on grounds of formal excellence rather than by their likeness to the stuff of life; (2) the images must assist in imitation conceived as involving the artist's *ordering* of nature; the success of his interpretation depends on its coherence and the appropriateness of the images to the poem's basic purpose; (3) the images must assist in the revelation of truth, concerned with the conveying of concepts and not simply the creation of orderly patterns.[22] We cannot deny that the imagery of this sonnet is vividly sensual; indeed, it is one of the principal and appealing features. But the images are also artful constructs whose formal excellence is due to the wit informing them; thus the images appeal both to the senses and to the mind. In the fourteen lines there are concentrated a number of conceits, most of them derived from commonplaces; and, except for the final one, based on paradox or equivocation, they are all metaphorical. The remarkable thing is the way these conceits are linked. Because of this organic construction, the entire sonnet is a compound conceit. Baltasar Gracián distinguishes between that wit which produces unrelated conceits and that which produces linked conceits:

Unhampered wit is that in which, though three, four, or even more matters pertaining to a subject are brought up . . . they are not in unity with themselves but are raised freely and discussed without correlation . . . wit that is linked to an artifice is that in which the matters are united with each other as parts in order to compose an artful, mental whole.[23]

For Gracián the creation of a harmonious compound conceit is the perfect employment of wit: 'When all the circumstances and adjuncts of the subject are adapted to the term of transfer, but without violence and with such consonance that each part of the metaphor is a lustrous conceit, the compound device reaches its greatest exaltation.'[24] The sonnet's images are not only artificial but perfectly united in an organic ordering of nature. In this order each of the images is appropriate in the amplification of the beloved's beauty. Finally, this order assists the artist in the revelation of truth, the lover's agony. He is in love with a beautiful woman who excites his passion for sexual union but who insists on a chaste relationship. The impossibility of satisfying his desire, therefore, causes the lover emotional and psychological torment. This universal truth is the poem's cause.

It may well be that the inability to discover the poem's cause is the reason why some critics have unjustly criticized this type of poetry. This critical myopia stems from a prejudice against *conceptismo*, and reflects the romantic notion that a poem cannot be emotionally sincere if it involves an active participation of the intellect. For such a critic the poem is merely a showcase for wit. A critic of modern literature, however, might see in the sensuous vivacity of the imagery the immediacy of an emotional experience. Neither of these critics has discovered the poem's cause. The first does not care about the cause because, for him, the poem is not sincere. The poet could not possibly have been in love with the subject if he wrote a 'love poem' in which the intellect dominates over feeling; therefore, the poem's cause is poetical showmanship. The second may not question the poet's love, but confuses cause with the representation of experience (Tuve, p. 12). The imagery does indeed convey the poet's perception of a particular experience, but it does not by itself constitute sufficient cause. Rather, the amplification of the beloved's beauty through imagery, Renaissance or Baroque, leads to the revelation of a truth shared, at one time or another, by all lovers: the pain of frustrated desire. The *subject* of the poem is the beloved but it is *about* the lover.

While the function of the sonnet's imagery follows Renaissance poetic theory, there is something about the imagery that is uniquely Baroque, and which reveals something about Quevedo's experience. A. A. Parker, in his study of sonnet 449, 'En crespa tempestad del oro undoso,' emphasizes that Lisi's hair is not by progression 'frothy tempest, wavy gold, gulfs of light, sea of fire, golden path,' but all of these simultaneously.[25] Similarly in sonnet 465 Lisi is not progressively, but at once, 'burning gold, resplendent light, gleaming skin, pearls, rubies, diamond, scarlet lightning-flashes of laughter.' The conceits open up a world of human experience, revealing a poet reacting to life with his feelings, passion, intelligence and moral judgment. This intensity of living is what Parker calls 'Baroque tension' (1952, p. 353). The poet reacts passionately to Lisi's beauty, desiring physical union. He also reacts with his intelligence, artistically reconstructing a vivid sensual impression; furthermore, his intelligence vies with his passion, and here he has to contend with his moral judgment. The tension experienced is expressed in a sonnet of great intensity, and this is what the poet is all about.[26]

The expression of this tension would not have been possible without the economy and force provided by the organic conceit, nor could it have been possible without the framework of the Petrarchan idiom, which provides, as it were, a poetical shorthand which the poet uses to develop and concentrate his conceits. So we see that the strain or tension of this poetry also has something to do with foreshortening or compression.

The emergence of *conceptismo* in the poetics of the seventeenth century is due to that 'mechanism of sensibility' which T. S. Eliot pointed out in the English Metaphysicals. Similarly, for their Spanish contemporaries thought and feeling were not separate phenomena, rather they were amalgamated in a sensibility that allowed them to think what they felt and to feel what they thought. We note, then, that the sonnet is not 'more witty than passionate' (Mérimée, 1931, p. 238), but on the contrary both witty and passionate.

Contributing to the sonnet's tension, and part and parcel of the *conceptista* outlook, is the ludic element. By means of *conceptismo* and the element of play, the *conceptista* and the Metaphysical can accommodate simultaneously levity and seriousness, aesthetic distance and emotional attachment, wit and passion: 'canto de amor con donaire, / unidos gusto i tormento' ('I sing of love with elegance and wit, / pleasure and torment united').[27] Warnke says that 'play' is an inadequate word to denote the cast of mind underlying the work of such figures as Marvell, Donne and Quevedo. Touching on Eliot's observation, he suggests that this sensibility or cast of mind 'has something to do with a radical sense of the power of an aesthetic conception to hold in solution all manner of opposed conceptions which are, however opposed, mutually valid. Such a sense informs the conceits, paradoxes, and ironies of the Metaphysical poet' (1972, p. 122).

Such an aesthetic conception informs Quevedo's sonnet, where the poet's wit gives meaningful form to his emotions. On the one hand the imagery reveals an intense sensual reaction to Lisi's splendor, and on the other it is imagery put in logical harness conveying a particular experience and leading to a universal truth. At the heart of the sonnet lies an existential torment. The imagery also points to a devastating irony brought to a subtle point by the repeated 'traigo,' 'I bear.' The phantasmagorical amplification of the imprisoned beloved results in the smoldering diminution of the lover. At the conclusion we can ask: 'Who, indeed, is the prisoner?'

DREAMS, 'DESENGAÑO' AND DEATH-IN-LIFE

The employment of 'external Petrarchan conceits' does little to relieve the poet's courtly burden. The model of physical perfection he re-creates only makes him more aware of his obsession with desire. For him the treatment of external conceits leads to the revelation of internal ones: the effects of love.[28] In another effort to escape momentarily from the conflict between the reality of the senses and the abstraction of courtly love, the poet attempts to discharge his tension through the traditional safety valve of the dream. Sonnet 337, however, reveals how even imagined intercourse gives him no consolation. On the contrary, reality pervades his dreams, turning them into nightmares of tormenting desire:

> ¡Ay, Floralba! Soñé que te . . . ¿Dirélo?
> Sí, pues que sueño fue: que te gozaba.
> ¿Y quién, sino un amante que soñaba,
> juntara tanto infierno a tanto cielo?
>
> Mis llamas con tu nieve y con tu yelo,
> cual suele opuestas flechas de su aljaba,
> mezclaba Amor, y honesto las mezclaba,
> como mi adoración en su desvelo.
>
> Y dije: 'Quiera Amor, quiera mi suerte,
> que nunca duerma yo, si estoy despierto,
> y que si duermo, que jamás despierte.'
> Mas desperté del dulce desconcierto;

74

> y vi que estuve vivo con la muerte,
> y vi que con la vida estaba muerto.

[Alas, Floralba!, I dreamt that [I was] . . . Shall I say it? Yes, for it was a dream: that I was making love to you. And who, except a lover who was dreaming, could combine such a hell with such a heaven? My flames with your snow and ice were being mixed by Love, as he is wont to do with the opposing arrows of his quiver, and he mixed them chastely, as is my adoration in its wakefulness. And I said: ' May Love, may my fate will that I never sleep, if I'm awake, and that if I'm asleep, I never wake.' But I did awaken from the sweet discord; and I found that I was alive with death, and I found that with life I was dead. (ER)]

The poet evokes Floralba, telling her that in a dream he enjoyed sexual union with her. It is only in this way that a courtly lover can join his fiery passion with a divine woman. This is possible because dreams are sweet lies that do not offend the beloved.[29] They allow the suspension of the rules, permitting the lover to enjoy briefly his sweet fiction. In the dream contraries can be reconciled, so Love can mix the lover's flames with the beloved's coldness, as he mixes in the same quiver the arrows of love and hate. The poet, therefore, can enjoy his fantasy knowing that their love remains chaste. He achieves momentarily a resolution of the contradictions that afflict him in his wakeful hours. He can suspend the adoration of his beloved and enjoy earthly love.

This cherished union with Floralba puts the lover in ecstasy. He does not know if he is awake or asleep; thus he beseeches Love and fortune to let him remain awake, if not sleeping, and if asleep, never to awaken. Reality undermines his 'dulce desconcierto,' and he is shaken from his ecstasy. The sudden confrontation with reality and the paradoxical nature of life and death is reinforced by employing a chiasmus to convert the oxymoron of line thirteen into a second oxymoron in the final line. This double paradox is driven to a point through repetition of the verb, ' vi,' and the heroic prosody. The same words, or close variants, are stressed but the meaning has changed completely. In contrast to sonnet 359, where sleep deprives the lover of his vision of the beloved, here sleep has brought him a dream in which he *saw* that he was alive while dead, that is, while asleep. In the dream he enjoyed intercourse with Floralba, and this fulfillment gave him life. Yet when he woke up, he *saw*, realized, that in life, in the real world, she was not his. The denial of this satisfaction brings him a death-in-life.[30]

The sonnet begins in a light and playful mood, gains intensity in the second quatrain, climaxes in the first tercet in which the poet experiences ecstasy, and ends with the crushing note of *desengaño*. Ultimately, the brief delight granted him through the oneiric experience only makes him that more aware of his real sexual deprivation. Furthermore, if he feels alive only in a dream, then life, real life, must be a torment. In short, to awake is to die.

Death-in-life is a theme in Quevedo's love poetry. The frequent use of this metaphorical death in courtly lyrics gradually exhausted the topic. However, with Quevedo, if we pay attention to its context and expression, invariably we will find an intensity behind it which infuses the topic with thematic import. In effect, death is more agonizing experienced as a state of mind than actual physical death. In 'Sentencia 972' Quevedo says of death, 'De los que tienen vehemente la imaginación dice Plotino que padecen más en la memoria de la muerte representada, que en la separación actual del alma y el cuerpo; quizá es ésta la ocasión de que a las personas entendidas les hace más guerra la buena imaginación que su mala fortuna, porque el daño actual toca a la parte sensible, el imaginado en la entendida.' ('Plotinus says of those who have vivid imaginations that they suffer the image of death more than the actual separation of the soul and the body; perhaps this is why intelligent people are more beset by their good imagination than by their bad fortune, because real harm affects the sensitive part of the body, and imagined harm affects the mind'). Furthermore, if we consider Quevedo in the context of a period of national decline and moral depression, in which existence becomes a lifetime of despair, of living death, 'vivir muriendo,' then the courtly topic of death-in-life gains existential impact. What he experiences through love poetry, and feels in his heart and imagination, intensifies the solitude and despair experienced in life's activities. Returning to the sonnet, we perceive that the poet's disillusionment is felt as a reversal of life, a life-draining depression. The realization that a life-giving act is a fantasy confirms a state of existence that can only be experienced as moribund.

The poet's emotional collapse is expressed in sonnet 358. The dream escape valve fails to vent his carnal frustration.

> A fugitivas sombras doy abrazos;
> en los sueños se cansa el alma mía;
> paso luchando a solas noche y día
> con un trasgo que traigo entre mis brazos.
> Cuando le quiero más ceñir con lazos,

y viendo mi sudor, se me desvía,
vuelvo con nueva fuerza a mi porfía,
y temas con amor me hacen pedazos.
    Voyme a vengar en una imagen vana
que no se aparta de los ojos míos;
búrlame, y de burlarme corre ufana.
    Empiézola a seguir, fáltanme bríos;
y como de alcanzarla tengo gana
hago correr tras ella el llanto en ríos.

[(See pp. 6, 10 for trans. of octave.) I try to take revenge on a phantom image [of her] that never leaves my sight; she tricks me, and runs away proud of her mockery. I start to chase her, I lack the strength; and since I yearn to reach her, I let my tears run after her in rivers. (BB)]

The sonnet is a forceful expression of the poet's frustration with an unbearable ideal. Now he cannot entertain even briefly the fantasy of union with the beloved; his diurnal obsession haunts him at night, turning his dreams into nightmares. The initial line concisely states the poet's dilemma: the phantoms he attempts to embrace are not only intangible, they flee from him. The rest of the poem amplifies this futility and depicts the poet's state of mind and spirit.

In the first quatrain the hopeless lover struggles night and day. His desire, denied satisfaction while awake, breaks loose in his dreams; and his soul, yearning for spiritual love, tires in its struggle with the flesh. The vehemence of his emotional and psychological state rendered by non-consummation causes him to see his lady as a 'trasgo,' a sort of goblin–poltergeist, which he has within his arms but cannot grasp. Here the poet gives substance and meaning to a jaded convention. The comparison of the beloved to a 'trasgo' is an indication of a change in the conception of the woman in the literature of this period. The courtly tradition had idealized her into a goddess vying with the sun's splendor. Despite the fact that the medieval social structure which had created and fostered this ideal had changed, the ideal of courtly love continued, reinforced by the optimism of the Renaissance and perpetuated by the genre itself. But in Quevedo's time *desengaño* sets in, idealism is shattered and reality topples the lady's pedestal. This reality does not prevent the Spanish Baroque poet from sustaining an illusion, or, because of a genre's pressure, from continuing to hyperbolize her; yet, at the same time, he is more aware of her as a person of flesh and blood. A poet like Quevedo becomes critically aware of the difficulty of sublimating his desire into the fantasy of an abstraction; it runs counter to his

feelings and perception of reality. As a 'trasgo' the courtly idealization of the beloved becomes distorted and diminished. This
diminution however, does nothing to alleviate the lover's grief; rather
the latter becomes more intense. If in the courtly tradition the
beloved was unattainable because she was an ideal, the fact that she
remains out of his grasp as a creature of flesh and blood, or as a
diminished but taunting 'trasgo,' is doubly agonizing.

The second quatrain illustrates the nature of the struggle. When
the lover attempts to girdle the beloved, she becomes alarmed by the
sweat on his face and eludes him. This image of 'sudor' intensifies the
'lucha' and is an indecorous but expressive metonomy of the lover's
lust. He does not give up; yet, despite his increased efforts, he is
defeated. Here the full significance of 'trasgo' becomes evident. A
'trasgo' causes mischief at night, shattering dishes and upsetting
furniture;[31] however, since the poet's lady taunts him by demanding a
chaste relationship, she *shatters him*: 'y temas con amor me hacen
pedazos.' This outburst reveals the marrow of the poet's anguish: the
conflict between desire and love, between *querer* and *amar*. The
persistence of this conflict is emphasized by a Spanish proverb which
comes immediately to mind: 'cada loco con su tema,'[32] and indeed
the poet is driven crazy by his affliction and shattered by it. The
popular expression 'me hacen pedazos' is very fitting in this context.
In rhyme position it culminates the shattering trajectory of the first
half of the sonnet: 'abrazos–brazos–lazos–pedazos.'

This sonnet brings up an important stylistic point. In serious love
poetry there was no considerable innovation as regards rhyme.
Rhyme was by and large standardized; for example, *frías–mías,
ausente–fuente, divertido–gemido, desatado–descaminado, hermosura–locura,*
etc. The reason for this standardization is that dissonance was
considered indecorous. By the seventeenth century, Quevedo feels the
need to insert a prosaic expression or a 'non-lyrical' word to provoke
a contrast with the mellifluous sonority of traditional love lyrics,
which in the twilight of the tradition had covered up a paucity of
thought and feeling. Through his innovative diction Quevedo elicits
from the reader a psychological and emotional response different
from that which had become customary to a mentality and sensibility
subjugated to a convention. From a different perspective a deep
feeling and experience are dynamically communicated. The surprising word or expression not only stirs the reader with the force of
meaning and emotion, but also radiates the same to the other words,

breathing life into them. The lover's shattered psychological and emotional state is expressed semantically by 'pedazos,' and is sonorously reinforced and affectively communicated by the dissonance created by the end rhyme -*azo*, a suffix often used in pejorative augmentatives. The rhyme set up by 'abrazos,' fully conventional, does not strike us as dissonant until we reach the vulgar 'pedazos'; then, without realizing it, we instantly relate the previous rhyme words to it, and a sort of disassociation sets in. Suddenly the rhyme is set off from the words carrying it, and the resulting dissonance has a shattering effect, which is assuredly the poetic intention.

The force created by this dissonance provokes an energetic response. No longer do we passively receive a characteristic and meaningless courtly complaint of the lady's disdain, but respond to a man existentially tormented by the burden of courtly love, which his lady and conscience expect him to shoulder, but which his flesh and emotions want to cast off. In a reaction against an absurd ideal, he strives to seize a woman of flesh and blood, not an abstraction, a 'fugitiva sombra.' We note, then, that the poet's harsh diction is structurally and thematically related, organic. It is *indecorous* in the stream of a genre's tradition but *fitting* within the framework of context and structure. With the organic utilization of such expressions as 'harto–muerdo' (360), 'sediento' (311), 'hambriento' (485), 'bestia' (379) and 'necio' (478), the poet was instrumental in the revaluation of a poetic diction concerned with a noble subject. This innovation communicates a feeling which a traditional poetic was no longer capable of expressing. Quevedo was within that vanguard which would eventually declare there was no word essentially unpoetical.

In the initial tercet the poet is once again determined to catch his prey. This time he will take vengeance on an 'imagen vana' that will not elude him. Again the poet intensifies the incorporality of the subject and simultaneously enriches our conception of her. To the meaning associated with 'trasgo,' we now add 'haughty'; and with this attitude she mocks the lover and runs away. The concluding tercet is a gem of rhythmic construction and moving sentiment. The mimetic nature of the rhythm accentuates the alternating moods of determination and disheartenment, and emphasizes the rushing force of the line. After the innovation of the quatrains and the subsequent defamiliarization, this image of 'llanto–ríos' comes as a surprise because it is unexpected, because it is so common yet defamiliarized as well. Quevedo revives a dead metaphor and uses it to express his emotional collapse. In sonnet 337 there is a single wave of emotional intensity building to a climax in the first tercet, and then a rapid descent. This sonnet has several emotional crests and falls. The repeated fluctuation between hope and despair, especially as it is concentrated in the final tercet, is another reason why the final image is so effective.

The dream safety valve has given him no relief; indeed, it is questionable if it is even intended as an escape mechanism. Rather, the dream is a nightmare, a chilling, intensified drama of the poet's state of mind and a startling manifestation of his haunting obsession. In it we find no idealization of the beloved nor resignation to a sweet affliction leading to perfection; instead, we have the poet's utter frustration with the concept of unsatiated desire. The pity is that the convention is expected of him, 'y viendo mi sudor, se me desvía,' but it is unrealistic, and therefore unbearable. The insubstantial nature of the images of the beloved emphasizes this point. This incorporality also emphasizes an important distinction. Although his lust is a motivating factor, the poem deals essentially with the poet's frustration with an abstraction. Struggling with the courtly code, he desires to put his hand on a tangible reality. It is this deprivation that provokes a cry of existential torment.

THE ABSURDITY OF COURTLY LOVE

In the discussion of sonnet 490, 'Puedo estar apartado, mas no ausente,' we recall that the lover's separation from his lady was conducive to the experience of human love. The distance facilitated the spiritual and rational contemplation of the beloved. This level of amorous sustenance, however, is an exception; as noted in sonnet 474, '¿Qué buscas, porfiado pensamiento?', separation likewise causes anguish. Sonnet 374 also deals with the lover's separation, but in this instance the evocation of his lady leads to a demoralizing awareness of courtly love's absurdity:

> Solo sin vos, y mi dolor presente,
> mi pecho rompo con mortal suspiro;
> sólo vivo aquel tiempo cuando os miro,
> mas poco mi destino lo consiente.
> Mi mal es propio, el bien es accidente;
> pues, cuando verme en vos presente aspiro,

no falta causa al mal porque suspiro,
aunque con vos estoy, estando ausente.
   Aquí os hablo, aquí os tengo y aquí os veo,
gozando deste bien en mi memoria,
mientras que el bien que espero Amor dilata.
   ¡Mirad como me trata mi deseo;
que he venido a tener sólo por gloria
vivir contento en lo que más me mata!

[Alone, without you and [with] my present grief, I tear my breast with a lethal sigh; I am only alive as long as I see you, but hardly does my fate allow it. My ill is my own, the good is accidental; since, when I aspire to see myself present [in your eyes], there is no lack of cause for the pain which makes me sigh, although I am with you [even] when absent. Here I speak to you, here I have you, and here I see you, enjoying this good in my imagination, while the good I hope for is deferred by Love. See how my desire treats me: I have come to hold as the only [glorious] happiness to live contented with what most destroys me! (BB)]

The sonnet begins with a lamentation on the beloved's absence which causes the lover to suffer an emotional death. It ends, however, on a surprising note, demonstrating that his death has a different and more agonizing cause. The initial quatrain presents the immediate dilemma: the lover laments the absence of the beloved and the presence of his grief. This grief causes his chest to heave a lethal sigh, for he only lives when he sees his lady, but this is a rare occasion. The quatrain presents the following argument: the lover is alive only when he sees the beloved; seeing her is a rare occurrence; therefore, he is dead most of the time. In this expression it is important to note the effects created by the use of connectives, and especially, the adverbs: 'sólo,' 'cómo,' 'más' ('only,' 'how,' 'most') give emotional emphasis to the conflicts they introduce. Further impact is created by the emphatic distribution of the stresses in the third line, where the stressed 'sólo' foreshadows a systematic use of stressed adverbs in the final lines.

The second quatrain tells us that death, the affliction caused by love and the beloved's absence, is the lover's essential characteristic. Seeing her (that is, being alive) is an accident, a chance occurrence. When he succeeds in evoking the beloved's presence, his affliction does not lack a cause to release another sigh. Although he is with her in his imagination, in reality he is separated from her. The word play on 'aspiro,' meaning 'to desire vehemently' and 'to inhale,' suggests the urgent need to evoke the beloved in his imagination. Despite this effort, it falls short of her real presence; hence 'aspiro' results in the exhalation of grief. Nevertheless, the lover succeeds in vividly evoking her presence: 'Aquí os hablo, aquí os tengo y aquí os veo.' The anaphora emphasizes the momentary calm that has come over the lover.

It has been noted that the senses most conducive to virtuous love are the spiritual senses of sight and hearing. Separated from the beloved and deprived of the benefit of these senses, the lover can still enjoy virtuous love through his thoughts. Nobili sustains that memory of the beloved, although weaker, is a worthwhile compensation for her absence. Lavinello is more optimistic about the evocative powers of thought and imagination:

chance and fortune may frequently cut our desires off from these approaches to their goal since . . . neither eye nor ear will serve us when we are far from what we love; therefore the same nature which provided these two senses has likewise given us the faculty of thought, with which we may enjoy both kinds of beauty when we please. By thought . . . we may recapture them and relish them unhindered at any hour that we wish (Bembo, pp. 157–8).

In the sonnet the lover is regenerated, enjoying his beloved's beauty in his thought, memory and imagination.

In the middle of this spiritual experience, the beloved's presence suddenly elicits, in line eleven, an unexpected response, stimulated perhaps by the sexual connotation of 'gozando,' 'enjoying.' This arousal of the sexual appetite will shatter his reverie and initiate a reaction that will end in *desengaño*. There are three different *bienes* treated here: the *bien* of the beloved's real presence bringing life to the lover; the *bien* with the stress on 'deste,' 'this,' which is her imagined presence, and the *bien* of sexual satisfaction. The latter the courtly lover attempts to sublimate in a rational and spiritual reverence for his lady's physical and spiritual beauty.

In the love sonnets of this period an imperative at the beginning of a tercet often concludes a linear exposition of thought and opens a different line of development (Brown, 1979, p. 30). Such is the case in the final tercet, where, after a moment of silence, the poet releases the cry of 'Mirad.' He realizes that he has fallen into the absurd situation of courtly love. The arousal of desire has shaken him back to reality. He becomes aware that he has allowed himself to become a courtly lover, loving his lady from a distance, evoking her in his imagination and enduring the agony of unsatisfied desire. Is living contentedly as a courtly lover his only glory? It is no glory at all. Here we note the special role of the affectively charged adverbs: 'cómo,' 'sólo,' 'más' are all in stressed position, giving impact to the poet's anguish. 'Cómo' prepares us for the poet's emotional reaction; 'sólo' puts 'gloria' in an ironical perspective, and with 'más' these adverbs give a dynamic emphasis to the *desengaño* that devastates the poet.

Quevedo also uses multipartition to realize a gradation. Each quatrain begins with a bipartite line framing an antithesis, then the initial tercet commences with a tripartite line marked by a stirring repetition:

> Solo sin vos   y mi dolor presente
> Mi mal es propio   el bien es accidente
> Aquí os hablo   aquí os tengo   y aquí os veo

On this emotional peak the poet enjoys human love. Yet with line eleven the thought of sexual satisfaction arises, carrying over into the transition to the concluding tercet. In this period of silence the poet comes to a realization, and abruptly voices an exclamation to shatter his reverie and to proclaim the absurdity of courtly love.

The sonnet ends on a surprising note. The poet thought his emotional death was caused by the absence of the beloved, but in his evocation of her he suddenly realizes that the real cause of his death is the indefinite postponement of sexual gratification. Even if she were actually present, he would still die because she would deny him the satisfaction he desperately desires. Again he is a phantom trapped by his afflictions. This disillusion becomes more apparent if we compare the last two lines with the third. The 'sólo vivo aquel tiempo cuando os miro' becomes the questionable glory of 'vivir contento en lo que más me mata.' The poet is condemned to an indefinite death-in-life; even her vision offers no relief. But the situation is even more pathetic. The poet is especially disillusioned with himself because he has allowed himself, 'he venido a tener,' to fall for the folly of courtly love.

The sonnet's conclusion presents an interesting turn of events. Before the seventeenth century there were occasional protests against the restrictions of courtly love in serious poetry, but rarely such an outburst as Quevedo's against its *absurdity*. Courtly love had so pervaded the mentality of those who wrote and practiced it that even what reactions there were against it were themselves absorbed by the convention. Quevedo's sonnet is an indication that courtly love has essentially collapsed. It demonstrates that a transition has taken place, allowing the poet to reflect critically on a tradition. Like Nobili he is aware that human love cannot completely satisfy the lover; yet he is writing in a genre that compels the affirmation of this ideal. He revives the convention, but in his heart of hearts he realizes that courtly love runs counter to his reason and feelings, and he chides himself for pursuing it.

This absurd state to which the poet has been reduced manifests a type of ludic element that approaches the grotesque. Warnke has perceived a kind of ludic hyperbole in some of Quevedo's love sonnets which 'go beyond the traditional Petrarchan exaggeration of the lover's suffering to achieve something like the grotesque: the speaker becomes ludicrous, even if his emotion does not, and the poems establish a tension between his real and painful emotion and his self-conscious perception of the state to which he has been reduced' (1972, p. 103). The poet's *anagnorisis* gives an ironical twist to the sonnet, revealing the poet as a fool to himself; but his subjection to the courtly code is no laughing matter.

Sonnet 485 of the Lisi cycle is one of Quevedo's most accomplished works, the poem which, Gonzalo Sobejano affirms, expresses love's anguish with incomparable and penetrating vehemence:[33]

> En los claustros de l'alma la herida
> yace callada; mas consume, hambrienta,
> la vida, que en mis venas alimenta
> llama por las medulas extendida.
>   Bebe el ardor, hidrópica, mi vida,
> que ya, ceniza amante y macilenta,
> cadáver del incendio hermoso, ostenta
> su luz en humo y noche fallecida.
>   La gente esquivo y me es horror el día;
> dilato en largas voces negro llanto,
> que a sordo mar mi ardiente pena envía.
>   A los suspiros di la voz del canto;
> la confusión inunda l'alma mía;
> mi corazón es reino del espanto.

[In the cloisters of my soul the wound lies silenced, but it consumes hungrily the life nourished in my veins by a flame extending through the marrow [of my bones]. The fiery heat is drunk by my hydropical life which now, as loving and debilitated ashes, a carcass of the beautiful blaze, displays its expired light as smoke and darkness. I shun people and find horror in the day; I draw out in long cries my black tears which to a deaf sea my burning grief does send. I gave the voice of music to my sigh; confusion floods my soul; my heart is the kingdom of terror. (BB)]

This sonnet is a profound, lugubrious plaint. The texture is a tight fabric of fire, darkness and woeful sounds. The diction is precise, yet allows for tenebrous associations conjuring up the poet's psychological and emotional torment. There are abundant pauses, momentary silences caused by syntactical breaks, producing short, penetrating rhythmic bursts. These cadences express the poet's internal probing and ultimate confusion, a *tanteo interior*. The imagery is intense, making immediately perceptible the poet's consuming passion. This 'power of interiorization' is what Sobejano considers to be Quevedo's greatest poetical gift (1971, p. 469).

The sense of the initial quatrain is: 'In the cloisters of my soul the wound (of love) lies silent, but it ravenously consumes my life, which in my veins (blood) is nourished by the flame (of passion) extending through my marrow.' The spatialization of the poet's soul, 'claustros,' apparently coincides with the 'composition of place,' as set forth by St Ignatius Loyola in his *Spiritual Exercises*. This composition is a prelude in which the 'eyes of imagination' see the place for the meditation on visible or invisible things. This practice was especially cultivated by the Metaphysicals, lying behind the graphically imaged openings of their sacred love poetry, and carrying over into poetry of profane love (Martz, pp. 27–31, 212–16). With the sonnet's opening image, the poet vividly figures forth the depths of his being; and with these cloisters we associate four ideas: contemplation, silence, solitude and darkness.

In sonnet 375 love is described as 'herida que duele y no se siente.' It is a wound causing pain but it cannot be felt, that is, it is not perceptible. Here the poet intensifies this experience: love is a wound which lies silent but which is devouring his life. The expression 'yace callada' suggests death, as if a cadaver were lying in a tomb, an idea that will be developed in the second quatrain. The wound is silent, love's anguish is unknown to others; but it is also silenced by him, as love is to be suffered in silence, 'callamos los volcanes florecidos' ('we silence our flowering volcanoes,' 302). Yet this silent wound is devouring his life. With the adjective, 'hambriento,' the poet dramatically expresses the ravaging effects of love. It is like a ravenous beast, it is like a cancer that devours the heart, 'landre que ... mata los corazones' ('Sentencia 1111'). The consumptive nature of love is developed in lines three and four. Here the life in his veins, his blood, is nourished by his passion extending like a flame through his marrow. The poet is devoured by love, yet he is, in turn, sustained by his passion. In other words, the only thing that sustains him in love's spiritual and physical consumption is the thought of requited love. In this quatrain the poet presents his soul, veins, blood and marrow, his *entrañas*, the vitals of his spiritual and physical being. To express this he utilizes a probing, increasingly profound rhythm highlighted by two enjambments. These enjambments do not produce a rapid effect, but maintain a slow, internalizing effect. This is accomplished by the hiatus in 'la herida,' which draws out the length of the enjambment producing a temporal sensation – the wound is not only profound, it has afflicted him for some time – and by the assonance of the *a*, again giving a sensation of length and time. The deep, dark sounds sonorously conveying the profound effects of love are attributable to the assonance of the *u*, 'cl*au*stros–cons*u*me–med*u*las.' In conjunction with the rhythm and the imagery, this particular assonance in stressed position emphasizes the accumulative effect of this quatrain. With 'medulas' we are vicariously in the marrow of an anguished existence, the expression of the most intimate channels where the fire devastatingly burns (D. Alonso, p. 570).

The lover is paradoxically both consumed and sustained by his passion. In most of Quevedo's poetry it is the former that is usually expressed,[34] but the latter is also true. In 387 love so blinds Plato 'que le hizo beber por agua el fuego' ('that it made him drink fire for water'), and in 450 the poet compares himself to a salamander, 'cuando en incendios, que sediento bebo, / mi corazón habita y no los siente' ('when in flames, that thirstily I drink, / my heart dwells and feels them not'). These instances help us interpret line five as 'My hydropic life drinks the ardor (flame).' Recalling 'nave sedienta' from 311, the line expresses an obvious sensuality. The poet burns from the fever of desire and, lacking relief, he is forced (hydropic) to continue drinking the very thing that causes his illness, the flame of his passion.[35]

Unrequited love makes life unlivable. This state of death is expressed in line six. On the inside he has been burned to enamored ashes, and on the outside his body is withered, 'mi semblante macilento' (451). Love has destroyed him physically; he must go through life as a cadaver. Smoke and darkness are the remains of his passionate existence; they are signs singling him out as a perished lover. The final tercet of 473 expresses this idea:

> Yo me seré epitafio al caminante,
> pues le dirá, sin vida, el rostro mío:
> 'Ya fue gloria de Amor hacerme guerra.'

[I shall be my own epitaph for the traveler, since, lifeless, my face will say to him: 'This was Love's glory, to war against me.' (BB)]

Sobejano has noted that the sonnet is composed of three phases: consumption, negation, inundation (p. 461). In the first phase, the quatrains, the syntactical structure is dominated by hypotaxis. The extended subordination of phrases and the numerous pauses account for the slow cadence. The second and third phases, the poet's psychological destruction, are expressed in the tercets,[36] most of whose lines are composed of brief and independent syntactical units. Line nine is bipartite, composed of two such units; and although line eleven is a dependent clause, it relates a single and complete idea. The effect of this parataxis is juxtaposition and enumeration, and an increased tempo. Each line is an emotional outburst (particularly so in the final tercet), conveying the poet's state of shock and confusion.

In line nine the poet can no longer bear his solitude among people. He is no longer the lover who can 'con soledad entre las gentes verse, / y de la soledad acompañarse' ('encounter solitude among people, / and with solitude accompany himself,' 367). Lisi's mental image previously accompanied him in his solitude (490); now Lisi has caused him such grief that he cannot bear to be seen. Here the syntax suggests the poet's subjective state. Daytime seems horrible to him. He has died inside, he is filled with darkness, he cannot bear the light of day, and each day prolongs his anguished existence. He is now a nocturnal creature housing death, a 'sepultura portátil' ('portable sepulchre,' 12).

Lines ten and eleven proclaim the poet's grief. The parallelism in the pre-position of the adjectives creates charged epithets. This passage begins with an expressive verb. The poet does not say that he releases a cry of grief, rather black tears swell out of him in long and loud shouts. He no longer can contain his silence. Out of his marrow, veins, soul and heart swells a black grief, a black mourning in a chilling wail. The poet gives a lugubrious dimension to the 'llanto' commonplace. With the 'negro' adjective it becomes more expressive, striking an emotional chord and setting off tenebrous associations. He does not say that his weeping has become a stream of tears; this is implied, but there is more to it than this. His tears are not a babbling brook, rather a black, wailing current that his burning affliction sends to a deaf sea. 'Mar' is required by the implied river, and, since in quatrain two his life is reaching death, here sea is the traditional symbol of death: 'envío / mi vida oscura: pobre y turbio río / que negro mar con altas ondas bebe' (30: 'I send my obscure life: a poor, turbid river which a black sea with high waves drinks,' ER). The sea is traditionally deaf because it does not heed the sailor's plea to spare his life; however, since the 'llanto' is caused by or addressed to Lisi, in her aspect of death-bringer she is also the sea. On the metaphorical level the poet is shouting the news of his death to an aloof and inaccessible beloved. By returning his love, she can give him life, but by remaining inaccessible, deaf to his pleas, she causes his death.

The negation phase is followed by inundation and damnation. He can no longer voice his plaint, only sighs remain. The poet has wasted away inside, he is psychologically devastated, yet must face existence. His beloved has scorned him, he avoids people, he shuns day: the confusion inundates his soul. Essentially he is dead. Heaven has rejected him, so he must bear the torment of hell. The accumulative force of the enumeration climaxes in the final lines. This impact is abetted by the increasingly affective gradation provided by the structure of this tercet. Line twelve contains a transitive verb with two objects; the transitive verb of line thirteen has a single object; finally, line fourteen is a predicate nominative: the poet's heart *is* a reign of fear.

Sobejano affirms that the amorous expression of this sonnet transcends love poetry, attaining such intensity and universal projection that the suffering of such intimate love, faced with such distant indifference and within such domineering terror, is the same for a woman as for the whole of humanity, for the world, the truth, an idea, an illusion, hope or God. Even more, this poem reveals excessive suffering, all suffering (p. 462). The sonnet is an expression of universal suffering but it is provoked by a woman's denial of her love. It expresses an anguished human experience and an intensely personal one.

The intensity of this suffering discovers a tone different from that voiced in the previous sonnets studied. In lines ten to eleven we detect a vehement, protesting tone. The voicing of the poet's death to an indifferent beloved is more than a courtly complaint. The epithets 'negro llanto' and 'sordo mar' point to an embittered attitude towards his lady's relentless virtue. For the modern reader, the epithet is often no more than a decorative figure; for Quevedo's contemporaries, although it (*epitheton*) 'garnishes and provides grace and majesty, its functions are value stating, not descriptive' (Tuve, p. 10). Because of the continual denial of the good desired, this lover ceases to be humble and silent, and voices his anger, as Quevedo states in 'Sentencia 46':

Del amor del bien ausente nace deseo del bien presente, gozo y alegría. Otrosí, del aborrecimiento que tenemos al mal ausente nace temor; del mal presente nace tristeza. Y estas seis pasiones que son amor, odio, deseo, temor, tristeza y alegría, llaman los filósofos la parte concupiscible de nuestra ánima. Del deseo del bien ausente juzgado por dificultoso o por imposible, nace desconfianza y desesperación; y si es muy grande el deseo, nace otra pasión, que es animosidad, la cual atropella por grandes dificultades; pero si todavía se atraviesan estorbos, y nos impiden lo que deseamos, o nos sacan de la mano lo que poseemos, se enfurece la irascible, que es otra parte de nuestra ánima.[37]

[From the love of absent good is born the desire for present good, joy and happiness. Furthermore, from the abhorrence we feel for absent ills, fear is born; from the present ills, sadness is born. And these six passions which are love, hate, desire, fear, sadness and happiness, are called by the philosophers the concupiscent attributes of the soul. From the desire of absent good judged difficult or impossible, uncertainty and desperation are born; and if the desire is very great, another passion is born; this is boldness which rushes to overwhelm great difficulties. But if other obstacles still have to be crossed, and deny us what is desired, or take it out of our grasp, then the irascible passion becomes enraged, and this is another attribute of the soul. (BB, JO)]

This bitter attitude is supported by the negative aura surrounding 'ceniza amante,' emphasized in turn by 'cadaver.' 'Ceniza' is a leitmotif in Quevedo's love lyrics, and in most instances it expresses an affirmation of his enamored existence and the vehement desire that his passion endure beyond death. The 'polvo enamorado' ('dust in love') of sonnet 472 is a positive expression of love's transcendence and of immortal passion. The motif in this sonnet expresses abject solitude, torment and total disillusionment.

The sonnet demonstrates an acceptance of suffering and of death-in-life, but certainly an embittered one. The poet's indignation goes beyond Lisi to reproach life itself. It is in this guise that his anguish is more than a lover's complaint. He is bitter that love and life *have to be* as they are. It is not a resigned acceptance of suffering, rather an anguished acceptance of the absurd in its deepest existential sense. Although Quevedo is pursuing a genre that demands adherence to the courtly ideal, we are left with the feeling that, in his heart of hearts, he cannot reconcile himself to its ethos. This impression has been given in other sonnets analyzed; this sonnet confirms it. Philosophically and existentially, courtly love causes him unrelenting torment.

4

Quevedo and Neoplatonic love

The study in chapter 2 of sonnets 457, 484, 458 established Quevedo's *prima facie* recognition of Neoplatonic love. By this 'new' ideal the virtuous lover aspires to a further purification of his love; and by making it intellectual he also attempts to overcome the corporal affliction caused by the courtly tradition. In a good majority of Quevedo's love lyrics, however, we note that the poet cannot deny his corporal passion, nor in his conscience can he embrace an ideal attempting to overcome it. Most of his poetry dealing with Neoplatonic love, therefore, either treats it with irony or expresses the grief caused by its too abstract nature.

CORPORAL REACTION AND IRONY

González de Salas has given sonnet 331 the title of 'Amor que sin detenerse en el afecto sensitivo pasa al intelectual' ('A love which, without delaying at the sensitive level, passes on to the intellectual'):

> Mandóme, ¡ay Fabio!, que la amase Flora,
> y que no la quisiese; y mi cuidado,
> obediente y confuso y mancillado,
> sin desearla, su belleza adora.
>   Lo que el humano afecto siente y llora,
> goza el entendimiento, amartelado
> del espíritu eterno, encarcelado
> en el claustro mortal que le atesora.
>   Amar es conocer virtud ardiente;
> querer es voluntad interesada,
> grosera y descortés caducamente.
>   El cuerpo es tierra, y lo será, y fue nada;
> de Dios procede a eternidad la mente:
> eterno amante soy de eterna amada.

[Flora commanded me, alas Fabio, to love her and not to want her; and my caring love, obedient and confused and tarnished, without desiring her,

adores her beauty. What human affection feels and laments, the understanding enjoys, love-struck and wooed by the eternal spirit, imprisoned in the
mortal cloister which treasures it. To love is to know ardent virtue; to want is
an act of selfish will, gross, degrading and perishable. The body is earth, and
shall be, and was nothing; from God the mind proceeds to eternity: eternal
lover am I of an eternal beloved. (BB)]

The poet talks with himself through his *persona*, complaining that
Flora, the beloved, has ordered him to love her spiritually and
intellectually ('amar') and not physically ('querer'). The poet's
reaction to this mandate is registered in a tone of sharp disappointment. The poet's love, stained by sensual desire, is bewildered by this
unexpected demand but is obedient and commences to adore her
beauty. This is the first step in the process of Neoplatonic love; the rest
of the sonnet is a consequence of the intellectual adoration of beauty.

In the second quatrain we note that the beloved's beauty, painful
on the sensual level, is enjoyed by the most noble part of the soul, the
intelligence, which perceives through corporal beauty the greater
beauty of the beloved's soul. The soul is in love with God, the eternal
spirit; but it is imprisoned in the body, 'claustro mortal,' which
treasures it. Nonetheless, through the intellectual contemplation of
beauty, the soul aspires to transcend its earthly confinement and
unite with the beloved's soul. Ideally this Neoplatonic process should
continue and culminate in divine love, union with the eternal spirit.
The first tercet continues to emphasize the difference between the two
types of love. To love intellectually is to know pure virtue; carnal love,
on the other hand, is selfish, base, uncourtly and transient. The final
tercet rejects the body as earth and nothing, while the mind derives
from God and is eternal. This leads to the conclusion: since his and the
beloved's souls are eternal, he is an eternal lover of an eternal beloved.

Green contends that Quevedo relates the theory without wholeheartedly embracing it; most of the poem is 'pure León Hebreo,' and
the final tercet echoes a passage from *Gli Asolani*, 'Good love is not
only a desire for beauty, but a desire for true beauty' (*CLQ*, pp. 27–8).
Green is essentially correct; there seems to be a lack of conviction on
the affective level. Although Quevedo at times appears to adopt a
conventional pose, he handles courtly and Platonic theories critically,
fully aware of their implications, and often giving them an ironical
twist. We shall now consider the sonnet from the perspective of
affective expression and irony.

On the surface of the sonnet there is a condemnation of physical love and a praising of intellectual love. By so loving, the poet will be able to enjoy a noble existence; and, because the soul is eternal, this love will endure forever. We hesitate to accept the poetical truth of this conclusion. There are certain elements of discord which merit examination. When we compare this type of eternal love with those poems in which the poet expresses a belief in an eternal love experienced by both the body and the soul, we will note a decided difference. In the latter he concentrates his poetic resources. Through gripping conceits and intense, emotional language and rhythm, he attempts to convince the reader and himself that the love experienced by the body and soul in life will endure after death. For him the body's passion is not subordinate to the love of the soul. In this sonnet the poet sets forth an *enthymeme*, a type of fallacious argument used especially by *conceptistas*. The enthymeme will be discussed in the next chapter; suffice to say that here it argues that 'The soul is eternal; my soul loves my beloved's soul; therefore, my love is eternal.' The eternal love expressed by this conceit is conceived as primarily spiritual, and is concluded on the basis of a discourse on the theory of Neoplatonic love. We will note a marked difference when we study this type of conceit in the context of sonnet 460, 'Si hija de mi amor mi muerte fuese' ('If my death were the child of my love'). In the latter the conceit yokes a complex of dualities: temporal–eternal and corporal–spiritual. The poet's major preoccupations are present, and he gives full poetic force to their expression. In sonnet 331 the important corporal element, projected eternally, is missing; therefore, there appears to be a lack of emotional reinforcement.

Communication on the affective level, however, is not entirely lacking, and noting where it occurs will help in evaluating the sonnet. Considerable emotion is expressed in the first quatrain, where the poet is ordered by the beloved to love her intellectually. Instead of voicing an objection, the poet's suffering love, 'cuidado,' finds itself perplexed and obeys her. Nonetheless, his immediate reaction is a sharp disappointment which continues as an undercurrent of discord beneath the surface of Neoplatonic love. In the rest of the sonnet expression on the affective level declines, in spite of the conceit of the last line; yet there is emotion here, but only if we perceive a sense of irony. The detection of irony often depends on our awareness of the poet's manipulation of language. In addition to 'confuso,' we have the ambiguous verb 'gozar'; one can spiritually enjoy God or physically enjoy a woman. We also note the expression 'amartelado de,' meaning 'in love with.' D. Alonso registers admiration over the use of this extra-poetical diction, especially at the moment when Quevedo is about to express the highest human yearning (p. 546). This choice of diction over *enamorado de*, which has the same meaning and is metrically equivalent, broadens the scope of interpretation. The expression can also mean *galantear*, 'to woo'; thus the poet's intelligence is both in love with and wooed by the eternal spirit. Equally important is that *amartelar* can also imply 'torment.'[1] This ambiguity on the linguistic level complements the despair on the affective level, producing irony. The sonnet could thus be given the interpretation suggested by Terry:

The anguish lies in being compelled, against the passionate nature of his feelings, to love platonically because this is commanded, not only by conscience and reason, but also – alas! – by the woman herself . . . for Quevedo there is an agonizing conflict between body and mind, since the latter both 'woos' and 'is wooed by' God, but his summons to divine love is a torment to man while his understanding is still imprisoned . . . in the body . . . Seen in terms of this conflict, the courtly love references fall into place, as if the speaker were saying: 'I know all about Platonic theory, which says that physical love is only a stage on the way to divine love. I know also that the body dies and the mind is eternal; therefore, if I am forced to love the woman with my mind, I am condemned to being an eternal lover.' And the implied comment is 'How absurd, and what a torment' (*Anthology*, II, pp. xxvi–xxvii).

This sonnet is open to interpretation. On the one hand there is a slackening of emotion after the first quatrain, as Green perceives, followed by a Neoplatonic discourse, and ending with a neat conceit with little emotional depth. On the other we encounter a considerable degree of irony, and the complexion of the conceit changes. It now expresses a subtle mockery of Neoplatonic love. In either case we note an implied dissatisfaction with an abstract and idealistic love. But we cannot pass over the obvious and most important revelation. The poet lusts for Flora's body; yet she commands him to love her platonically.[2] Attempting to compensate for sexual frustration, he tells himself why he should heed Flora's command and follow the path of true love. Nonetheless, he proceeds against his will; in his heart he is not entirely convinced by his intellectual cover up for sexual failure.[3] Intentionally or not, the sonnet conveys a feeling of despair.

The implied irony of sonnet 331 is made explicit in 448, 'Comunicación de amor invisible por los ojos,' where Quevedo gives an ingenious sensual account of the Platonic contemplation of his beloved.

> Si mis párpados, Lisi, labios fueran,
> besos fueran los rayos visüales
> de mis ojos, que al sol miran caudales
> águilas, y besaran más que vieran.
> Tus bellezas, hidrópicos, bebieran,
> y cristales, sedientos de cristales;
> de luces y de incendidos celestiales,
> alimentando su morir, vivieran.
> De invisible comercio mantenidos,
> y desnudos de cuerpo, los favores
> gozaran mis potencias y sentidos;
>   mudos se requebraran los ardores;
> pudieran, apartados, verse unidos,
> y en público, secretos, los amores.[4]

[If my eyelids, Lisi, were lips, the visual rays of my eyes would be kisses; they would gaze at the sun as golden eagles, and kiss more than they see. Your beauties, hydropically, they would drink, and as crystals thirsting for crystals, for lights and celestial fires, by feeding their death they would live. Sustained by invisible intercourse, and stripped of body, my faculties and senses would enjoy your favors; in silence our passions would woo each other; separated they would be united, and in public our love would be secret. (BB, JO)]

The sonnet is based on the Renaissance theory of perception that the eyes send out invisible beams which carry the object's image back to the spectator. As poets became increasingly interested in the mechanisms of love, this theory quickly became a commonplace. By means of the 'optics of love,' the beloved's image was lodged in the lover's heart or impressed on his soul.

The sonnet begins with a novel conceit based on a correspondence of form: 'párpados–labios.' The poet tells Lisi that if his eyelids were lips, his visual rays would be kisses. The intensity of this vision is amplified by a second comparison. It was believed that a golden eagle, 'águila caudal,' could fly the closest to the sun (*Dicc. Auts.*), and, since it was also believed that eagles could look straight into the sun and not be blinded (Covarrubias, *Tesoro*), then the poet's visual rays are many 'caudales águilas,' able to bear the splendor of Lisi's beauty. However, because his eyes are lips, they are inclined to kiss more than they see.

The second quatrain again demonstrates the poet's skill in compressing expression. The adjectives 'hidrópicos,' 'sedientos' qualify the conceit, 'párpados (eyes)–labios.' If we straighten out the syntax and fill in the ellipsis, lines five and six read, 'My hydropic eyelids would drink your beauty, and, thirsting for crystals, would drink your crystals.' Line six contains a foreshortened image; Lisi's skin is as clear and sparkling as water, therefore like crystals. Here we have an instance of what Lope de Vega called 'metaphors of metaphors' (BAE, 38, p. 146). If we extend the conceit's scope of function, the poet's eyes, as thirsty lips, not only kiss but also drink in her beauty and crystalline fairness. In line seven 'cristales' refers to Lisi's eyes, which as crystal balls reflect the light and fire of heaven. The simultaneous referents of 'cristales' are held together by extending the conceit along the line of the malady of dropsy. On the one hand the poet's eyes cannot quench their thirst for Lisi's physical beauty, 'cristales.' The consequence of this is expressed in the conceit 'alimentando su morir.' Because his malady causes him to drink incessantly Lisi's beauty, he ironically nourishes his death. Thus, while he lives to satisfy his thirst for Lisi, sensual insatiety paradoxically causes his death. On the other hand, through her crystal eyes, which are the mirrors of her soul, he sees reflections of heavenly splendor. This vision instills in him, 'alimentando su morir,' a yearning to transcend his corporal limits. With the end of the second quatrain, by means of the conceits of 'ocular osculation'[5] and ocular nourishment, Quevedo establishes an equilibrium between two realms of experience: the beloved's beauty excites him both spiritually and sensually.

This spiritual and sensual equilibrium is reinforced in the tercets by a deliberate ambiguity. 'Invisible comercio' means 'invisible communication,' but implies invisible sexual intercourse.[6] 'Los favores' can refer to Lisi's spiritual beauty or sexually to her physical favors.[7] As noted before, 'gozar' is likewise ambiguous. In the sense of sexual enjoyment, it develops the conceit, pointing to an implied figurative saying, 'comer con la mirada' ('devour with the eyes'). Since the object devoured is the beloved, the carnal implication is quite obvious. 'Potencias' refers to the three faculties of the soul, but in the singular it can have a carnal implication. Finally, 'desnudos de cuerpo' means stripped of the body, that is, without the barrier of the body; yet it implies 'cuerpos desnudos,' naked bodies. The expression is a conceit of opposition in that it suggests the opposite of what it says. This ambiguity creates two levels of meaning, one corresponding to the soul, 'potencias,' and the other to the body, 'sentidos.'

Consequently, the poet enjoys the beloved either in Platonic contemplation or in the imagination of sexual intercourse or both. The final tercet is a threefold logical extension of the conceit. Because of the 'invisible comercio,' the lovers could woo each other in silence; separated they could be united; and in public they could make secret love.

A conventional employment of this topic of the optics of love would have led only to the union of the lovers' souls. Quevedo develops its witty potential to express a unique experience. In this Platonic contemplation of the beloved, we encounter a fusion of two souls with all the delights of sexual union. On the surface Quevedo 'plays' with a topic, developing it to render a sensual account of Neoplatonic love; indeed, the sonnet is a burlesque of this ideal. Yet the levity, by contrast, emphasizes the sonnet's serious intent. The simultaneous expression of two different loves suggests that intellectual love, of itself, is not sufficient for the poet. Like his metaphysical contemporary John Donne, who expresses the same idea in 'The Exstasie,' Quevedo does not desire a bodiless union of the lovers' souls.[8] The body and soul together form 'That subtle knot, which makes us man'; consequently, the divided pursuit of intellectual or corporal love unties this knot, and, in truth, is not the human way to love. Rather, the soul and the body should participate jointly as equal partners in the experience of love. Such a love would be ecstasy.

An awareness of the sonnet's serious intent, in turn, uncovers and underlines a tension between the vying realities of life and art. Deprived of *real* physical union with Lisi, the poet creates a poetical reality to achieve a precarious equilibrium of soul and body. The conceit's poetical argument, which attempts to resolve a conflict between the spiritual and the corporal, is at the same time an attempt to cover up a bitter truth: in life such a resolution is not possible. The experience the sonnet constructs is even more idealistic than Neoplatonic love. The real force of the sonnet lies in what it momentarily avoids. It points to an existential anguish rather than to a consolation.

THE PILGRIM OF LOVE

Quevedo's ironical and even humorous treatment of Neoplatonic love reveals a basic antipathy to an ideal that pretends to disassociate the soul from the body. Beneath the irony and humor there is a reluctance to become the victim of an absurd torment. The feeling of despair implicit in this poetry will become more evident in the following sonnets. In these we shall see that, while Neoplatonic love may assist the courtly lover to overcome his corporal affliction, for the poet it causes an agonizing alienation. The soul may delight in the intellectual contemplation of the beloved, but the body is condemned to wander in an existential void. The ultimate and bitter irony is that Neoplatonic love, in freeing the soul, returns the poet to his death-in-life existence. He becomes a pilgrim of love, *peregrino de amor*, lost in an emotional wasteland.[9]

The pilgrim's quest for requited love becomes in sonnet 478 an existential burden:

> Cargado voy de mí: veo delante
> muerte que me amenaza la jornada;
> ir porfiando por la senda errada
> más de necio será que de constante.
>   Si por su mal me sigue ciego amante
> (que nunca es sola suerte desdichada),
> ¡ay! vuelva en sí y atrás: no dé pisada
> donde la dio tan ciego caminante.
>   Ved cuán errado mi camino ha sido;
> cuán solo y triste, y cuán desordenado,
> que nunca ansí le anduvo pie perdido;
>   pues, por no desandar lo caminado,
> viendo delante y cerca fin temido,
> con pasos que otros huyen le he buscado.

[I'm loaded down with myself: I see before me death threatening my journey; to insist on following a mistaken route is more the act of a fool than of a faithful man. If to his hurt a blind lover follows me (for misfortune is never single), alas!, let him come to his senses and turn back: let him not take a step where steps were taken by so blind a wayfarer. See how mistaken my way has been, how lonely and sad, and how disorderly, for never has a misguided foot so wandered; because, so as not to retrace my course, seeing a fearful end ahead and close, with steps which others avoid I have sought it. (ER)]

The lover's hope for requited love has diminished, yet he persists in his quest because it is too late to turn back. Love's journey has become a way of life.

In the exposition love's pilgrim carries a great burden, his own self; before him death lies in wait like a highwayman threatening his journey. In these lines Quevedo combines two sources. The first is an imitation of Boscán, 'Cargado voy de mí doquier que ando' ('I'm

97

loaded down with myself wherever I go'); the second is Petrarch, 'la morte vien dietro a gran giornate' ('and death comes after me by great stages,' 272). By associating these sources with a verbal cluster of perception and place, 'veo delante,' the poet gives a spatial dimension to life's solitary journey. His entire existence is determined by love, and it has become a burden. The lover is tired and defenseless; therefore, to continue obstinately along the wayward road of passion is a sign more of sheer folly than of constancy in love, 'necio en ser – mi daño porfiado' ('a fool to persist in my harm,' 379).

The *peregrino* motif is associated with a familiar commonplace, *escarmiento*: the lover's plight should serve as a warning to others who would follow his senseless way. Led by his folly, he encounters *desengaño*, and points out how confused his life has been. The repetition of the adverb 'cuán' stresses the magnitude of his folly. Never has a lover been so lost, a conviction similarly emphasized in 475: 'y en mí se escandalizan los perdidos' ('the lost lovers find in me their scandal').

Instead of changing his way, love's pilgrim declares in the final tercet his willingness to proceed on the errant road. He looks back down this twisted road and, seeing all his errors and follies, emits a casual 'pues.' This insignificant word introducing the final tercet is an emotional understatement. It contrasts with the anguished tone preceding it, communicating completely his resignation to a fate chosen by himself. The lover has been disillusioned; nonetheless, he laconically states his intention of not straightening out his life, even in the face of death, 'Antes muerto estaré que escarmentado' ('I shall be dead before I learn from experience,' 371).

The *peregrino de amor* thought he was on the road of love, but realized too late that it was the road of death. He contemplates his condition and confesses how taxing his journey has been. His life has become a burden to him, and he suffers from an existential exhaustion. Too tired to turn back, he seeks a different destination: death will relieve him of his burden. The entire poem is characterized by verbs of movement, volition and perception. The lover *goes* on his journey, he *sees* what lies ahead, and he *proceeds*. He is now motivated by the search for death.

The pursuit of the road of errant love is impelled by carnal desire, and the pilgrim realizes that his grief is a consequence of this burden. Relief can be sought either in death or in the death of desire. To achieve the latter, the lover feels that his pilgrimage must become a

Neoplatonic quest for intellectual love. Only by striving to this end can he hope to overcome the agony of the flesh. In sonnet 292 he relates this new journey:

> Fuego a quien tanto mar ha respetado
> y que, en desprecio de las ondas frías,
> pasó abrigado en las entrañas mías,
> después de haber mis ojos navegado,
> merece ser al cielo trasladado,
> nuevo esfuerzo del sol y de los días;
> y entre las siempre amantes jerarquías,
> en el pueblo de luz, arder clavado.
> Dividir y apartar puede el camino;
> mas cualquier paso del perdido amante
> es quilate al amor puro y divino.
> Yo dejo la alma atrás; llevo adelante,
> desierto y solo, el cuerpo peregrino,
> y a mí no traigo cosa semejante.

[A fire, spared by a great sea and which, in spite of the cold waves, has survived within the shelter of my vitals after sailing in my tears, is worthy of being raised to heaven as a new issue of the sun and time; and among love's constellations [worthy] to burn fixed [nailed] in a nation of light. The journey can divide and separate, but any step taken by the forlorn lover is a perfection to pure and divine love. I leave my soul behind; I go on ahead, deserted and alone, [with] my pilgrim body, and I have nothing [left] which resembles my [former] self. (BB)]

Carlos Blanco Aguinaga regards this sonnet as 'almost a good poem,' maintaining that the elaboration given to the idea that the beloved's fire has reached his heart via the eyes, with the additional metaphorical treatment of the latter, is too long and mannered. After the quatrains culminate with two magnificent lines, interest (he says) declines in the tercets, which initiate a different and obscure argument. He adds that the poet's declaration that the fire *deserves* to be transported to the sky is a tentative expression in comparison to the absolute and radical affirmation of sonnet 472. Blanco Aguinaga concludes that the reader is left doubting the clarity of the poet's intuition (pp. 71–2). This judgment is derived from a comparison of this sonnet with 472, 'Cerrar podrá mis ojos' ('My eyes may be closed'), on the basis of an image they seem to share. The image of eternal love, 'nadar sabe mi llama la agua fría / y perder el respeto a ley severa' ('my flame is able to swim across the cold water and disobey a harsh law'), is regarded by the critic as similar to the image expressed in the first quatrain of 292. His judgment of this poem is colored by his critical preoccupation with 472, causing him to see the former in the light of the more highly regarded sonnet. This similarity of expression supposes for him a similarity of intuition, which, because of a structural weakness in 292, is not clearly defined. Conceptually, the two images have nothing in common. The intuition of a love enduring after death is not the *cause* of this sonnet, which, on the contrary, clearly delineates the poet's intuition through an admirable, organic structure.

The initial quatrain expresses meaning on two metaphorical levels. On the first, the simplest, the fire–water antithesis expresses the idea that separation and distance have not diminished the pilgrim's love for his lady. On a long voyage, the expansive sea respected this 'Fuego'; the pilgrim scorned the cold waves' power to extinguish a love[10] that was sustained and protected in the center of his being. On a more complex level, 'Fuego' is the beloved whom the pilgrim's copious tears, 'mar,' have respected. The tears he has shed are a consequence of a courtly affection, 'respetado,' treated with disdain. The tears flowed into a sea of disdain in which his eyes had to navigate, that is, function. Nevertheless, the sea's cold waves could not extinguish his love, which swam over them and was received by the eyes, then passed into the warm protection of his heart and soul, the 'entrañas' of his being.[11] With this nautical dramatization, the poet fuses two commonplaces: the sea of love and the optics of love. Here the fire–water antithesis expresses the idea that neither the pilgrim's tears nor the beloved's disdain can put out the fire of love.

Blanco Aguinaga's description of the sonnet, a 'mannered elaboration,' leaves a negative impression; we should prefer the term *artificio*, 'artifice.' The poet develops an artificial allegory to express two related experiences: the pilgrim's unrequited love and his devotion during separation. The allegory depends on a familiar conceit called an *equívoco*, 'pun.' The double meanings of 'desprecio' and 'respetar' are structurally critical, being the pivotal puns in a complex conceit involving two metaphorical levels of meaning. Yet we must not pass over the literal level crucial to the dramatization of the *peregrino* motif. This level fixes the space of land and sea in which the pilgrim, embodying the idea of constant love, wanders.

Syntactically, the initial quatrain consists of a subject, 'Fuego,' and a series of descriptive, subordinate clauses. The relative pronoun of the first clause suggests a personification of this subject, and the adjective in the succeeding clause, 'abrigado,' confirms it.[12] This expository method creates a gradation to the predicate, 'merece ser,' held back for emphasis to the second quatrain. The pilgrim's love has endured despite separation and the beloved's disdain. As a reward for this devotion, it deserves to be transported to the sky. His love is a fire ignited by the beloved, 'sol,' and which daily suffering is purifying. Because of this constancy and grief, it deserves to be converted into a star and blaze in the eternal hierarchy. The expression 'las siempre amantes jerarquías' reflects a Neoplatonic conception of the universe. The quatrains express an aspiration to ascend from the sublunary world to the celestial realm of the *anima mundana*.

The desire to become a blazing star is an amplification not of a love-after-death wish but of a Platonic ascent, as noted in 458:

> La llama de mi amor, que está clavada
> en el alto cenit del firmamento,
> ni mengua en sombras ni se ve eclipsada.
> Las manchas de la tierra no las siento:
> que no alcanza su noche a la sagrada
> región donde mi fe tiene su asiento.

In comparing his love to a fixed star, the pilgrim is referring to the fixed stars of the eighth heaven, as opposed to the lower order of wandering stars. Thus, in addition to amplifying a Platonic ascent, the metaphor also emphasizes a constant, fixed love as opposed to his wayward life on earth, 'perdido amante.'

The envisioned ascension of love is contrasted in the tercets with the pilgrim's terrestrial wandering; however, these tercets do not initiate another topic, as they are a continuation of the peregrination established in the first quatrain. In the first sonnet of this *peregrino* cycle, the lover's quest for requited love ended in disillusion and a yearning for death. To overcome physical and mental torment, he now follows the road of purification and perfection leading to intellectual love. He has a definite goal in mind, yet he considers himself a 'perdido amante.' This element of discord goes against the mood of anticipated spiritual bliss established in the quatrains. The epithet means more than a loss of direction; it strongly implies condemnation, as if love has been his perdition. In the light of this dissonance, line eleven strikes us as ambiguous. It seems uncertain whether the poet is referring to two types of love, the *amor purus* of courtly love and Neoplatonic love – as if the first were a step to the second, or only one of these. If it is Neoplatonic, why all the agony? Indeed, this love was intended to overcome the anguish of the flesh.

THE LOVE POETRY OF FRANCISCO DE QUEVEDO

The process of suffering seems to be that of courtly love, yet the Neoplatonic references in the second quatrain make it evident that the poet has in mind intellectual love. Here he uses 'divino' in the sense of 'incomparable excellence' (*Dicc. Auts.*), making it function as a synonym of 'puro' to emphasize the ideal love which the pilgrim seeks.[13] The tercet reveals an important consideration. For the pilgrim the road to this ideal love requires a mortification of the senses and flesh. The 'perdido amante,' therefore, becomes more than a courtly commonplace: it expresses the poet's personal reaction to the consequences of intellectual love.

It is not expected that Neoplatonic love can cause grief. If we trace the pattern of the imagery, we shall find that it confirms this conclusion. The first quatrain posits two fundamental ideas: physical separation and devoted love. The latter is characterized by the equally important idea of the unity of body and soul. Despite separation body and soul act in unison in the experience of love. The poet's diction is precise on this point. He does not say that love is in the pilgrim's soul or in his heart; rather he uses 'entrañas,' a metaphorical term embracing both. Another point to keep in mind is that the pilgrim has attempted to keep this love on a courtly level, but it is causing him grief. With the second quatrain we witness a cleavage between the body and soul. The pilgrim now identifies his love with the affection of the soul, and envisions its ascent as a star to the sphere of the intelligences. His grievous courtly love attempts to become Neoplatonic. Line nine reinforces this pattern: the road separates him from his beloved but it also divides. Instead of proceeding on the courtly road, he takes the Neoplatonic one, taking the way of the soul and forsaking that of the body. The quatrains and initial tercet constitute the first two stages of a pattern which can be formulated as union–division–desolation. The final tercet relates the pilgrim's harrowing desolation.

The pilgrim leaves his soul with his beloved, since this is where it functions (Nobili, fol. 28r), and in his solitary wandering he takes with him his deserted body. Love has wrought in the pilgrim a complex alienation: 'alma, cuerpo, yo.' The soul is left behind, and the body wanders on as a shell to which is attached a consciousness. The assonance of the *o* affectively emphasizes and sonorously defines his hollow being and the spiritual void in which he is left to wander. I. A. Richards has noted that a technique of metaphysical poets is to take commonplaces seriously; thus, by taking seriously such daily expressions as 'That man is not himself' or 'is beside himself,' the poet expands them, making their implications explicit (pp. 82–3). This alienation of the body and the consciousness also recalls that psychological phenomenon whereby one develops a center of perception that seems to be outside the body, a split into one who observes and into one to whom things happen (Kahler, p. 84). The result is an overwhelming desolation.

Love can be a devastating force. As Bembo declares in *Il cortegiano*, it causes the lover to endure

anguish, torments, sorrows, sufferings, toils; so that to be pale, dejected, to be in continual tears and sighs, to be always silent or lamenting, to long for death, in short, to be most unhappy, such are the conditions that are said to befit lovers. The cause, then, of this ruin in the minds of men is chiefly sense (p. 338).

Carnal desire is the cause of the lover's affliction, so he embarks on the new journey of intellectual love. Yet this way causes equal torment. It is obvious that the concepts of Neoplatonic love as set forth in *Il cortegiano* and *Gli Asolani* differ considerably from the poet's treatment of it. Instead of a process through which the torment of the flesh is avoided or overcome, the pilgrim's suffering seems to be a requisite of intellectual love: 'mas cualquier paso del perdido amante / es quilate al amor puro y divino.' In his pilgrimage to cast off the demon of sensuality, the lover's 'Neoplatonic' journey is causing havoc to his mind and body. He is sacrificing his corporal and emotional needs for the sake of intellectual love. This note of sacrifice, on which the sonnet ends, suggests an additional perspective to the 'arder clavado' image. Previously the adjective reinforced the intellectual nature of the pilgrim's love, making explicit that his soul was fixed in the sphere of immobile stars. From a different perspective, the adjective, in the literal sense of 'clavado', suggests the idea of Christ nailed to the cross, and now reinforces the impression of sacrifice and suffering. This same impression is given in 401:

> Si amasteis en la vida
> y ya en el firmamento estáis clavadas,
> pues la pena de amor nunca se olvida,
> y aun suspiráis en signos transformadas

[If you loved in life and are now to the firmament nailed, since the suffering of love is never forgotten, and you sigh even when transformed into constellations (BB)]

This perspective, in turn, causes us to see 'esfuerzo,' 'effort,' in a different light. It is as if, owing to the beloved's disdain and the grief caused by courtly love, he were forced to become a Neoplatonic lover.

By expressing a longing for a Platonic bliss gained at the expense of considerable sacrifice, the poet communicates an idea running counter to the traditional concept of an intellectual love that *transcends* the body, achieving a tranquility of the senses. This treatment of Neoplatonism suggests the possibility of irony, but it is not a deliberate irony, for it is a consequence of the shaping of an intuition. It has been suggested that the intuition of the sonnet, its cause, is vaguely defined. A first reading perhaps gives this feeling, as the tercets move in a direction different from that assigned by the quatrains. But a close attention to the sonnet's structure reveals a clear delineation of its cause, which is an indication of a well-conceived intuition and its execution. Yet it is reasonable to assume that this is not the case, and herein lies the sonnet's special merit. The sonnet gives the impression that the poet began with a preconceived idea, a yearning for intellectual love, expressed quite artificially, even 'mannered' in a depreciatory sense. In the course of its expression, the structure gradually brought to the surface an unconscious intuition, causing a visceral reaction to the aspiration of Neoplatonic love.[14] The pattern of the imagery leads to a feeling of desolation caused by the split of the soul from the body. This cleavage is also reinforced by the dissolution of the elements of fire, air, earth and water. According to Hebreo's Empedoclean doctrine the four elements are harmoniously bound by their amity (p. 87). Intellectual love breaks up the pilgrim's elemental composition; the lighter element of the spirit, the flame of love, rises to the ethereal region, while the heavier, the body, remains below on earth and water.

Bereft of his soul, the pilgrim suffers a desolating alienation.[15] It is because of this agony that he believes his love *deserves* to be granted the bliss of intellectual love. And here lies the pathos. The sonnet is an anguished revelation of the tension between what the poet yearns for and what, in reality, he has to endure. If we are to judge the merit of a poem on the basis of how well the artistic expression succeeds in the revelation of experience, then we would have to consent that this is an admirable poem. It may not be as good as 'Cerrar podrá mis ojos,' but it is more than 'almost a good poem.'

Sonnet 292 reveals an ambivalent attitude towards Neoplatonic love. This intellectual transcendence brings spiritual bliss, but at the cost of psychological alienation and corporal enervation. Neoplatonic love involves a sacrifice which the poet is reluctant to make. The result of this conflict is a death-in-life, as becomes apparent in sonnet 473:

> Éstas son y serán ya las postreras
> lágrimas que, con fuerza de voz viva,
> perderé en esta fuente fugitiva,
> que las lleva a la sed de tantas fieras.
> ¡Dichoso yo que, en playas extranjeras,
> siendo alimento a pena tan esquiva,
> halle muerte piadosa, que derriba
> tanto vano edificio de quimeras!
> Espíritu desnudo, puro amante,
> sobre el sol arderé, y el cuerpo frío
> se acordará de Amor en polvo y tierra.
> Yo me seré epitafio al caminante,
> pues le dirá, sin vida, el rostro mío:
> 'Ya fue gloria de Amor hacerme guerra.'

[These are and indeed will be the final tears which, with the strength of a loud and live voice, I shall cast off in this fleeting stream, which takes them to thirst of so many beasts. Fortunate am I if, on foreign shores, as food for such elusive suffering, I should meet a merciful death to raze such a vain structure of fantasies! Naked spirit, pure lover, above the sun I shall burn, and my cold body will remember Love when dust on earth. I shall be my own epitaph for the traveler, since my lifeless face will say to him: ''Twas Love's glory to war against me.' (BB)]

The pilgrim says he is done with weeping. He emphatically announces that the tears he sheds are the final ones he will lose in the fleeting fountain of life, which takes them to the insatiable thirst of his bestial affliction. The expression 'voz viva' compresses two meanings. The first is 'viva voz,' meaning 'out loud'; thus these tears are the final ones he will shed with cries. The second is 'with a live voice'; anticipating his death, he states these are the last tears he will emit. The sense of the lines is similar to that of 'dilato en largas voces negro llanto' (485). The pilgrim has been sapped of energy and the will to continue living. His journey has brought him to foreign shores where he hopes to encounter a merciful death that will topple his tower of illusions. In this context 'playas extranjeras' also points metaphorically to the shores of the river of death. The search for requited love has been an illusion and the cause of unmitigated grief. The first quatrain dramatizes the destructive effects of his sensual affliction. The pilgrim's tears feed a river where beasts come to drink. As they drink up his tears, so does his animal passion; and, although the tears feed this passion, they do not quench its thirst. Extending the image's range, we have the beloved, the 'fiera,' who consumes him, taking but giving nothing in return. In the second quatrain his afflictions are chimaeras, monsters of illusions feeding on his hopes. Death will be merciful because he will no longer have to nurture and sustain them.

The tercets relate that death will separate the soul from his body, and his spiritual love will burn above the sun while his cold body will remember love in dust and on earth. He will remain as an epitaph to the traveler, as his lifeless face will tell him that it was love's glory to cause him strife. Here we realize the pilgrim has not been talking of actual physical death but of death caused by love. Nonetheless, since this type of death causes complete enervation it is experienced as a separation of soul and body; thus, for him, it is as devastating as physical death.

In this sonnet the *peregrino de amor* has come to the end of his journey, where he paradoxically finds both purification and death. He states he has been weeping and feeding an insatiable illusion. He has been unable to rid himself of the thought of sensual satisfaction. This burden has been too great and has finally succeeded in causing his death, which he now regards as merciful because it relieves him of his carnal chimaera. Released from its corporal prison, the soul will ascend above the sun, where it will become a pure lover and delight in the contemplation of intellectual beauty. The body will remain on earth as dust, not because it has decomposed but because this is its essence, 'polvo ciego' ('blind dust,' 308). The soul will take the flame of love, and the body will turn cold; still, it will remember the disruptive experience of love. Since Love causes the pilgrim's death, the *yo*, the I, perishes; therefore, his body will have to speak for him. It will become a walking tomb and an epitaph telling others he was Love's victim.[16]

In a sense the pilgrim has achieved what he set out to accomplish. Whether the carnal appetite is overcome through spiritual purification or perishes from frustration, the result is the same: the liberation of the soul. But at what cost? Considering the sonnet in this context, we discover the poet's attitude towards intellectual love. Quevedo aspires to a love in which body and soul can participate as equal partners. Such a love will give substance to his life, and in death he will lament their separation:

Siento haber de dejar deshabitado
cuerpo que amante espíritu ha ceñido;
desierto un corazón siempre encendido,
donde todo el Amor reinó hospedado. (479)
[I regret having to leave uninhabited a body which has enclosed a spiritual
love, to leave deserted a heart always aflame where nothing less than Love
reigned as a lodger. (BB)]

However, he will attempt to find consolation in the belief that even in
death the body will continue to feel the passion which it so ardently
experienced alive:

Llevara yo en el alma adonde fuese
el fuego en que me abraso, y guardaría
su llama fiel con la ceniza fría
en el mismo sepulcro en que durmiese. (460)
[I would carry within my soul wherever it went the fire which consumes me,
and I would keep its faithful flame with my cold ashes in the same sepulchre
where I might sleep. (BB)]

C. M. Coffin has noted the interdependence of the soul and body in
Donne's love poetry. His observation can apply as well to Quevedo,
who shares with Donne

an intense love for real experience combined with an ardent belief in the
reality of the spiritual. In the greater world these two spheres exist as matter
and spirit; in the lesser world, in man . . . they are conjoined as body and soul
. . . Here they are known to exist, as death proves, yet in some way joined and
mutually dependent . . . truth derives not from the separate experiences of
body and soul but from the experience of both conjointly (p. 285).

In the achievement of intellectual love the body cannot participate.
Deprived of the experience of love, the body suffers a death-in-life as
real as physical death, and is condemned to wander as an empty shell
that can only remember an experience it no longer shares. The lover's
consciousness accompanies his body; yet, as in 292, they are alienated
from one another. Intellectual love will be achieved but at great
sacrifice. This is the tone that reverberates in the final line. Such a
love is not regarded as a positive experience, for it has cost him his
psychological and physical well-being.

With the projection of the self through the persona of the *peregrino de
amor*, the poet adheres to a tradition. The pilgrim continues to be a
symbol of anxiety and suffering caused by an impossible and
unrequited love (Vilanova, p. 434). His restless wandering along the

road of love and life dramatizes the lover's confused existence. This role-playing also allows the poet to dramatize an intimate experience (Warnke, 1972, pp. 40, 136). Against the backdrop of a tradition, the poet plays out a particular love experience dealing with his reaction to Neoplatonic love.

Most courtly poets tacitly accepted the Neoplatonic ideal. They knew in their conscience that, while some sort of intellectual apprehension of God ought to have been their ultimate goal, they settled, perhaps never quite seriously, for an intellectualization of their love for the beloved. Quevedo's treatment of Neoplatonism, humorous and serious, reveals an intense personal and philosophical involvement. While we feel that he would prefer a love permitting the full participation of body and soul, this is impossible because of the pressure of the genre and, primarily, because it goes against that part of his conscience framed in the conviction that spirit is higher and nobler than matter, and continence more spiritual than indulgence. Compelled by tradition and conscience, he aspires to an intellectual love that will alleviate corporal agony. This road does not lead the pilgrim to the outcome we would normally expect; instead, the soul's victory causes in sonnet 292 an intense visceral reaction – which comes through especially in the shaping of the sonnet's intention – and produces in 473 total enervation, a spiritual lobotomy. The poet's treatment of the ideal involves, not corporal transcendence, but corporal sacrifice. It reveals a tension between a conscience aspiring to sublime love, and another conscience aware that the ideal is absurd and a source of torment. Neoplatonic love involves a sacrifice which, in his heart of hearts, he is reluctant to make.

BODY AND SOUL

Neoplatonic love is not compatible with the poet's most ardent feelings. Early in this study we noted his attraction to it, and on one occasion, sonnet 458, 'Por ser mayor el cerco de oro ardiente,' he seems to be on the threshold of an ethereal experience. This atmosphere, however, is too rarefied, and, furthermore, he cannot forget for long the real presence of the body. Either this corporal concern is at the root of his deliberate ironical treatment of intellectual love, or it colors his conception of it. In the latter case it becomes a road of suffering leading to a death-in-life just as surely as the anguish caused by unsatisfied desire. This is to be expected, since both have in common the denial of the body's needs.

Torn by two contradictory realities, Quevedo feels he must make a claim for the provisional truth of the body in the face of the absolute truth of the soul. Probing intellectually into the mystery of his passions, taking in an amorous tradition from the perspective of his metaphysical sensibility, he becomes concerned with love, as Warnke says of Donne, 'as a *coincidentia oppositorum* – body and soul have their respective claims, each claim excludes the other, and yet both claims are undeniably, however mysteriously, valid' (1961, p. 8). The precarious balance in Quevedo's sonnet 448, 'Si mis párpados, Lisi, labios fueran,' 'is no facile synthesis of sexual urge and Platonic rationalization; it is an assertion of the equal truths of mutually exclusive attitudes . . . a truth of experience in the face of all logic.'[17] Quevedo avails himself of the only resource left to a metaphysical poet in his quest for total experience. By means of the conceit he creates a poetical reality affirming the participation of both body and soul in the experience of love. This shared, unifying experience is central to his philosophy of love. Another important factor is his conception of beauty, as expressed in sonnet 321:

> No es artífice, no, la simetría
> de la hermosura que en Floralba veo;
> ni será de los números trofeo
> fábrica que desdeña al sol y al día.
> No resulta de música armonía
> (perdonen sus milagros en Orfeo),
> que bien la reconoce mi deseo
> oculta majestad que el cielo envía.
> Puédese padecer, mas no saberse;
> puédese codiciar, no averiguarse,
> alma que en movimientos puede verse.
> No puede en la quietud difunta hallarse
> hermosura, que es fuego en el moverse,
> y no puede viviendo sosegarse.

[No, symmetry is not the craftsman of the beauty which in Floralba I see; nor can a structure, indifferent to the sun and day, be the triumph of numbers. It is not the result of musical harmony (with due respect to the miracles performed by Orpheus), for my desire does indeed recognize in it a secret majesty by heaven sent. It can be endured but not known, it can be coveted yet never grasped, this soul which only in movement reveals itself. In death-like stillness beauty cannot be found, for it is a fire in motion, and whilst alive it cannot rest. (BB)]

Neither symmetry, proportion or harmony are the true sources of Floralba's beauty; rather, it derives from a hidden majesty sent from heaven and recognized by the poet's desire. In *Gli Asolani* Lavinello relates this definition of beauty:

Beauty is a kind of grace which is born of proportion and the harmony of things; the more nearly perfect it is in its embodiments, the more lovely it renders them to us, and in human beings it is an attribute of the mind no less than of the body. For as that body whose members are proportionate is beautiful, so is that mind whosè virtues meet in harmony; and each enjoys its share of beauty according to the grace which informs us and reconciles its parts (p. 157).

According to this Neoplatonic conception of beauty, because the soul informs the body, the latter's beauty is a reflection of the soul's. In line eight the poet makes evident that the soul's beauty is what he has in mind, yet he does not agree with the Pythagorean and Platonic explanations of external beauty.

The poet says Floralba's beauty can be suffered but not known, and it can be coveted but never grasped. Finally, he gives the answer to his riddle: beauty is the soul which can be seen only in movement. On the one hand this definition of beauty seems to coincide with the traditional Neoplatonic progression from the attraction of the senses to corporal beauty, and thence to the contemplation of intellectual beauty: 'so knowledge of sensible beauty is good and is the source of love and pleasure in so far as its end is in knowledge of intellectual beauty and induces love and enjoyment of the latter' (Hebreo, p. 397). But beauty is not just the soul, it is the soul in movement. Yet this revelation begs a question: how can the soul's movement be seen? The answer must be tied up with the body; indeed, the poet seems to have in mind Hebreo's definition of beauty: 'Beauty is grace which delights the mind which recognizes it and moves it to love' (p. 264). But only through the beloved's moving grace is her beauty perceptible. 'Quiere que su hermosura consista en el movimiento' ('He wants beauty to consist of movement'), states González de Salas in the sonnet's epigraph; thus, in dead stillness there can be no beauty. If we now turn to Nobili, the sonnet's meaning will become even clearer:

Perhaps by the word 'grace' the proportion of the members is often meant, when it results from the movements of the body; for, without fail, movement is an act to cause in a body a different proportion of the parts from that which it had in repose; so that on occasion it will delight us when it moves, and it will offend us by being still; or, on the contrary, it will bring us pleasure when still, and annoyance in motion. So that he who, according to common usage, should call beauty motionless grace, and grace beauty in motion, would not err exceedingly.[18]

There are two types of grace. Static grace is what the sculptor achieves in the creation of a statue, whose beauty can be measured, but the poet can find no beauty in this dead stillness. Quevedo's marginalia in his copy of the treatise indicate that this passage was significant. The first notation is 'Las tres gracias en romance son verdad, alegría, splendor'; and the second, 'Esta tercer gracia, que llaman gentileza de aire, y en español mujer airosa y que tiene donaire, consiste en movimiento que anima de gracia viva todo el cuerpo'[19] ('The three graces are in Spanish truth, happiness, splendor. This third grace, which is called "gentility of behavior," and in plain Spainsh "a lively and spirited woman," consists of the movement which animates with sparkling grace the whole body'). Beauty for Quevedo requires movement, revealing itself through the body's dynamic grace. The sonnet points to the bodily movement but needs a metaphor to fuse spirit and matter, a metaphor that moves and excites. Beauty is a moving fire which, living, cannot rest.

Quevedo departs from traditional concepts of beauty because either they consider only corporal beauty or they make a distinction between it and spiritual beauty. Lavinello states the body's beauty is a sign of the soul's beauty. The grace of one is a revelation of the grace of the other, but they move in their own sphere of activity. As a Christian Quevedo believes in the beauty and perfection of the soul; it is an 'oculta majestad que el cielo envía.' But for Quevedo, the lover and poet, beauty is the fusion of the soul with the beloved's body.[20]

The importance of this sonnet lies in the revelation that the poet cannot abide solely in the Neoplatonic progression from the contemplation of the beloved's corporal beauty to the contemplation of her soul. This is impossible because it would result in the contemplation of a soul completely abstract and static, and, therefore, deprived of beauty. The soul and the body are both important and cannot be separated. Together they are a fire exciting the poet and moving him to love. In this context 'deseo' ('desire') is 'an affect [passion] of the will aimed at the coming to be or the coming to be ours of a thing we judge good'; love, then is 'an affect [passion] of the will to enjoy through union the thing judged good' (Hebreo, p. 12). That which is esteemed to be good is the beloved's beauty, a dynamic grace; thus, the poet desires to 'possess the beloved's grace' (Nobili). This leads to an important revelation: to unite with the beloved's body is to unite with her soul. By virtue of this union he would enjoy her grace. The crowning achievements of this union would be to 'generate in beauty' (Nobili).[21]

For Green the sonnet 'seems to lack emotional depth and to be merely a toying with Platonic ideas on the nature of beauty' (*CLQ*, p. 26). On the contrary, the emotion comes through in the never-slackening rhythm. Four instances of enjambment add a forceful continuity to this rhythm, and twice they put into relief the central idea of beauty, 'hermosura.' This emotion is intensified in the first tercet through effective parallelism and accumulation. All these lines are emphatic, climaxing in the flowing line, 'alma que en movimientos puede verse.' The ten instances of alliterated sibilants musically amplify this dance of the soul. Finally, the poet crystallizes his anti-Platonic feelings in the fire's dancing flames, defining beauty with an image we can grasp. It is spiritual and visual, kinetic and exciting. Fire is a dynamic motif in his poetry. It is a symbol of his intensity, of life and love, of passion and the beloved, and now of beauty. Spirit and matter together make fire. This is the beauty the poet sings. This is the fire in which he would burn. Quevedo is a poet of fire.

5

Love and death

Death is one of Quevedo's major themes. In his prose it is often considered with a stoic and Christian conscience,[1] by which death is regarded not as a destructive force, but as a vital transition. Characteristically, the most frequently repeated aspect of this theme is the interchangeability of life and death; life is a living death, 'vivir muriendo,' and death is a passage to a better life, 'mejor vida' (*Epistolario*, p. 257):

es . . . la vida un dolor en que se empieza el de la muerte, que dura mientras dura ella. Considéralo como el plazo que ponen al jornalero, que no tiene descanso desde que empieza, sino es cuando acaba . . . Todo lo haces al revés, hombre: al cuerpo, sombra de muerte, tratas como a imagen de vida; y al alma eterna dejas como sombra de muerte . . . y cuando llega la hora postrera . . . hallas que el cuerpo te deja, y que tu mejor parte es el alma . . . Empieza, pues, hombre, con este conocimiento, y ten de ti firmemente tales opiniones: que naciste para morir y que vives muriendo, que traes el alma enterrada en el cuerpo, que cuando muere, en cierta forma resucita; que tu negocio es el logro de tu alma (*La cuna y la sepultura, Prosa*, pp. 1193–5).

[Life is a sorrow in which that of death has its beginning, and which lasts all through life. Think of it as the term the laborer is subjected to; he has no rest from the moment he begins, but only when he is done. Oh mortal, you do everything backwards! You treat your body, which is the shadow of death, as an image of life; and your eternal soul you abandon as the shadow of death. And when the final hour arrives you discover that your body leaves you, and that your best part is your soul. Oh mortal, begin with this knowledge and hold firmly to these ideas: that you were born to die, and that you are dying while you live; that you carry your soul buried in your body, which upon dying is resurrected in a pure form; that the work you have cut out for you is the salvation of your soul.]

In his lyrical poetry, however, we often find an attempt to overcome a fear of death:

> Breve suspiro, y último, y amargo,
> es la muerte, forzosa y heredada:
> mas si es ley, y no pena, ¿qué me aflijo? (30)

113

[A brief sigh, a final bitter one, is death, our inevitable heritage: but if it's the law, and not a penalty, why do I complain? (ER)]

Death is a bitter pill to swallow, but since it is a *law* common to all men, as heirs of Adam's fall, it is a legal and acceptable inheritance. Death is a condition of our existence; and, 'if we take adequate steps, its bitterness can be avoided, that is, if we make it our law, not our punishment' (Wilson, p. 25). Much as the poet may feel in his conscience that life is both a burden and an illusion, he still laments the slipping away of time and dreads death's destruction:

> ¡Cómo de entre mis manos te resbalas!
> ¡Oh, cómo te deslizas, edad mía!
> ¡Qué mudos pasos traes, oh muerte fría,
> pues con callado pie todo lo igualas! (31)

[How you slide from between my hands! Oh, how you slip away, my life! What mute steps you take, cold death, for with silent foot you make all things equal! (ER)]

Despite the belief that the eternal life of the soul is the true life, Quevedo fears death and loves this corrupt existence:

> Temo la muerte, que mi miedo afea;
> amo la vida, con saber es muerte:
> tan ciega noche el seso me rodea. (47)

[I am in dread of death, which my fear disfigures; I love life, knowing it to be death: so dark and blind a night surrounds my mind. (BB)]

Death, which is attractive because it can release him from an oppressive existence, is made ugly by the poet's fear of it, while life, putrid and senseless, is rendered beautiful by his intense love of it. Existence, then, becomes a state of perpetual darkness in which he confuses the values of death and life. Here we have a notable illustration of the seventeenth century's obsession with death, time and destruction. Poulet affirms that the seventeenth century is the epoch in which the individual discovers his isolation. As opposed to the poet or thinker of the Renaissance, who experienced the 'joy of being in time,' and felt himself capable of self-realization in duration and by duration felt the fullness of existence, the human consciousness of the succeeding century, 'isolated from exterior time,' feels itself separated from the modes of its existence, 'finds itself reduced to existence without duration. It is always of the present moment.' Poulet points out that all the thought of this century had been one long meditation on the phrase of Saint Augustine, 'If God should

114

withdraw his creative power from the things he created, they would fall back into their primal state of nothingness.'[2]

The Baroque sees life through a prism different from the Renaissance's, perceiving in the budding rose the seed of death. This simultaneous perception of antagonistic forces in practically every instance of existence can produce a tension the expression of which occasionally achieves a metaphysical note. The constant anticipation of life's destruction diminishes the quality of life itself, revealing the latter as an illusion that only the reality of death can shatter. Consequently, death is conceived as a positive transition and, paradoxically, as life:

> Llegue rogada, pues mi bien previene;
> hálleme agradecido, no asustado;
> mi vida acabe, y mi vivir ordene. (8)

[Let her come sought-for, since she prepares my own good; let her find me grateful, not frightened; let her end my life and bring order to my living. (ER)]

Yet Quevedo is reluctant to embrace his final death because, as he sees from experience, annihilation is abhorrent. The destruction of the most trivial is a constant portent of his own corrosion; and, faced with his inevitable reduction to nothingness, he prefers to cling to his solitude-in-life. Thus, on the one hand the metaphysical poet yearns for death's release from his isolated, moribund existence, and on the other he is tantalized by life's illusions. He lives under the tension of death and death-in-life. Much of Quevedo's poetry, then, is permeated by death, and is often an attempt to come to grips with it.

The courtly concept of death-in-life has a profound resonance in Quevedo, for the grief caused by unrequited love is a manifestation of the *vivir muriendo* which characterizes his existence. Quevedo invests the courtly topic with metaphysical profundity, not only expressing a lover's tortured heart, but, more importantly, expressing a state of being. Through love poetry he expresses his existential situation; and, ultimately, he strives to believe that love can be a way of transcending death's annihilation.

In poem 423, a *romance*, Quevedo extolls the transcendent power of requited love:

> Contra el Tiempo y la Fortuna
> ya tengo una inhibitoria:
> ni ella me puede hacer triste,
> ni él puede mudarme una hora.

[Against Time and Fortune I already have a prohibition: the latter cannot make me sad, nor can the former change a single hour. (BB)]

In a life threatened by time and imperiled by the fluctuations of fortune, love elevates the poet from a quantitative to a qualitative existence. Requited love unburdens him of all preoccupations, even the thought of death. Embracing each other, Fabio and Florisa can hide from their annihilation: 'Escondidos estamos de la muerte, / pues es tan grande el gusto que poseo' ('Hidden are we from death, / so great is the joy I hold,' 412). Such expressions of love's power are found principally in poetry of the Middle Style. In the High Style, unless concealed by irony,[3] love must be virtuous. The dominant note of this poetry is a dolorous one, as the poet becomes tormented by desire and solitude.

When desire and death come together, Quevedo's love poetry becomes profound. The passion caused by unrequited love causes corporal anguish; yet even in moments of intense torment, the body manifests life: it feels. The elimination of desire, then, is either the result of death or caused by the separation of soul and body as a consequence of Neoplatonic love, in which case existence becomes a living death. In one instance even the attainment of the courtly ideal seems to result in a death wish. Sonnet 488, 'Mejor vida es morir que vivir muerto,' concludes:

> Y ya que supe amar esclarecida
> virtud, siempre triunfante, siempre hermosa,
> tenga paz mi ceniza presumida.

[It's a better life to die than to live as a corpse: And since I was able to love a resplendent virtue, always triumphant, ever beautiful, may my presumptuous ashes find peace. (BB)]

The poet seems to be saying, 'I have achieved pure love; my desire has expired; therefore, I have nothing to live for.' Instead of ending with an exclamation of joy over a goal achieved, the sonnet ends on a note of irony. In his description of Lisi's splendid virtue, the repetition of the adverb 'siempre' exudes a resentment against courtly love's conquest, because, in the process, her unassailable virtue, always triumphant, and her beauty, always unattainable, have emasculated him.

With the imminence of death something complex happens in Quevedo's love poetry, and if we stick strictly to the love theme, we shall miss the point. In his heart of hearts, despite all the travails,

Quevedo loves life and fears death. It is more to the point to say that he does not fear death as much as he fears the death of the body's capacity to feel. He believes in the soul's immortality, and he *wants* to believe in the immortality of the body's passion. He believes both the soul and the body ought to participate in the experience of love; however, death and intellectual love separate them, dissolving their interdependence. For the soul death is not a barrier, but it is a formidable one for the body. His problem is to encounter a means by which the body can transcend this barrier, to resolve in some way the immortality of one and the perdition of the other.

Love is the most powerful force he has ever experienced:

Es el amor la vida del corazón, y así como es imposible vivir el hombre sin vida, así es imposible estar sin amar el corazón. Es el amor una afección voluntaria de gozar con unión la cosa que es tenida por buena. Otros llaman a esto pasión, y dicen que es una complacencia que pone la cosa amada en la voluntad del que ama. Y asimismo es el amor principio de todas las pasiones, y que todos los afectos del corazón estriban en él, como fundamento, y nacen de él, como causa y raíz ('Sentencia 46').
[Love is the very life of the heart, and just as it is impossible for man to live without life, so it is impossible for the heart to be without love. Love is an affectation of the will, which wishes to enjoy union with the object deemed to be good. Others call this passion, and say that it is a complacency which subjects the beloved object to the will of the lover. And yet love is the first and foremost of all the passions, and all the concerns of the heart are borne by it and spring from it, as if it were their cause and foundation.]

On occasion it has given him happiness, but mostly it has caused him much agony; yet at each extreme he has been most consciously aware of existence. Love intensifies existence, causing either joy or grief. At the juncture of life and death he seizes upon love as a means of vital transcendence. If love is so intense in life, it may endure after death. And if so, then the body, informed by love, may also endure. L. Elaine Hoover confirms this observation: 'the acuteness of Quevedo's death-in-life, due to his eternal denial of . . . requital, determines the intensity of his ultimate glory, his life-in-death' (p. 139).

Faced with the inevitability of death he responds with his total being, and his poetry becomes metaphysical, transcending 'love poetry' and, especially, courtly love. In death the soul and the body will separate but they will be joined by an experience they shared in common: love. By virtue of this experience, although his body will decay to bones and dust, its passion will continue to burn.

WIT AND ETERNAL PASSION

In sonnet 479 the poet reveals he is not afraid to die. His only regret is having to leave a body that loved intensely; however, he finds consolation in the premonition that his love may endure after death.

> No me aflige morir; no he rehusado
> acabar de vivir, ni he pretendido
> alargar esta muerte que ha nacido
> a un tiempo con la vida y el cuidado.
>   Siento haber de dejar deshabitado
> cuerpo que amante espíritu ha ceñido;
> desierto un corazón siempre encendido,
> donde todo el Amor reinó hospedado.
>   Señas me da mi ardor de fuego eterno,
> y de tan larga y congojosa historia
> sólo será escritor mi llanto tierno.
>   Lisi, estáme diciendo la memoria
> que, pues tu gloria la padezco infierno,
> que llame al padecer tormentos, gloria.

[To die does not distress me; I have not rejected an end to my life, nor have I sought to prolong this death which was born at once with my life and love. I regret having to leave uninhabited a body which has enclosed a spiritual love, to leave deserted a heart always aflame, where nothing less than Love reigned as a lodger. My fervor gives me a sign of an eternal fire, and for such a long and anguished story only my gentle weeping will be the chronicler. Lisi, my memory keeps telling me that, since I endure your glory as hell, I should call the suffering of torments glory. (BB)]

The sonnet begins with the declaration that death causes the poet no anxiety; he has accepted the end of life. Neither has he attempted to prolong the death which was born simultaneously with life and love. The expression of these ideas is particularly meritorious. Quevedo frequently uses enjambment to emphasize concepts, especially as these are manifested through substantives (Navarro, p. 155). Infinitives also are an important stylistic feature. It is not uncommon for him to begin a poem with an infinitive or place it after an enjambment to accelerate action, stress its meaning or highlight its emotional value. Such is the case in this quatrain where the poet combines this technique with parallelism to shape an idea. The quatrain is composed of three structurally similar negative statements. The first succinctly posits the idea of facing up to death: 'No me aflige morir.' The second says the same thing but in a different way: 'no he rehusado / acabar de vivir.' Here the enjambment and prosody give

118

additional emphasis to this shading of meaning and progression of emotion. This shading is important as it is clear the poet is expressing not the commonplace of death caused by love, but physical death. The emotion accompanies meaning, is highlighted by the double negatives and is made forceful by the contrast between 'morir' and 'vivir,' each receiving prosodic stress. The third negative follows the same pattern as the second: negative + predicate + enjambment + infinitive, but with a notable difference. The first two negatives are expressed in brief syntactical units; the third runs on for two and a half lines whose length mimics the meaning of 'alargar.' This length provides an ironic contrast between what the poet asserts and what he is experiencing. He has not attempted to prolong the death caused by life and love; nonetheless, this is how it has been. This death refers to two aspects of experience. The first is life, which, as perceived by the Baroque mentality and the poet's stoic conscience, is an illusion. Life is really death, and true life begins with the end of living. The second is love's tormenting passion.

The compelling feature of this quatrain is that Quevedo is not speaking only as a love poet. Death, life and love come together, and he speaks as a man and a lover. The *vivir muriendo* experience takes in both the existential and amatory planes; 'vida' and 'cuidado' come together. We are not listening to Quevedo, the courtly aspirant, but to a man who happens to be in love. He accepts death as he accepts life. He does not seek a premature end nor does he desire to extend existence. He accepts the agony of life and love.

The contrast between life and death reveals the essential conflict confronting the poet: the body and the spirit. The poet does not fear dying but he regrets having to leave uninhabited a body that housed his spiritual love. The perfect tense 'ha ceñido' gives a sense of indefinite duration to the poet's love, as if to say 'I have loved all my life; my life is love.' *Ceñir* can also mean 'to embrace' (358); hence line six figures forth the meaning by presenting the body and soul as embracing lovers that only death can part.

With restrained emotion, the poet matter-of-factly states his acceptance of an inevitable reality, in the expression of which he employs melodic lines. When he gets to the heart of the conflict, in the second quatrain, he resorts to an emphatic prosody to stress his sorrow affectively. Furthermore, the enjambment isolates the source of his sorrow: the body. He will have to leave deserted a heart that was always aflame, a heart where Love reigned and lodged. The progression from 'deshabitado' to 'desierto' intensifies the poet's grief. We have noted that *ausencia*, absence, is a leitmotif in his love poetry. He regrets the absence from his beloved, and mourns the cleavage of soul and body caused by intellectual love; but, when he contemplates the very real separation of soul and body which death will bring, *ausencia* is profoundly experienced. Despite the agony, love has exalted his existence. Laín Entralgo's comments on the quatrains are apposite:

Life, death and love are essentially joined in man's existence; Quevedo knows this well. He also knows that human existence is capable of magnification through love: his memory and heart so tell him. Therefore, without diminishing his serene acceptance of death, he regrets leaving uninhabited his body and deserted his heart (p. 36).

After death the body will decay, but the poet has a premonition that, perhaps, its passion will live on: 'Señas me da mi ardor de fuego eterno.' In this longing for eternal love, the poet avails himself of the 'inferno of love' motif, investing it with his wit. On this occasion the motif is employed as a vision of a real abyss where lovers suffer torment as punishment for their amorous excesses (Post, p. 76); consequently, since the poet has taken the errant way of love, he will be condemned to hell for his *truancy*. In this eternal fire the only writer of his grief will be his tears. Suddenly he avails himself of a rationalization. Reason, he declares, tells him that since Lisi's glory causes him to suffer a burning hell, he will be able to call his torment heaven. The conceit involves two processes. The first is based on the double meaning of 'gloria.' Lisi's splendor, virtue and nobility make her triumphant, and the poet's love for this glory causes him hell. When 'gloria' and 'infierno' are contrasted, however, the former's sense changes into 'heaven'; therefore, the love of such a person, although causing torment, will be heavenly.[4] Second, his love for Lisi causes him to burn as if he were in hell; hell is eternal; consequently, his love will burn forever. The conceit, then, lies in the contradiction between heaven and hell, and the conversion, by the force of love and wit, of the latter into heavenly immortality. He may be in hell, but because he enjoys the beatific vision of the beloved, it will be heaven. The poet is actually expanding the courtly concept of suffering.

Suffering, even to the point of morbidity, is an intrinsic courtly trait. He who can endure more pain than others is esteemed the more worthy courtly lover. In sonnet 486 Quevedo demonstrates a difference between himself and courtly lovers:

Todo soy ruinas, todo soy destrozos,
escándalo funesto a los amantes,
que fabrican de lástimas sus gozos.
[I am all ruins, I am all destruction, a dreadful and scandalous example for
lovers, who fashion their joy out of misery.]

He cannot be a meritorious courtly lover who can devise mental
orgasms from grief; instead, the pain caused by sexual deprivation
shatters him. As a courtly lover he is a failure, a scandal to his coterie.
We noted in sonnet 374, 'Solo sin vos, y mi dolor presente,' this
exaggeration of suffering to the point of ludicrousness and the double
perspective it implies. If Quevedo is aware that courtly love is
ludicrous, it is equally, if not more ludicrous, to follow the tradition.
The irony, and the real source of his agony, is his vexing awareness
that he has been reduced by an absurd convention to a situation
worse than that of the *fin amant*. Yet, if he suffers more than these, then
he ought to be envied:

Los que han de ser, y los que fueron antes,
estudien su salud en mis sollozos,
y envidien mi dolor, si son constantes. (486)
[Let those future lovers, and those of the past, learn about their welfare from
my tears, and envy my suffering, if they are constant. (BB)]

In the present sonnet Quevedo takes a different perspective to the
courtly concept of suffering. It not only proves his love, but is a sign
that it will live forever. According to Christian teaching, if one sins in
life without repenting, the soul will be condemned to suffering;
consequently, persistence on the sinful trail of desire is cause for
damnation. It is popularly believed, as Dante illustrates, that the
punishment meted out corresponds to the nature of the sin committed; thus the poet seems to be saying, 'If I suffered in life because of
love for you, is it not conceivable that I shall likewise suffer in hell? I
shall endure torment, but because I love you hell will be heaven and
my passion will be eternal.' Death is acceptable but it presents a
problem. The poet's spirit will have to leave his body, which
experienced a deep and passionate love. Inquiring metaphysically
into an emotional conflict, he ponders how to take his passion with
him. In this context heaven and hell, salvation and damnation, point
to a conflict between the eternal and the ephemeral. This conflict is
resolved through wit and the intensity of his love experience.

DEATH, THE CHILD OF LOVE

As we have noted, one of the most frequent commonplaces in love poetry is the theme of death caused by love. Beginning with the troubadours, this death was a metaphor for the psychological and emotional state of the afflicted lover, a death-in-life. When Petrarch used the phoenix as a symbol of this state, he expressed an additional dimension of love: not only could it cause the lover's death, but it could also resurrect him. By the seventeenth century this topic had become another lifeless expression. But in the twilight of a tradition, Quevedo gives it new life. For him it is no mere commonplace; unrequited love is a torment, and the endeavors to sublimate this grief through courtly love or rationalize it by Neoplatonism have a shattering impact on his existence.

In the face of death, and incited by his desire for immortality, love's anguish becomes a force against his corporal destruction. He desperately wants to believe that, in some way, his body will also achieve eternal life. It is for this reason that he looks forward to experiencing love beyond death. If this is possible, then the passion felt by the body in life will continue. Furthermore, the soul, which participated in this experience, will take with its spiritual love the memory of corporal love. Through love's power Quevedo attempts to overcome death's destruction. Death will release him from the demon of carnal desire, the major cause of his grief, but bestow immortality on his passion. Death will bring freedom by resolving the conflict between corporal and spiritual love that torments him in life.

In sonnet 460 Quevedo, in the fashion of metaphysical poets, takes a commonplace seriously. What would happen if love really caused death?

> Si hija de mi amor mi muerte fuese,
> ¡qué parto tan dichoso que sería
> el de mi amor contra la vida mía!
> ¡Qué gloria, que el morir de amar naciese!
> Llevara yo en el alma adonde fuese
> el fuego en que me abraso, y guardaría
> su llama fiel con la ceniza fría
> en el mismo sepulcro en que durmiese.
> De esotra parte de la muerte dura,
> vivirán en mi sombra mis cuidados,
> y más allá del Lethe mi memoria.

Triunfará del olvido tu hermosura;
mi pura fe y ardiente, de los hados;
y el no ser, por amar, será mi gloria.
[If my death were the child of my love, what a most fortunate birth would
my love give in exchange for my life! What a glory if death were born of love!
I would carry within my soul wherever it went the fire which consumes me,
and I would keep its faithful flame with my cold ashes in the same sepulchre
where I might sleep. In the other realm beyond harsh death, my love and
care will live in my shadow, and beyond Lethe my memories [will live]. Your
beauty will triumph over oblivion; my pure and fervent faith [will triumph]
over the Fates; and not to be, for love, will be my glory. (BB)]

The first quatrain posits the conceit on which the sonnet is based. If
the poet were to die of love, his death would be the child of a most
fortunate birth. This conceit causes a shift in perspective, making us
perceive quite differently the idea that death is the birth to a greater
life, and that life, as Quevedo laments, is only a constant progression
of stillbirths:

En el hoy y mañana y ayer, junto
pañales y mortaja, y he quedado
presentes sucesiones de difunto. (2)
[In my today and tomorrow and yesterday, I couple a diaper and a shroud,
and I remain as present successions of a dead man. (JO)]

In such a concept we usually give to the meaning of birth a figurative
sense; it expresses the idea of passing from one stage to another.
Through the conceit, and especially the word 'parto,' the poet shifts
our attention to the literal meaning of birth. The juxtaposition of an
earthy, life-giving process with an abstract concept of life after death
is fascinating. Love's labor gives birth to a child. The child is the
lover's death, but it is a new and eternal life as opposed to his
ephemeral existence. The poet's euphoria is like that of a jubilant
father voicing the arrival of his newborn child, a glorious blessing:
'¡Qué gloria que el morir de amar naciese!'
For the poet such a death would allow the soul to take with it the
fire of love in which he at present burns, and the body would keep its
eternal flame in the cold dust of the tomb. Ceniza, like the Latin cinis,
was frequently used to designate the ashes of a cremated corpse. By
also taking literally the conventional flame of love, the body would
therefore be consumed to ashes, which would sustain the now
metaphorical flame. Wherever the soul may go, 'adonde fuese,' it will
take his love. In the shadow of rigid death his passion will continue to

live, and beyond the waters of oblivion his soul will retain the memory of corporal love. This quatrain develops a parallelism similar to the one the poet perfects in sonnet 472, 'Cerrar podrá mis ojos'; lines five and six correlate with line eleven, and seven and eight with lines nine and ten. Because the beloved's beauty is impressed on the lover's soul, it is not forgotten; thus, her beauty is immortalized and triumphs over oblivion. The poet's pure and ardent faith in love's power will also triumph over the Fates. Here we have an amplification of the conceit. According to Greek mythology, the Fates (or *Moirai*, the 'Alloters') were believed to be birth-spirits who visited a newborn child to determine what his portion in life would be. In this case, however, since death is the offspring of Love, it is a child over which the Fates have no dominion. This amplification introduces the joyous reiteration of the conceit which initiated the sonnet: 'y el no ser, por amar, será mi gloria.' What a contrast this is with Quevedo's *Poemas metafísicos*![5]

> La vida nueva, que en niñez ardía,
> la juventud robusta y engañada,
> en el postrer invierno sepultada,
> yace entre negra sombra y nieve fría. (6)

[My new life, which blazed in childhood, my robust and deceived youth, buried in final winter, lies among black shadows and cold snow. (ER)]

What a difference love makes! Instead of destruction and nothingness, it creates a 'vida nueva,' an eternal love.

Even though it causes death, love instills in him a feeling of immortality. It is a positive force because now his death is the birth to a new existence where the experience of love will be infinitely richer. Death is the fruit of love. Having established this, the poet continues arguing that, like his eternal soul, his cold dust will be immortal and sustain faithfully the flame of love. Of course, the proof of this argument is not demonstrable, and from the point of view of Christianity it is not only fallacious, but perhaps even sacrilegious. Love can transform life and may even cause death, but it is unlikely that it endures after death. The conceit develops an argument that is plainly false. According to Emanuele Tesauro, a seventeenth-century Italian theorist of *conceptismo*, this would be a perfect conceit because it is founded on metaphor (child–death) and takes the form of 'arguments urbanely fallacious.'[6] The specific mode of argument is through an enthymeme, a fallacious and rhetorical syllogism intended to create beauty and not to investigate truth; it is what we today would call the 'logically expanded metaphor' (Mazzeo, 1951, p. 248). The urbanity of the argument, its rhetorical beauty, lies in the witty force of the paradoxes. Since death is love's daughter, love gives birth to death. This is a state of *gloria*, meaning 'heaven' and 'salvation' as well as 'exaltation.' Therefore, since love achieves heaven (or heaven is won by love), then heaven is non-life, not to be: 'el no ser.' Love brings extinction, but also salvation; fallacious, but poetically beautiful.[7] Because the conceit produces a fallacious argument, this does not mean the conclusion is false; rather, it is a truth of a different order. Such a conceit gives poetical truth precedence over conceptual truth (Donato, p. 27). Faced with the reality of his annihilation, the poet responds with a poetical truth sustaining love's triumph over *nothingness*, 'el no ser.'

James Smith detects in this type of poetry a certain air which he calls the 'metaphysical note,' a note of tension (p. 21). This tension or 'high strain' arises, in the first place, from the metaphysical conceit, usually a metaphor, and is due to the 'sharpness' with which its elements are opposed (pp. 24, 33). In terms of the mode of operation it is similar to that of the extravagant or ornamental conceit, but, once experienced and contemplated, the distinguishing feature of the latter is that the 'elements come together only for a moment, at that moment cause surprise and perhaps pleasure, and then immediately fly apart' (p. 34). The metaphysical conceit, on the contrary, tends to the sphere of argument, and its elements are such that they can 'enter into a solid union and, at the same time, maintain their separate and warring identity' (p. 36).

Terry has augmented Smith's study by distinguishing the function of the organic conceit, 'illuminating a particular theme or idea which is important, either for the poem as a whole, or for a substantial part of it,' and of which the metaphysical conceit is a particular kind whose peculiarity is 'not in its mode of operation, but in its content' (1958, pp. 213–14). We have noted the organic conceit in various sonnets, for example, 359, 311 and 465. While this type of conceit lacks the tension of the metaphysical conceit, the discovery of its function can illuminate a tension within the poem as a whole; that is, the conceit, once comprehended, is seen as an expression or dramatization of a tension experienced by the poet. In the case of Quevedo, the organic conceit often discloses the tension between his conscience and the genre's demands, and his passion and feelings, between what reason knows to be true and what the heart wants to believe, between the beloved's beauty and the effects of her beauty.

With the metaphysical conceit, the reader is aware of both the unity and the discord of its elements. Terry adds that this 'sense of "unity within discord"'... is not present in the organic variety. If the latter contains a contrast (it need not), then it is not a philosophical one, and is likely to contain elements derived from a particular literary tradition' (1958, p. 215). What most distinguishes the metaphysical conceit, then, and what contributes the most to its tension, is that it is concerned with metaphysical problems, that is, problems which entail oppositions differing in essence, such as the one and the many, body and soul, the temporal and the eternal (J. Smith, pp. 24, 36–7). At the same time that it 'offers something unified and "solid" for our contemplation . . . even when it is being dwelt on by the mind, tension between the elements continues. That is the most striking thing about it' (pp. 34–5).

In this sonnet Quevedo presents an astonishing metaphor of child–death, amplified by the act of birth. Here we have sharply opposed elements, which already tend to reconciliation because of our familiarity with the belief that death is the beginning of an eternal existence. It does not take any stretch of the imagination to see that the child is a metaphor for a particular type of existence. Yet what fascinates us is the perspective, the approach that Quevedo takes. By taking a commonplace seriously, we see death in a novel light. It is generally conceded that a child is the fruit of love, but since the poet's love for Lisi causes his death, then death is his child and fruit of love. Because of a universal familiarity with this expression, we are also susceptible to the poet's argument, which, with the poetic force, seizes the imagination and the mind so that we stop thinking in terms of problems and 'reality.' We suspend our disbelief and make ourselves emotionally vulnerable. A factor in this suspension is that the sonnet begins hypothetically; the quatrains form an extended 'if' clause in the subjunctive mood. In the tercets, however, the poet switches to the future indicative; his wish for a love experience beyond death ('¡Qué gloria, que el morir de amar naciese!') becomes an anticipated reality, 'y el no ser, por amar, será mi gloria.' In the transition we are subtly deluded, as the switch from the subjunctive to the indicative is not all that apparent. Unawares, with our disbelief suspended, in a flash of poetic revelation we find ourselves 'duped' into accepting the poet's conclusions: the reconciliation of two sets of metaphysical oppositions. Since death is love's child, the poet's love will not end with his own mortality; the temporal is projected into the eternal.

Furthermore, since soul and body shared in the experience of love, love's immortality guarantees that, while the body will decay, the soul will take into eternity its passion, sustained by the memory of the beloved's corporal beauty.

When the poetical force and emotion begin to wane, we realize the deception and note warring identity between the conceit's elements. The metaphysical oppositions start to strike us again with their brutal duality. We also become aware of a different tension between what the poet wants with all his heart and soul to believe, and what reason compels us to believe. As a result disbelief begins to set in. We know the limits of reality, and, after all, the poet's argument is really hypothetical. Yet the reality of the poetic experience, its beauty, is not discredited. The conceit, aesthetically and emphatically, affirms his fervent desire that love transcend temporal and corporal existence. And from the point of view of his mortality, love transforms his existence because he does not fear death.

The sonnet contains yet another fascinating manifestation of metaphysical wit, which derives from a definition of love as proposed by Plato and related by Nobili: 'Plato reasonably denied Love to be desire of beauty, not because in Love one does not desire to see the beautiful, which one ardently desires, but because this was not the principal end of amorous desire; rather, one seeks to achieve immortality through the birth of one's children.'[8] In addition to taking seriously the commonplace of death by love, Quevedo takes seriously this realistic definition of love, but gives it a witty inversion. Lisi has denied him her love, and he cannot, as Nobili says, 'generate in beauty' and attain immortality through the propagation of a child.[9] Nonetheless, by love of her, of her beauty, he will gain eternal life by propagating his own death. By dying for the sake of love, that is, by giving birth to the child of love, death, he will engender his immortality, 'con pretensión de fénix . . . intenta que su muerte engendre vidas' ('With the ambition of a phoenix [my heart] tries to make his [Icarus's] death engender lives,' ER). This is a prodigious poetical feat worthy of our highest admiration. The poet takes a literal and practical definition of love, executes a metaphysical inversion, and then amplifies it through a literal application of the metaphor of death by love. This is a remarkable example of the poet's wit. The result is the development of a conceit which is both urbanely fallacious and metaphysical. This combination is the product of the highest order of wit and the revelation of a profound experience.

BAROQUE DEFIANCE

Quevedo's most famous love sonnet is 'Amor constante más allá de la muerte' ('A love constant beyond death'):

> Cerrar podrá mis ojos la postrera
> sombra que me llevare el blanco día,
> y podrá desatar esta alma mía
> hora a su afán ansioso lisonjera;
>   mas no, de esotra parte, en la ribera,
> dejará la memoria, en donde ardía:
> nadar sabe mi llama la agua fría,
> y perder el respeto a ley severa.
>   Alma a quien todo un dios prisión ha sido,
> venas que humor a tanto fuego han dado,
> medulas que han gloriosamente ardido,
>   su cuerpo dejará, no su cuidado;
> serán ceniza, mas tendrá sentido;
> polvo serán, mas polvo enamorado.

[My eyes may be closed by the final shadow which will take away from me the bright day, and this soul of mine may be freed by an hour indulgent to its anxious longing; but it will not, on the further shore, leave the memory in which it used to burn; my flame is able to swim across the cold water and disobey a harsh law. A soul which has been imprisoned by no less than a God, the veins which have supplied the moisture to so great a fire, the marrow which has gloriously burned: it will leave its body, not its [loving] anguish; they will be ash, but it will have feelings; they will be dust, but dust which is in love. (ER)]

While not denying the sonnet's greatness, Mas has attempted to abate the 'too modern interpretation' of Quevedo's poetry, particularly this sonnet. Mas sustains that the energy does not come from *what* the poem says but from *how* it is said. Essentially this is true of all poetry; however, he makes a distinction between form and content which does not apply to poetry of this period.[10] Form is an extension and revelation of content, and we shall discover that the sonnet's formal intensity is a pristine revelation of the intensity of its cause. It is a faithful verbal extension of a vehement sentiment.

The sonnet and Mas's comments have drawn the attention of Blanco Aguinaga, who handles Mas's objections quite well, contributing in the process an admirable exegesis.[11] Yet Blanco Aguinaga makes some generalizations, which seems to be the fate of the criticism of metaphysical poetry.[12] Such a statement as that describing the sonnet as 'an absolute metaphor' (p. 71), is beautiful and compelling, but of little value in understanding the sonnet unless it is applied to, or results from, actual analysis. A great deal of attention has been given the sonnet, yet it can be rightly maintained that some of this attention is polemical; in addition, critical analysis has been hampered by textual considerations questioning González de Salas's edition. Since most criticism of the sonnet is based on it, Blecua's recent edition not only demands that we take another look at the sonnet, but also makes possible a keener appreciation.[13]

The sonnet begins with the poet's show of respect for death's power to end his life. This respect is complemented by a solemn tone set off by the inversion of the verb in the future and the infinitive. The inversion slows down the cadence which accelerates only slightly with the normal order of verb and infinitive in line three. The alternating emphatic lines following enjambments isolate the poet's two adversaries: Death and Time. Death is the final shadow which will close his eyes and take away white day. Time will untie the soul from the body, slipping the subtle knot that makes him man. Respect and solemnity are structurally important and are emphasized through tone and alliteration. The *r*s evoke the chilling and awesome power of death; conversely, the soul is weary of life and longs to be freed. The sibilants evoke the fluttering of the soul's wings, as it anxiously awaits its freedom. Respect is also implied through the value-stating epithet. With the epithet 'la postrera sombra' the poet reinforces his respect for death's power. In opposition the fullness of life is implied by the epithet, 'el *blanco* día.' He has lived existence fully; life and love have brought light, and death will take it away. The quatrain, therefore, expresses the oppositions of death and life, and of the soul and the body, all of which will be subsequently developed. Respect, solemnity of tone and the overall majesty of the quatrain exalt the power of death and time to end life and loosen the soul's ties to the body.

In this double-dealing capacity of death and time we note two attitudes towards mortality, each expressed through corresponding images. The first is the death which submits man to perpetual darkness and oblivion, and which is anticipated with fear. The second is the release of the soul from worldly tribulations (Naumann, p. 334). Implicit in the latter is the topic of the desire for death as a liberation from erotic torment. Yet, for Quevedo, complete liberation from his passion implies corporal extinction, which he is at pains to accept. The sonnet, then, is geared to a conclusion which will accede to death's power to take away his life and free his soul to a better life; but the latter, in violation of a severe law, will take with it a substance of his corporal being: the memory of his love. Overcoming death, assuring some sense of corporal immortality, consists of not forgetting his love (Naumann, p. 334).

The stage is set for an act of defiance. The negative 'mas no' is asserted with force in stressed position. As Blanco Aguinaga notes, from the first line and the future 'podrá,' we anticipate what lines five and six will declare, 'Cerrar podrá . . . y podrá desatar . . . mas no . . . dejará' (p. 74). The soul will not forget the passion of love experienced in life.[14] Life, already expressed in 'blanco día,' is affirmed with extraordinary understatement as 'esotra parte.' The soul will leave behind that *other part*, the body.[15] In a compelling dramatization the soul will leave the body on the shore of life, but it will not forget its passion. It burned in the body's flames; 'en donde' is another spatial reference to the body, which will be developed in the sextet. The poet, then, affirms that the soul shall not forget where it experienced love. Aflame with love's passion, the soul can *swim* the cold waters of oblivion, losing respect for a severe law. The traditional fire–water antithesis is invigorated through presentation and context. The poet does not use the infinitive *cruzar*, 'to cross' (metrically equivalent), but *nadar*, which is concrete and emphasizes the soul's contact with powerless oblivion. With this image the poet intensifies the exhausted oxymoron into a formidable catachresis expressing love's determination. Leander swimming the Hellespont is a personification of love determined and ill-fated (311). Here the poet drops all mythological amplification (except the allusion to Lethe) and intensifies determination into realization. We have seen this image in a different context –

> Fuego a quien tanto mar ha respetado
> y que, en desprecio de las ondas frías,
> pasó abrigado en las entrañas mías . . . (292)

– in which the allusion to Lethe's waters emphasized that, despite distance and separation, the poet did not forget his beloved. The association of death was not relevant; here death and forgetfulness are both equally important. He projects into eternity the knowledge that in life he could not forget the experience of love, and the fire–water antithesis is transferred to a different context. He switches from the future to the present tense, 'nadar sabe,' because he can affirm, through belief and experience, that his love can defy oblivion. The future tense would attenuate the sonnet's emotional impact, since it would imply reservations with regard to love's power. The cold waters no longer refer to separation from the beloved, her coldness or his tears, but to the very frontier of life and death, and to the real separation of soul and body. He respects death's power to snuff out his life, but not to extinguish his love.[16]

The second quatrain ends with the major image, the theme, of Quevedo's love poetry. Love is a fire. W. Naumann confirms that no other image obsesses Quevedo more, captivating his soul both as marvel and horror, than fire. Since Quevedo experiences life in the same manner, as fire, then love and life are one in his existence. It is in this way that his fire imagery transcends the sentiments of an amorous tradition, and becomes, as well, the expression of an existential anguish.

Regarding theme and structure, Blanco Aguinaga sustains that there is no conventional development of the initial declaration of love's immortality; rather, the sonnet is divided in two parts, with the tercets declaring more emphatically the idea expressed in the octave. He further maintains that the sonnet is comprehended instantaneously with the first reading, which is experienced like a 'flash of lightning' simultaneously illuminating everything and eliminating the sonnet's temporal dimension (pp. 73–4). Blanco Aguinaga has grasped the sonnet's force, but the energetical relation between structure and theme still begs for more elucidation. Contrary to what he states, the sonnet is not divided into two well-defined parts, and it has a development proper to the sonnet form. The development of exposition, proposition, proof and conclusion is perfect. He further maintains that, from the conceptual point of view, the poet says the same thing twice. Yes and no. The principal concept is that love will endure after death, but there is more to it than this. The concept is related to the poet's experience in life. In the first quatrain we have the exposition that death will end life, and time will free the soul. The next quatrain proposes that, despite this, his love will cross the river of oblivion. The other terms of the oppositions, life and the body – expressed in 'blanco día,' implied in 'desatar,' reiterated in 'esotra parte' and in 'en donde' – will be developed in the sextet. Without them the central concept has no justification. Furthermore, the tercets will amplify the central image of love as fire. The poet affirms that his love will endure precisely because of what he so intensely experiences in life. It is this which will now be developed and which constitutes the poetic proof of the proposition. While it is true that the sonnet is comprehended instantaneously, this comprehension may not be achieved in quite the manner claimed by Blanco Aguinaga. We certainly experience in this sonnet what T. S. Eliot meant when he said that a 'genuine poem can communicate before it is understood' (p. 200). Quevedo's poem achieves much of this communication through a pattern of imagery and an intense rational and affective development that captivate us from beginning to end. At the conclusion, we immediately experience this 'communication,' the instantaneousness of which may be sensed as eliminating time. However, time, thematically opposed by the sonnet, is more effectively defeated by an astonishing structural innovation.

The first tercet is a parallelistic structure of extraordinary force and beauty. The lines are formulated as subject + relative pronoun + perfect tense. The poet describes life as a state in which his soul has been Love's prisoner, in which his veins have given humors to, have fed, his passion, in which his marrow has gloriously burned. The enumeration of 'Alma–venas–medulas' goes from the center of his spiritual being to the center of his physical being. The first two subjects are emphatically enumerated, but in 'medulas' the poet shifts the stress to the dark u. This rhythmic modulation intensifies the tercet's emotional swell. The modulation also results from a transition from enumerated superlative adjectives, 'todo–tanto,' to a functionally superlative adverb, 'gloriosamente.' With this adverb, echoing the conceit of 'gloria' in sonnet 479, 'gloriosamente ardido' expresses a fiery passion felt as heavenly, eternal. In this respect the enumerated perfect tense functions qualitatively, underlining the poet's state of existence, and communicating a sense of indefinite duration. The poet feels as if he has been in love all his life, and, because this experience has been so intense, he feels that it is timeless; therefore, he believes that his love will burn after death.

It has been current to read line nine as 'Alma que a todo un dios prisión ha sido,' the sense being that Love is the soul's prisoner. This version fails to take into consideration lines three and four, in which the soul anticipates its freedom from the body and its return to God. It is logical to assume that the soul is the prisoner, not only of the body (religious terminology), but also of Love. The latter has possessed both body and soul, and as the lover's body is consumed by passion, so the soul is Love's prisoner.[17] The idea of subordination or victimization is consistent in both lines. It would be remiss, however, to consider the soul as an unwilling victim. The experience of many of Quevedo's love poems emphasizes the contrary: the soul shares the body's passion. The concept expounded in this sonnet can be made clear by comparing it with sonnet 331:

> Lo que el humano afecto siente y llora,
> goza el entendimiento, amartelado
> del espíritu eterno, encarcelado
> en el claustro mortal que le atesora.

The soul is like a woman courted by two lovers: God and Love. Rightfully she belongs to God, but is possessed by Love. In order to get her back, God woos her, but she cannot resist the attraction of Love. While she is in the body, the latter has considerable power, making him a powerful god, 'todo un dios'; but with death she will be freed from her captivating suitor and return, 'a su afán ansioso,' to her rightful owner, but not without taking the memory of her corporal experience.

This distinction between prisoner and captive should not be understood as taking place exclusively in the metaphorical space of a prison. All criticism of this sonnet restricts 'prisión' to its usual sense of cárcel, 'prison';[18] but it can also be used in the sense of prisiones,[19] 'bindings' or 'fetters' ('La red que rompo y la prisión que muerdo,' 360). This is a meaning employed in a letter written by Quevedo around 1632, when he was in his fifties, in which he pleads for his soul's release from the bonds of carnal appetite:

Dice Mercurio Trimegisto, antiguo teólogo . . . que 'el amor del cuerpo es causa de la muerte, y que quien no aborreciere el cuerpo no se podrá amar a sí; porque es el cuerpo vestidura de ignorancia, fundamento de maldad, ligadura de corrupción, velo opaco, muerte viva, cadáver sensitivo, sepulcro portátil y ladrón de casa, que mientras halaga, aborrece; y mientras aborrece, invidia.' Desta condición es la casa que traemos con nosotros mismos. Él nos lleva tras sí porque no veamos el decoro de la verdad; él embota la vista de los sentidos exteriores y la ciega, y con la materia pesada los ahoga. Embriágalos con abominables defectos, por que nunca oigamos ni veamos aquellas cosas que se deben oír y mirar.

He includes himself among these unfortunate souls and prays for his release:

Señor, si piadoso ordenas favorecer mis deseos, pues criaste para ti mi alma a tu imagen y semejanza, y después contigo mismo la separaste, desátala de las ligaduras, donde en república mortal se ve sujeta a leyes de apetitos desordenados. Baste Señor, el tiempo que, ciega con la nube del cuerpo, vaga y errante, es forzada a obedecer albedríos tiranos. Desnúdame, Señor, destas prisiones (*Epistolario*, pp. 257, 259).

[The ancient theologian Mercurius Trimegistus says that 'love of one's body is the cause of death, and whoever will not hate his body will never be able to love himself; because the body is a cloak of ignorance, a base for evil, a ligature of corruption, an opaque veil, a living death, a corpse with feeling, a portable sepulchre, and a common thief; and while it flatters us, it despises us; and while it hates us, it envies us.' Such is the condition of the house we carry with us. This love drags us behind it so that we cannot see the propriety of truth; it covers the sight of our external senses, and makes us blind, and stifles our senses with its heavy burden. It stupefies them with abominable defects, so that we never hear or see those things which we ought to hear and see. Oh Lord, if it please thee to heed my prayers, since thou didst raise unto thee my soul in thy likeness and image, and thence from thyself didst separate it, release it now from the bonds of this mortal republic, where it is subject to uncontrollable appetites. Oh Lord, let cease the time of waiting, during which my soul, blinded by the cloud of my body, disordered and errant, is forced to obey tyrannic wills. Divest me, oh Lord, of these shackles.

With this additional meaning we can now see what the organic function of 'desatar' points to.[20] Death and Time will also slip Love's knot, freeing the soul to its spiritual lover, but the soul cannot regret having been Love's captive. With this image of 'prisión,' Quevedo condenses what has been his reality. Untying love's fetters also means the end of life. Love and life are one in his existence; and if the soul informs the body and the soul is in love, then love also informs the body. It makes his life, and this neither he nor his soul wants to forget. This belief is what the sextet is developing and affirming.

The poet expresses his mode of existence through many stylistic devices: parallelism, dynamic prosody, superlatives, expressive verbs, enumeration and accumulation. With these he also achieves another purpose. He whets our curiosity, forcibly underlining the sonnet's continuity through anticipation. Reading the first quatrain, the future tense gives us the sensation that an objection, a defiant act, will be made against death and time. The transition to the following quatrain is an anticipation fulfilled. We expect and are rewarded with, 'mas no . . . dejará.' A more intense anticipation occurs at the close of the initial tercet. Here the enumeration of three subjects, each characterized through a subordinate clause, leaves us at a peak of anticipation. Syntactically and ideologically, we expect a plural verb complementing the subjects and binding them into a single idea. But the poet upsets this expectation, surprising us with a verb in the singular. We are rationally disturbed by the break of rhetorical continuity; yet, because of the accumulated energy and the additional dynamism provided by another parallelistic stucture consisting of enumeration and bipartite lines, we proceed to the conclusion and are emotionally rewarded. In this sense the sonnet communicates before it is understood, reaching us through our emotions. However, we have to return to the sextet in order to supply a missing element,[21] at which time we discover a perfect correlation. The antecedent of each line of the concluding tercet is found in a similar position in the previous tercet. Line nine correlates with line twelve, ten with thirteen, and eleven with fourteen. We also note the sextet's structure is similar to the octet's: affirmation + objection + affirmation. In the octet the poet affirms a universal reality, then makes an objection in order to affirm an exceptional spiritual reality. In the sextet he affirms a *qualitative* state of being, whose intensity incites him to object to its complete demise, and to affirm love's transcendence. Through the rhetorical discontinuity, however, the structural formula is compressed, and the concept, or rather the conceit, attains tremendous emotional impact. The initial tercet builds up our anticipation; then, in the final tercet, each line, each hemistich drives home a point. Correlating the lines, we see that the soul, which has been Love's prisoner, will leave the body but not its passion. The body, anticipated all through the sonnet, is finally declared. The veins, which have nourished the intense fire of love, will be ashes but they will have feeling (or meaning); the marrow, which has gloriously burned, will be dust but dust in love. The final word, 'enamorado,' sums up his existence, mortal and eternal.

With this rhetorical discontinuity Quevedo anticipates modern poetry. Roger Shattuck, in his study of Apollinaire, describes the effect of what the French poet called 'simultanisme':

In poetry it . . . means an effort to neutralize the passage of time involved in the act of reading. The fragments of a poem are deliberately kept in a random order to be reassembled in a single instant of consciousness . . . Simultanism means a telescoping of time, a poetic technique that achieves the opposite effect from the regulated flow of music (p. 310).

Quevedo does not disperse the sextet's lines randomly, but correlates them in an A–B–C, A_1–B_1–C_1 pattern. By separating each member and upsetting the anticipated progression, he makes the reader return to A, B and C to pick up the rhetorical progression to their respective members. Blanco Aguinaga's idea of the defeat of time is based on captivation. When one is enthralled by an object's beauty, one is oblivious to time. This is the magic of intense aesthetic experiences. But what makes possible the sonnet's aesthetic temporal release is that the theme of time's defeat by love is structurally realized. The correlation of the dispersed lines facilitates their instant reassembly. Through this method of closure we apprehend the sonnet spatially, in a moment of time, rather than as a sequence.[22] Time's defeat comes in an instant, giving way to the poet's exultant reaffirmation of love's conquest. This is a type of poetry which, as Ezra Pound states, 'presents an intellectual and emotional complex in an instant of time,' thereby striking the reader with 'that sense of freedom from time limits and space limits; that sense of sudden growth, which we experience in the presence of the greatest works of art.'[23]

The technique of rhetorical discontinuity is an original contribution to that predilection metaphysical poets have for preventing the reader from gliding through a poem. The sonnet deals with love after death, but Quevedo will not have us breeze through an abstraction. Instead, he contrives to clutch our minds and emotions, momentarily detaining us at critical junctures and making us read lines twice so that the significance of what he has to say will jolt us. All of the sonnet's elements contribute to this end, and aside from the technique of the tercets, the imagery is particularly efficient. In order to make us feel what he has to say, he presents his ideas as concretely as possible. The sonnet contains twenty-six substantives, of which only eight are abstract. The rest are either concrete or rendered so through tropical language. Furthermore, there are only two lines, four and five, without a verb, of which there are fourteen. The sonnet, then, is a dynamic organic structure. Its concreteness and many verbs make it a poem of action, an action against death and time.

Blanco Aguinaga sustains that love's immortality was what Quevedo's predecessors were attempting to express. On the contrary, there is a radical difference between such poets as Garcilaso, Cetina, Herrera, Lope, and Quevedo.[24] The difference is that the former are still bound to the love theme; with them we have the feeling we are reading *only* love poetry. More important is that their concern with death is characterized by Renaissance equanimity and spirit. Theirs is either a serene resignation to the death of love and the beloved, or a *tentative* affirmation of love's victory (which points more to the acceptance of love's mortality than to its infinity); or else love's eternity is envisioned as a paradise, a perfection of the Renaissance world where the lovers stroll hand in hand through infinite green meadows; thus love's transcendence is envisioned in terms of this world, even in death. With regard to the Renaissance expression of love and metaphysical love poetry, Hoover affirms:

Love, be it human or divine, rarely finds its articulation in the Baroque lyric or in the amorous poetry of Donne and Quevedo as the supreme manifestation of transcendence in terms of this world. As major representatives of the Baroque, Donne and Quevedo express, rather, love's essential role as the omnipotent adversary of time, death, and oblivion . . . Their metaphysical orientation, like their Baroque obsession with death, bestows on the amorous relationships expressed in their poetry a unique significance far beyond that of ordinary love. Mutability, transience, and death thus yield to the expressed transcendence of the sublunar emotion of love, primarily because of the poets' irrepressible human yearning for immortality . . . Sexuality no longer reflects life's joyous vibrance, but rather the fundamental human urge toward the transcendence of death. In the Baroque, love's emotion is directed toward the unknown, toward mortality, whereas in the Renaissance it was directed toward the celebration of life, toward the known. Hence, the clarity of Renaissance confidence yields in the Baroque to the dark musings of poets who wander in an alien land, beset by doubts and despair, having lost contact with the center of their being, of nature, and of the cosmos. In their search for transcendence, they nevertheless courageously direct themselves toward the ultimate question which, although it remains unanswered, paradoxically defines the human condition (pp. 86–7).

Because of Quevedo's metaphysical orientation, 'Cerrar podrá' transcends love poetry, incorporating the same obsession with death which permeates his *Poemas metafísicos* and *Heráclito cristiano*. We can agree with Blanco Aguinaga that the sonnet transcends its amorous tradition, becoming metaphysical (p. 76), but it is doubtful that Quevedo's predecessors had such a goal in mind or were capable of expressing it. The courtly lover sought perfection in this world, but death brought an end to both love and life. For Quevedo love is not looked on as a means of personal improvement, but rather as an exaltation of existence in the face of solitude and annihilation. The transcendence experienced in life thus becomes a portent of love's transcendence in death.

Another distinction between Quevedo and the courtly poets is the intensity of his corporal love. Naumann calls the sonnet a pure pagan poem (p. 333). Pablo Neruda sees its intensity as an extension of the poet's intense carnal passion, adding that nowhere in the history of the Spanish language has there been such a lyrical debate of such furious magnitude between heaven and earth; only to Quevedo can death concede love's power.[25] It is the intense corporal experience of love, developed in the tercets, that justifies his belief in eternal love. Only such a carnal attachment could give impetus to the metaphysical projection of the body's passion.

In such sonnets as 460, 'Si hija de mi amor mi muerte fuese,' and 448, 'Si mis párpados, Lisi, labios fueran,' we have noted that Quevedo attempts to resolve the dualities of life and death, soul and body, through the enthymeme. By means of this persuasive conceit, he alleviates his afflictions, finding consolation in the expression of a poetical reality. In this sonnet, however, the poet does not propose an argument, but affirms a vehement belief in love after death. The sonnet is an act of extraordinary defiance and volition. There are implied enthymemes. One is the same as that expressed in sonnet 460: 'Love is a fire which inflames the soul; the soul lives on after death; therefore, the fire of love continues to burn after consuming the body.' The other is ' My body is in love; my body will turn to dust; therefore, my dust will love.' These are important, but only marginally so because the poet does not rely on their conclusions to justify the persistence of love. The poem is metaphysical because of contrasts whose terms differ in essence. The eternal and the mortal, the spiritual and the corporal are joined under tension. If the sonnet relied solely on the fallacious logic of the enthymeme, the tension would be attenuated. On the contrary, here the tension between love's oblivion and its immortality is maintained by the poet's volition. He yields to death's destruction of the body, but not to the destruction of his love.

Death may not destroy the poet's love, and exegesis will certainly not kill the sonnet. Great poetry often defies definitive interpretation. Rich expressiveness and ambiguity can create multiple levels of meaning and perspective. Both elements are present in Quevedo's sonnet; here we shall deal with ambiguity. For most critics the poet's body, reduced to ashes and dust, will continue to feel, 'mas tendrá sentido.' We cannot refute this interpretation nor do we wish to; however, it is possible to attach a different meaning to the final lines by considering closely the ashes–dust motif.

Laín Entralgo says that the motif of the *ceniza enamorada*, enamoured ashes, is frequently repeated in Quevedo's serious poetry (p. 42). The motif actually has a wide range, from light lyrics to this *soneto grave*. In sonnet 308, on the occasion of Ash Wednesday, the poet tells Aminta that her eyes are capable of prodigious feats; since they are fire, they can reduce to ashes whoever looks at them: 'las hazañas de tus ojos: / pues quien los ve es ceniza, y ellos fuego.' In sonnets 420 and 380 he relates the curious practice of having lovers' ashes put into hourglasses, a morbid but concrete conceit of eternal love.[26] In these poems the ashes do not really feel; they figuratively have life and feeling because of their movement as they pour through the glass, which is an 'eterno afán,' eternal anguish. The ashes, being the lady's plaything, symbolize her eternal disdain and her victim's eternal love.[27]

In a more serious vein, confronted by the threat of death, the poet envisions the soul as taking his corporal passion, while his ashes will give evidence of the fire that consumed him and point symbolically to an eternal fire:

> Llevara yo en el alma adonde fuese
> el fuego en que me abraso, y guardaría
> su llama fiel con la ceniza fría
> en el mismo sepulcro en que durmiese. (460)

In sonnet 479 we noted the poet lamented leaving a body that housed Love and his 'amante espíritu.' He regrets having to abandon the body's passion; yet, by recourse to *agudeza*, he envisions its salvation:

> Señas me da mi ardor de fuego eterno,
> y de tan larga y congojosa historia
> sólo será escritor mi llanto tierno.
> Lisi, estáme diciendo la memoria
> que, pues tu gloria la padezco infierno,
> que llame al padecer tormentos, gloria.

His soul, tormented in life by Lisi's splendor, anticipates the flames of hell; therefore, he will burn in death as in life, and his passion will endure and hell will thus be heaven. The idea of eternal burning is also voiced in sonnet 471:

> Basta ver una vez grande hermosura;
> que, una vez vista, eternamente enciende,
> y en l'alma impresa eternamente dura.
> Llama que a la inmortal vida trasciende,
> ni teme con el cuerpo sepultura,
> ni el tiempo la marchita ni la ofende.

[It is enough to see great beauty once; and, once seen, it kindles an eternal fire which, stamped into the soul, lasts for eternity. A flame which transcends to immortal life need not fear entombment with the body, nor will it be weakened or destroyed by time. (BB)]

By extending the concept of the optics of love, the poet anticipates eternal passion. The beloved's resplendent beauty is transcendently impressive, burning its image on his soul. And because the soul is immortal, so her beauty will be eternal. By extension, then, his love for her will achieve immortality.[28] We see that, although the idea of the body experiencing love after death is more frequent, there is a progression to the aspiration that the soul will feel for the body, taking with it the experience and memory of corporal passion.[29]

The final lines of 'Cerrar podrá' seem to indicate that the body's remains will continue to feel; its ashes will have feeling ('sentido'). This impression is reinforced by the concluding line: his marrow will be dust, but dust in love. The adjective 'enamorado' logically communicates the capacity of feeling. Yet, from a different perspective, these lines express an additional significance. The poet, anticipating the end of life, fully realizes death's power and does not resort to a witty enthymeme to prolong his corporal passion. Nevertheless, he wants to believe that, while death will bring an end to his body, it will not end its passion. The soul will take love's flame across the river of death and oblivion. The reason for this is that he refuses to believe that such an intense experience can ever end. This is the meaning his existence has given him. Therefore, after death the soul will leave the body but not its love. Although the body's remains will no longer feel, they will not cease to have meaning. 'Sentido' also has the important sense of 'meaning'; this is especially the case when used with tener, 'to have.' Because of his intense existence his ashes will have meaning. It was not in vain that he loved. His dust shall not be the decomposition of just anyone, but the decomposition of a man who loved and experienced life intensely. Dust and ashes shall have more than material significance. They shall possess eternal meaning; they will be 'polvo enamorado.'[30] It is not overtly stated, but the implication is there. The poet's ashes will be relics testifying to a glorious love. This is the meaning they will have for those who look upon his grave or read this sonnet.[31] As saints' relics have meaning because they are reminders of their devotion and love of God, so the poet's ashes will testify to his intense love for Lisi. The profane transmutation of religious terminology, motifs and symbols began with the emergence of courtly love; yet in this context the relic motif seems to have been somewhat infrequent.[32] The cause of Quevedo's sonnet is love-in-death. This idea is expressed in the quatrains and subsequently reinforced in line twelve. The soul will take the body's passion, resolving his duality and desire for immortality. The principal function of the tercets is to justify his belief in eternal love by developing the equally important idea of love-in-life. His ashes will have eternal meaning. As relics they may symbolize love everlasting, but their major significance comes from pointing to an extraordinary existence. We should not see this sonnet solely in terms of love after death, but, just as importantly, as an affirmation of life given meaning by love.

6

Conclusion

No hay soledad ni hombre solo, si sabe
aprovecharse el alma de su cuerpo y el
cuerpo de su alma. ('Sentencia 488')
[There is no solitude nor a solitary man, if
the soul can·avail itself of the body, and the
body of the soul.]

With regard to Quevedo's stoically influenced poetry, Blecua perceives that the poet's originality and authenticity consist in his 'having
turned those ideas into flesh and blood (in having lived the stoic
"theory," if you will), in having made them his own with all his
passion and anguish' (1971, p. c). This statement applies with equal
vigor to Quevedo's love lyrics and to the 'theory' of courtly love.

Quevedo's love poetry makes use of many commonplaces, yet if we
accept these as poetic truth, the poetry can move us intensely. This is
due, first, to the style, which through conceits – organic and
metaphysical – can unify the disparate elements of experience and
disclose the paradoxes and tensions of love. It is due, secondly, to the
poet's ability to penetrate deeply into the particular from the general,
thereby reaching the heart of the personal anguish that the commonplaces conceal through their conventional lip service to the
ideal.[1] Quevedo's successful reworking and defamiliarization of
commonplaces is also often accomplished by moving them into other
contexts and areas of experience, with the result that the commonplaces have only a vestigial association with their models. They
acquire more depth and complexity, and the 'theoretical' is presented in a broader context, as immediate and experiential.

We can agree with Green that courtly love was a theme with which
Quevedo was philosophically concerned (CLQ, p. 8); but this does not
mean that it was an existentially irrelevant theme. By confronting on
an imaginative and philosophical level the conflict between the ideal
and the real, and by responding on this level with his feelings,
conscience and experience – learned as well as lived – Quevedo
produced profound and moving poetry.

Nothing in Nobili's view of reality supports the ideal of human love
as viable and applicable to man's highest aspirations: 'I do not see
how Nature could be excused if, for such a frivolous purpose ['the so

very narrow limits of a woman'], it had produced in us so noble an emotion as Love is seen to be.' This desire for transcendence and the experience of Eros is frustrated by the antinomy of body and soul. Human love cannot bridge this barrier. Complete felicity can be experienced only in the afterlife, with the soul's immersion in the Fountain of the Absolute; so Nobili has to redefine human love in terms of real and practical ends. Since pure love is impossible to maintain, for it cannot completely satisfy the lover, human love now seeks physical reciprocation because of the lover's desire for generation in the beautiful and the alienation of his soul. This tension between the ideal and the real, acutely noted by Nobili, is developed by Quevedo into a personal anguish.

What Nobili observes as impossible in life, Quevedo attempts to make possible in the reality of poetry. Quevedo reaffirms the ideal of pure love, and to this end he is stimulated by the courtly genre. Provoked by a conscience telling him that pure love is the greatest good, and operating within the ethical confines of the genre, Quevedo aspires to the courtly ideal; yet it becomes difficult for him to accept the idea that true love is an indefinite 'halagüeña dilación' (353) bringing spiritual rewards but not physical ones. There are very few poems in which Quevedo expresses satisfaction with the courtly ideal, and some of these are tinged with irony or disclose through their tone a *persona* attempting to rationalize erotic frustration by disguising it as moral prescription.

Quevedo discovers in his world of poetry what Nobili had ascertained in the world of reality: there are no Lavinellos who can satisfy themselves completely with the spiritual and physical contemplation of the beloved. Quevedo's poetry communicates a deep sense of anguish as the human being is torn between the absolute demands of the spirit and the irresistible claims of the body. The most moving poem in this courtly context, 'En los claustros del alma,' expresses a profound disintegration. Contributing to this anguish is the fact that, unlike his courtly predecessors, he is aware that he is following a convention, and yet he is compelled to reflect critically on it. Quevedo's courtly love poetry, therefore, reveals a tension between the aesthetic realization of the genre and the ethos it propagates.

Three major themes expressed in this courtly poetry are alienation, *desengaño*, and death-in-life, the very same themes that predominate in Quevedo's non-amorous lyrics. This coincidence helps to explain the intensity which he brings to his love poetry. Love and life are intimately articulated in his existence: 'Es el amor la vida del corazón, y así como es imposible vivir el hombre sin vida, así es imposible estar sin amar el corazón' ('Sentencia 46'). What he experiences in one area of existence is encountered and intensified on another level of existence. In the context of the courtly genre, the frequency of these themes reflects a constant subjection to the unavoidable reality of the senses and a sensibility increasingly at odds with the courtly ideal.

Ultimately, Quevedo recoils from the courtly ideal. In order to overcome the affliction of the senses, he looks to intellectual love; yet the cleavage the latter causes between soul and flesh occasions an intense reaction. In his Neoplatonic love poetry we find the above themes expressed with equal, if not more, anguish. Because of the more patent expression of the duality of body and soul, and the poet's subsequent reaction, it is in this poetry that we begin to perceive Quevedo's philosophy of love.

Although the courtly genre, his conscience and culture may tell him that spiritual love is the most noble love experience, Quevedo feels he must give equal consideration to corporal love. Where Nobili saw a barrier to the realization of the noble impulse of love, 'the so narrow limits of a woman,' Quevedo saw an undeniable truth of human nature that needed to be celebrated. Body and soul are no longer in his view antagonists, but allies in the most praiseworthy of human experiences.

Quevedo is fully aware of the ontological difference between body and soul. The whole concept of courtly and Neoplatonic loves resides in this recognition. In the former it is their separation that causes suffering, and it is this martyrdom which the courtly lover cultivates. The latter attempts to transcend corporal attachment and sensual grief. Quevedo is also aware that spiritual and corporal loves correspond to different aspects or needs of human experience. Social, moral and religious teachings establish a hierarchy of values. Man recognizes that the spiritual is the most noble, yet because of his obeisance to it, it can cause a schism in his existence.

Warnke has noted that such divisive experience causes the Baroque poet to 'thirst for the single reality behind the disparate appearances of experience'; no longer content with a double vision of reality – spiritual and phenomenal, eternal and ephemeral – he seeks 'not to reconcile the two worlds but to reduce them to one' (1972, p. 22). The Baroque sensibility includes a 'conviction . . . that ultimate reality is some kind of all-embracing unity, accessible to the human spirit, if at all, only in moments of intense passionate experience' (1972, p. 52). Through the passionate experience of love, Quevedo endeavors to reduce the vying realities of the spiritual and the corporal to one.[2] He goes beyond the courtly tradition by pursuing the metaphysical consequences of the duality of body and soul, and the lover's death. His philosophical concern with courtly love becomes the stage for the expression of an existential obsession. In the final consideration, his love poetry is the expression of a struggle to overcome solitude: the solitude of the individual in the chaotic climate of the seventeenth century, the lover's solitude, the alienation of body and soul, the solitude of death.

The defeat of solitude and the experience of unity do not depend on a passive surrender to passion, but on a ratiocination of passionate experience. Quevedo's endeavor to harmonize a duality gives rise to a corresponding tension. The grief caused by pure love gives way to an anguish whose source is the very effort to achieve this harmony. As he struggles with his solitude, his feelings, his conscience and the courtly ideal, the metaphysical conceit provides him with a means not only of illuminating a conflict, but also of confronting it. Only such an effort of the mind and the imagination can attempt a resolution of the essential opposition of body and soul.

In the development of courtly love, apart from Neoplatonism, there was one other reaction or escape mechanism, the pastoral. As reality increasingly emphasized the courtly illusion, the ideal was maintained by idealizing it even more. Lover and beloved became shepherds; and in an idyllic setting, removed from the preternaturality of pure love, the 'rustics' made natural love (Huizinga, pp. 134–45). The reality courtly love kept avoiding and sublimating came to bear squarely on Quevedo. The rift between the body and soul was a torment for him; yet, instead of indulging a fantasy but living in an age still professing the superiority of the spirit, he could only affirm what he felt or wanted to be true, his reality, poetically. By means of *agudeza* (wit) and its concrete expression, the *concepto* (the conceit), he strove to create a poetical world in which body and soul are bound together, 'cuerpo que amante espíritu ha ceñido' (479).

Metaphysical poetry is concerned with universal problems, but its occurrence is rare, apparently taking place at critical stages of civilization. Such a period is seventeenth-century Spain:

Metaphysical poetry, springing from a concern with problems with which the universe must always present mankind, is not confined to either one age or country. Yet the conditions in which it can be produced are by their nature somewhat rare in occurrence. Metaphysical distinctions must have been made; further, these distinctions must be so familiar that they are no longer felt merely as a challenge to the intellect. They must rouse an altogether different emotional reaction, tinged, perhaps, with a certain scepticism. It appears, therefore, only at high points of civilizations; perhaps only when that civilization is halting for a moment, or is beginning to decay. I find traces of it . . . in Virgil; in Tasso of the *Aminta* . . . but most of all . . . in the Spain of the Philips. There metaphysics was to be breathed in at the nostrils. In consequence, in some of the plays of Calderón not the language merely, but the action is a metaphysical conceit; it is at once fleshly and spiritual, and the one, it seems, because the other. In his *autos* he developed a form of allegory . . . which would well repay examination. For in them it is not, for example a beautiful woman who dies, nor is it Beauty that ceases to manifest itself on the earth; but Beauty itself, incredible as it seems, that dies (J. Smith, pp. 44–5).

Beauty will die but in sonnet 460 the love of beauty may engender eternal life. Incredible as it seems, death is the child of love.

The Spanish expression of metaphysical poetry, *conceptismo*, appeared at a time when the civilization was decaying. Political and economic decline, spiritual and moral turmoil, contributed to a mood of disillusionment, *desengaño*. Formally, the *conceptista* exploration of the metaphor is an extension of Renaissance poetics, a pushing to the limits of imagery and commonplaces.[3] In the context of its cultural and intellectual environment, this exploration reflects a search for meaning and order.

Mahood states that 'The Baroque style is based upon a *feeling for the need* to reconcile the seemingly irreconcilable (p. 145, italics mine). This reconciliation could only be achieved through *ingenio*, the creative faculty of the mind and imagination. While *agudeza*, as a creative activity, had a primarily aesthetic function – the aim of the *concepto*, according to Gracián, was to create beauty – at the center of this sensibility was the poetic of correspondence.[4] The *conceptistas* believed that a network of correspondences united every aspect of existence. In this guise God was the consummate *conceptista* who created and hid these correspondences, leaving them to be discovered by man. This principle of universal analogy was not new when cultivated by the *conceptistas* and the Metaphysicals; 'what was new is that the principle was used as the basis of a poetic for the first time' (Mazzeo, 1952, p. 89). This principle does not explain *conceptista* or metaphysical poetry, but knowing what these poets worked with gives us an insight into their world view and into the nature of their imagination.

The new aesthetic was a significant development. The Renaissance artist had worked in concert with Nature, or like Nature, to create an artifact; the creation was an ordering of Nature. With the increased importance of the imagination, with its autonomy in the creative act, the *conceptista* not only orders Nature but creates a Nature that vies with reality. The conceit, the metaphor, represents a metamorphosis of reality: 'Imagination stretches the mind, then, because it "stretches" reality by the linguistic means of metaphor. Given this, metaphor . . . is a thought in its own right.'[5] With *conceptismo* and metaphysical poetry, we now have *poiesis* instead of *mimesis*.

By discovering, perhaps inventing, a correspondence between things radically disparate, the *conceptista* may have achieved some sense of order and meaning in his world. This endeavor, noted by J. Smith, seems 'tinged with scepticism.' A metaphysical conceit does not, ultimately, supplant reality or modify a truth; yet the poet can take aesthetic, intellectual and emotional satisfaction, achieving this 'feeling' from the creation of a poetical reality, from forging what he would like to be true. One of the final impressions received from a poem like 'Cerrar podrá' is that it does not so much convey a meaning as constitute an experience, the imaginative experience of the resolution of opposing truths, of the reduction to one all-embracing reality of the conflicting realities of the body and soul, of eternity and corporal extinction.[6]

With this 'poetics' of *conceptismo*, we do not mean that behind every conceit there is an attempt to metamorphose reality or to find meaning and order in the world. The conceit can be merely frivolous and decorative, or it can be organic and illuminate a theme. On a more ambitious level, the conceit does more and can constitute an experience, 'because it alone can give order to the riot of the senses, control the clash of emotions and harmonize the dichotomy of ideas' (Parker, 1977, p. 80). The conceit can be an aesthetic means of existential integration.

Quevedo's conceits reflect the problems of living in a tumultuous age. They are often intense and tinged with anguish, dealing as they do with ideological and personal conflicts and the attempt to harmonize them. Allied with this is the element of tension, the metaphysical note. Taking into consideration that *what* the poet can say and *why* and *how* he can say it are partly determined by his culture, and to a good extent by his imagination operating within a particular place, time and environment, we have in the Baroque a set of cultural, personal and artistic conditions articulating in an exceptional manner. In this context Quevedo's expression of his cultural and personal experience is the revelation of a singular intensity of living.

The metaphysical note is frequently perceived in Quevedo's love poetry; but, with the exception of 449, 'En crespa tempestad,' it is not detected in those poems dealing with courtly love *per se*. It is only when courtly love begins to take on a Neoplatonic configuration or when death pervades the poet's experience that the metaphysical note starts vibrating. Its absence in his courtly love poetry possibly points to an attitude toward an ideal that he cannot wholeheartedly embrace.

Sonnet 448, 'Si mis párpados, Lisi, labios fueran,' is an extended conceit, a witty argument proposing, 'If my eyelids were lips, Lisi, I could kiss you with my rays of vision; therefore, every time I saw you, I could make love to you.' If we pay attention only to the correlation of form, not perceiving the serious dimension behind the ludic ambience, then the metaphor's terms come together, briefly entertain us, and fly apart. In other words, we note the similarity between eyelids and lips, and this is sufficient to entertain a 'farfetched' metaphor, which will disintegrate once the sonnet is concluded. On the other hand, if we consider what the metaphor's elements point to, taking into consideration the sonnet's double perspective, then this holds the metaphor up to contemplation. Neoplatonism tells the poet that only the souls should love, 'desnudos de cuerpo,' but his senses want to enjoy Lisi's physical favors. The poet attempts to resolve this conflict through the conceit, thereby satisfying both faculties simultaneously. His spiritual love is indicated by the eyes, his sensual love is pointed to by the lips; the poet longs for 'his eyelids to be the lips of the soul' (ter Horst, p. 47). The sonnet is born out of anguish because, philosophically and/or in real life, he is beset by a conflict. In the sonnet he achieves an ecstatic experience: two loves differing in essence are united. Reality is reconstructed into something ideal and beautiful, making life, if only momentarily and poetically, more tolerable. On the one hand reality pulls the conceit apart, and on the other a different reality, a poetical one, holds it together. The result of this particular tension is the metaphysical note.

We discover the metaphysical conceit again in sonnet 321:

Puédese padecer, mas no saberse;
puédese codiciar, no averiguarse,
alma que en movimientos puede verse.
No puede en la quietud difunta hallarse
hermosura, que es fuego en el moverse,
y no puede viviendo sosegarse.

Here the conceit is similar to the one in Donne's 'The Second Anniversary':

her pure, and eloquent blood
Spoke in her cheeks, and so distinctly wrought,
That one might almost say, her body thought.

This is the type of image that is startling, but, because it is plausible, not so startling: 'Here body accepts the attribute of thought, without ceasing to be body; and thought, persisting as such, immerses itself in body. And both gain thereby: for they appear no longer as abstractions, but as a reality that requires nothing further for its completion' (J. Smith, pp. 34, 37). In Quevedo's sonnet the soul can be endured but not known; it can be coveted but not understood; yet when it dances with the body, they 'both gain thereby': they make beauty. Alone one is not seen, the other is dead; together, spirit and matter make fire.

The metaphysical note vibrates intensely in the presence of death. The 'courtly' sonnet 449 expresses a conflict between reason and passion:

Con pretensión de fénix, encendidas
sus esperanzas, que difuntas lloro,
intenta que su muerte engendre vidas.

The heart asks if its ardent death in the fire of passion will not lead to a new life; is its passion not like the phoenix and capable of perpetual renovation? No, replies reason (Parker, 1952, p. 52). This distinction between reason and passion is not in itself a genuine metaphysical opposition, but it can become one to the extent that it is directed at the essential contrast eternal/temporal. Terry says:

'the heart acts as if love were eternal; the reason knows it is not'... though he may acknowledge reason to be in the right, the lover will continue to act as his passion demands. Thus the final effect, I would claim, is 'metaphysical' in Smith's sense of the term: in the phoenix image, the juxtaposition of eternal and temporal qualities is surprising, as any conceit must be, yet at the same time is not arbitrary. It is possible to speak of unity, even though the tension remains (1958, pp. 216–17).

In this sonnet reason vies with passion; however, when the poet contemplates the very imminence of death, mind, will and heart join forces.

In sonnet 479 we have seen that the poet accepts death, but regrets having to leave a body where love was housed. He wants his passion to endure, so he appeals to wit:

> Lisi, estáme diciendo la memoria
> que, pues tu gloria la padezco infierno,
> que llame al padecer tormentos, gloria.

The conceit involves an obvious *equívoco*, 'gloria,' and two commonplaces: the inferno of love and the heavenly beloved. The conceit is not startling; yet when we consider that the commonplaces are pushed to their limits so as to bridge the gap between mortality and eternity, then the conceit gains intensity.

The imaginative and rational inquiry into the mystery of his passions yields metaphysical propositions, but at this point Quevedo is not concerned with these propositions in themselves, philosophically; rather he is concerned with the lovers who are the soul and the body, who are two yet united by love, but who strive against each other because of an ontological difference, because God and conscience impose a higher law on Nature. He is concerned with the threat that death poses to these lovers, their eventual separation, with the consequences of corporal extinction and absolute solitude. In sonnet 479 we do not take literally the argument that the lover wants to go to hell so as to continue burning in his passion. The argument gives rise to a metaphysical strain because the poet attempts to eternalize love and the body's passion.

As we have emphasized, the metaphysical conceit is remarkably realized in sonnet 460, and again is the result of taking a commonplace seriously: love causes death. When this is associated with the common belief that death marks the birth to eternal existence, the idea that death is the child of love makes for a fascinating metaphysical conceit. The astonishing thing about it is that it sounds plausible, and, although it is abstract, it gives our mind food for thought.

Quevedo's metaphysical preoccupation with death gives a profound dimension to his love poetry. If he strives to make love a joint activity of body and soul, death threatens to destroy the body, subsequently bringing an end to love. The poet's obsession with achieving, in some way, corporal immortality hinges, therefore, on the possibility of loving beyond death. In other words, this metaphysical dimension involves the reversal of cause and effect. Faced with the reality of corporal extinction, by the power of love and the metaphysical conceit, Quevedo expresses the eternalization of corporal passion.

Sonnet 472, 'Cerrar podrá mis ojos,' is metaphysical because of conceits whose terms deal with oppositions differing in essence, creating a tension between these terms, between the oblivion of death and what the poet struggles to believe. The sonnet contains two closely connected conceits: 'nadar sabe mi llama la agua fría,' and 'polvo serán, mas polvo enamorado.'[7] The word play on 'ceniza' and 'tendrá sentido' are also important. The metaphysical oppositions involved are body and soul, the temporal and the eternal.

The first conceit is in itself complex because it contains three metaphors: 'llama' (immortal love); 'nadar' (determination and defiance); 'agua fría' (death and oblivion). The root of the conceit is the catachresis 'nadar,' which makes possible the linking of 'llama–agua fría.' 'Ceniza' compresses two meanings and traditions announced in the initial quatrain. The first is the ashes of the burial service, which reflects at once the fear of death, and the concept of death as liberation (see p. 129). The second is the ashes of the fire of love, expressing a mode of intensified existence, and pointing to immortality, 'tendrá sentido.'

In the second conceit, 'ceniza' and 'polvo' are conceptually related because of their mutual cause, 'fuego.' However, 'polvo' is more than a variant; it is a reiteration providing an uncomplicated perception of the final decomposition of the body. The epithet 'enamorado,' reintroducing the secondary meaning of 'ceniza,' qualifies 'polvo' in an extraordinary way. The temporal is made eternal by the action of love.

It is possible to discover in the sonnet a third conceit. Applying Smith's observation on Calderón's *autos* to the sonnet, we see that here as well the *action* is a metaphysical conceit.

In 'Cuando me paro a contemplar mi estado' ('When I pause to consider my state'), Garcilaso lamented the death of love:

mas cuando del camino esó olvidado,
a tanto mal no sé por dó he venido;
sé que me acabo, y más he yo sentido
ver acabar conmigo mi cuidado.

[But when I ignore the road, I don't know how I have reached such evil; I know I've reached my end, and I regret the more to see my [loving] sufferings end along with me. (ER)]

Quevedo's sonnet, on the contrary, defies the forces of death and oblivion. It is a conceit of action stated by the heart and will: 'Alma a quien todo un dios prisión ha sido, / . . . / su cuerpo dejará, no su cuidado.' But this is not enough for Quevedo, as he needs a metaphor that will crystallize this conceit, and he finds it in 'polvo enamorado.' In the Spanish Baroque's most compelling metaphysical conceit, the poet's transcendent theme is triumphantly accomplished: the yoking of physical and spiritual realities, even in death. The sonnet is metaphysical three times over. It is the exultation of an accomplishment impossible in life or death, but possible through poetry.

Quevedo's philosophical concern with courtly love goes beyond the convention when his love poetry moves into the area of his metaphysical preoccupations. The concept of pure love antagonizes the duality of body and soul, and love brings with it the threat of its destruction. One of the profound paradoxes of human nature is the increased awareness of death which love brings: 'to love completely carries with it the threat of annihilation' (May, p. 100).

In Quevedo's most intense love poetry dealing with these metaphysical preoccupations, the woman, the cause of love, disappears. She gives way to an anguished love affair between body and soul, and to an agonizing resistance to accepting the body's complete mortality. Here his poetry becomes intensely existential. At the core of his love poetry and lyrical meditations on death is the anguish of solitude, *la soledad*.

We have emphasized the tension in Quevedo's love poetry. This tension has different causes and manifestations. There is, first, the tension between the aesthetic realization of the courtly genre and the ethos it propagates. Second, we note the tension betwen the two points of view in those sonnets containing a ludic element. Third, there is a decided tension, the metaphysical note, arising from the poet's efforts to unite the separate realities of body and soul, and to survive his mortality. In the expression of these conflicts, much of this tension is contained within the metaphysical conceit, from the unity and discord of its elements. Ultimately, and underlying this conceit, we perceive the tension between what a metaphysical sonnet ecstatically declares and the despair that this same sonnet is attempting to overcome. This note of despair is most perceptible in

'Cerrar podrá.' After the poetic force of the sonnet has waned, we sense, alongside its transcendent statement, not only desperation but also something macabre about the conclusion. The very idea of dust and bones seems to vie with the attempt to make something blissful and enduring out of them. Poetical reality is *all* the sonnet is. It is a magnificent and noble expression, but a great illusion. At heart it is an anguished and desperate poem.[8]

Courtly love poetry effectively ended in Spain with the posthumous editions of Francisco de Quevedo's poetry in the mid-seventeenth century. The genre had essentially run its course by the close of the preceding century, but Quevedo invigorated the tradition. He inherited a fully developed yet exhausted lyric tradition with a repertory of amorous vocabulary and imagery, which served as the medium for the expression of his experience of love. Although he employed almost every aspect of the courtly convention, in many of his poems he was never conventional. His aesthetic and philosophical exploration of the genre led to the expression of a compelling personal experience that goes beyond the courtly tradition to address the profound preoccupations of human existence.

Notes

I INTRODUCTION

1. J. H. Elliot, *Imperial Spain*, pp. 293–5. For an insight into Quevedo in the context of national pessimism and *desengaño*, see H. Ettinghausen, *Francisco de Quevedo and the Neostoic Movement.*
2. The parallel between national illusion and the illusion of ideal love, both being a self-deception, has been pointed out by A. Zahareas and T. R. McCallum in 'Toward a Social History of the Love Sonnet: The Case of Quevedo's Sonnet 331,' *Ideologies and Literature*, 91–9. Sonnet 331 is discussed in chap. 4.
3. 'Ora quando senza offesa delle leggi il corpo della Donna amata intieramente godere non si può, chi chercherà di godere almen l'animo con esser contra cambiato in Amore, & di questo in gran parte s'appagherà, & di vederla, & di vdirla, e di pensar di lei, senza fallo humanamente amerà; ma più d'una volta maledirà la fortuna, che altrui habbia fatto possessor del corpo,' facsimile reprint, fol. 24r. This facsimile was published on the occasion of the tercentenary (1895) of Torquato Tasso's death, including the extensive marginalia the Italian poet recorded in his copy of the treatise. Quevedo's marginalia seem to be limited to two notes on fols 9 and 10 (discussed in chap. 4); however, he recorded eight poems on fols 1–4, four of which are love sonnets of the Lisi cycle. It is worth examining the attraction that such a minor *trattatista* as Nobili held for these two great poets. This study will deal with the attraction it held for Quevedo. His copy of the treatise is in the British Library, MS. Additional 12108. See J. O. Crosby, 'La creación poética en ocho poemas autógrafos,' in *En torno a la poesía de Quevedo*, pp. 15–42.
4. *Obras completas, prosa*, F. Buendía, ed., p. 136. The English title of this prose satire corresponds to the translation of the author's *Sueños*, *Visions*, by Sir Roger L'Estrange, 1667; reprint 1962.
5. The Junta de Reformación was established to bring about the 'regeneration of Castile' through moral and economic reform, and was convinced that the two were 'inextricably intertwined' (Elliott, p. 322).
6. The Marqués de Santillana (1398–1458) was the first to attempt this in his *Sonetos fechos al itálico modo*; but these 'formal exercises' reveal that he was unable to assimilate the dynamic and undulating rhythms of the hendecasyllable line because his poetic thinking was more attuned to the monotonous rhythm of the twelve-syllable *arte mayor* line.
7. E. Mérimée, *Essai sur la vie et les oeuvres de F. de Quevedo*, p. 397. This attitude prevailed at least to 1946 with A. González de Amezúa, *Las almas de Quevedo*, p. 16. For an overview of Quevedian criticism in this regard, see Otis Green, *Courtly Love in Quevedo*, pp. 3–9; henceforth *CLQ*.

8. *Quevedo*, p. 500; sonnet 358 from Quevedo, *Obra poética*, I, J. M. Blecua, ed., p. 525. Poetry from this source will be indicated by the poem number.
9. The 'dolorido desgarro' is difficult to translate. In this context 'dolorido' means 'painful' or 'suffering'; 'desgarro' literally means a 'rip'; 'desgarrado,' 'torn apart.' The idea is that of something, an emotion, that cannot be contained but is 'wrenched' from one, causing a painful wound.
10. The idea of putting this type of expression in a sonnet is already an indication of a move away from the principle of decorum: 'Es el *Soneto* la más hermosa composición, y de mayor artificio y gracia de cuantas tiene la poesía italiana y española'; Herrera, *Garcilaso de la Vega y sus comentaristas*, A. Gallego Morell, ed., p. 308.
11. 'Gotas' is a play on the meaning 'drops' (so that the woman gives herself to his tears, without payment), and on the meaning 'gout.' Since it was believed that gout was a rich man's disease, and he could afford treatment, the speaker's 'inflammation' has no money; hence, it cannot pay for relief.
12. The poet's 'chief fault' is 'the use of words and phrases that are low and essentially unpoetical'; G. Ticknor, *History of Spanish Literature*, II, p. 262.
13. For an excellent discussion of *conceptismo* and *agudeza* (conceit and wit), see A. A. Parker's introduction to the bilingual edition of Luis de Góngora's *Polyphemus and Galatea*, pp. 1–50.
14. L. Pfandl, *Historia de la literatura española*, p. 52. *Culterano* and *culteranismo* refer to the latinization of Spanish syntax and diction. They were applied to Góngora by analogy to 'Luterano'; that is, Góngora, vis-à-vis the tradition of Spanish poetry, was considered by many to be, like Luther, a heretic. See A. A. Parker, *Polyphemus*, pp. 10–11.
15. 'Yo soy contento a que ría el alba'; *Don Quijote*, I, 20; see also Calderón de la Barca, *La dama duende*, III, ll. 81–115.
16. 'Sentencia 474,' *Obras completas, prosa*, L. Astrana Marín, ed., p. 243. Subsequent 'Sentencias' will be from this source and will be indicated by number.
17. 'La "agudeza" en algunos sonetos de Quevedo,' *Estudios dedicados a Menéndez Pidal*, p. 356; quotation from Calderón, 'El hacer versos [es] una gala del alma o agilidad del entendimiento,' in E. Cotarelo, *Ensayo sobre la vida y obras de D. Pedro Calderón de la Barca* (1929), p. 287.

2 THE CONCEPTION OF AN IDEAL

1. 'Il nome d'humano in doppio significato prendiamo. Percioche alle volte significa quello, che comunalmente suole ne gli huomini hauer luogo, alle volte significa solamente quello, che all'honestà, & alle leggi è conforme; si come il nome etiandio del ragioneuole alle volte attribuiamo a tutti gli huomini, ma alle volte a quegli soli, che secondo la dritta, & buona ragion, viuono. Adunque nel primo sentimento tutti gli . . . Amori sono humani, ma nel secondo solamente i due ultimi, ciò è uno di hauer la sua amata per Moglie, & l'altro di goder l'animo, & la vista,' fol. 24r–v.
2. A. J. Denomy, *The Heresy of Courtly Love*, p. 20; see also P. Dronke, *Medieval Latin and the Rise of European Love-Lyric*; O. H. Green, *Spain and the Western Tradition*, I, pp. 72–95; C. S. Lewis, *The Allegory of Love*; F. X. Newman, ed., *The Meaning of Courtly Love*; P. Salinas, 'La tradición de la poesía amorosa,' in *Jorge Manrique o tradición y originalidad*; M. J. Valency, *In Praise of Love: An Introduction to the Love Poetry of the Renaissance*; R. Boase, *The Origin and Meaning of Courtly Love: A Critical Study of European Scholarship*, only came to my attention as this study was near completion.

3. There seems to be no recorded history documenting that the courtly ideal was ever maintained in life: 'How far did courting and flirtation during the fourteenth and fifteenth centuries come up to the requirements of the courtly system ... Autobiographical confessions are very rare at that epoch. Even when an actual love-affair is described with the intention of being accurate, the author cannot free himself from the accepted style and technical conceptions' (Huizinga, *The Waning of the Middle Ages*, p. 122). This is a noteworthy observation on the pervasive influence of a style on the mentality of several centuries.

4. With regard to individual poems, the terms 'cause' or 'intention' will often be used instead of theme. This is not to incur what in modern criticism is called the 'intentional fallacy'; rather, under Renaissance poetics a poem was required to *disclose* its intention; if it failed to do so, it was considered defective. In her study of Elizabethan and metaphysical poetics, R. Tuve states that *cause* 'combines the meaning of "poetic subject" and "poet's intention" ... Although close to the Aristotelian "final cause," it has, as used by Elizabethans, less of self-conscious calculation than our words *aim* or *purpose*' (*Elizabethan and Metaphysical Imagery*, pp. 12–13; see also Terry, *An Anthology of Spanish Poetry*, 1, p. xix).

5. Reference will be made occasionally to types of hendecasyllable lines. All have a constant stress on the tenth syllable, and vary in the distribution of the other two. An emphatic line stresses the first and sixth syllables; a heroic line, the second and sixth; a melodic line, the third and sixth; the sapphic line stresses the fourth and eighth syllables; and the *variante pura italiana* or anapestical stresses the fourth and seventh; see Baehr, *Manual de versificación española*, pp. 135–7.

6. On the function of imagery, see Tuve, p. 25, and Terry, 1, p. xxi; also the discussion of sonnet 465, p. 71.

7. L. Astrana Marín indicates the 'Fabio' identity in poem 432, 'Fabio, sobrenombre que se puso Quevedo en su época de estudiante en Valladolid, según su canción "Llaméme entonces Fabio"' (Quevedo, *Obras completas, verso*, Astrana Marín, ed., p. 744, n. 1). Although the identity of 'Fabio' is evident, the name was a commonplace in poetry of this epoch.

8. Denomy, p. 23; Lewis, pp. 13–14; Andreas, pp. 100–07.

9. The sense of the line is 'la gloria que se emplea en la posesión.' A similar hyperbaton, whereby the article is separated from the noun ('la ... cama'), is found in the twenty-seventh stanza of Góngora's *Polifemo*: 'Vagas cortinas de volantes vanos / corrió Favonio lisonjeramente / a la de viento cuando no sea. cama / de frescas sombras, de menuda grama.' See Parker, *Polyphemus and Galatea*, pp. 37, 143.

10. 'Peor' in this context means more readily, not worse. It can also be read as an ellipsis: 'peor sería la pérdida.'

11. 'non altrimenti potersi possedere la bellezza, che riguardando, & contemplando. Imperoche l'occhio, & la mente nostra altro modo non hanno da possedere, che questo,' fol. 13r.

12. 'Ariosto and Garcilaso,' 1962, p. 163; see also his 'Bembo, Gil Polo, Garcilaso, Three Accounts of Love,' 1966, p. 535, in which he criticizes Green (*Tradition*, 1, 1968) for propagating the ideal of courtly love.

13. '"Delante." Vale lo mismo que en presencia de alguna persona.' In the context of memory and imagination, 'delante' also points to 'poner delante. Phrase metaphorica, con que se explican las imagenes ù otras especies, que se suelen representar a la idea ... segun el estado en que por entonces se halla la imaginacion,' *Dicc. Auts.*

14. '[la lontananza] è stata riputata più tosto cote de accendere Amore, che acqua

per ispegnerlo, & giudicata oltre a ciò di maggior felicità all'Amante, che la presenza,' fol. 44v.

15. R. M. Price sees Neoplatonic considerations in the first tercet. This is a possible reading, given that the highest level of human love and the lowest one of Neoplatonic love overlap. Price's view is perhaps determined by his reading of the conclusion: 'The final tercet rejects any courtly considerations of reward or consolation; he aspires not to Lisi, but to heaven, the source of her beauty and her soul' (Price, *An Anthology of Quevedo's Poetry*, p. 114). It would seem, rather, that the poet rejects any guerdon in order to be the ideal courtly lover; furthermore, the final line is not a 'Not . . . but' construction, rather a comparative, 'less . . . than.' Lisi is less accessible than heaven.

16. An incomplete version of this sonnet is found on fol. 3v of Nobili's treatise; see Crosby, 'La creación poética en ocho poemas autógrafos,' in *En torno a la poesía de Quevedo*, pp. 13–42. It is also reproduced in Blecua's edition, p. 665.

17. 'Nel genere de gli enti,' Torquato Tasso, 'Discorsi del poema eroico'; discussed in *Poems of Góngora*, R. O. Jones, ed., p. 10.

18. 'Alma es del mundo Amor; Amor es mente' (332). A. Paterson reads this imitation of Torquato Tasso's 'Amore alma è del mondo, Amore è mente' as a parody; see '"Sutileza del pensar" in a Quevedo Sonnet,' pp. 131–42.

19. *The Mind's Wit and Art*, 1, L. H. Chambers, trans., pp. 94–7. 'Algún sutilísimo artificio, que . . . es el verdadero constitutivo del concepto . . . o correlación artificiosa,' Gracián, *Agudeza*, 1, p. 55.

20. 'Non troppo lungamente in questa contemplatione delle uniuersali, & eterne bellezze si fermaua; anzi quasi augelletto d'inferma piuma, che dal nido allontanarsi non ardisca, alla particolare di M. Laura tornaua,' fol. 25r.

21. 'chi più lo sperimenta meno della sua natura, & qualità conosce. Percioche prouandolo, o piacer vi sente, o dolore. Se piacere ne prende, troppo migliore il giudica, che egli non è, & con troppo maggiori lode il celebra che non vale. Ma se ne riceue martiri, il reputa dannoso & rio sì, che in biasimarlo trapassa fuor di misura la verità. Così ò tristo ò lieto ch'egli si sia, la passione gli torce gli occhi, & il fa trauedere,' fols 5v–6r.

22. 'Amore s'intende quel piegamento, & affettione dell'animo nostro verso il bello . . . Bellezza . . . è principalmente la attillata compositione delle parti del corpo humano, & la conueneuole proportione delle dette parti verso di se, & verso il tutto, con vaghezza di colore, & gentilezza d'aria; la qual gentilezza essendo una certa luce trasfusa dall'animo nel volto, et massimamente ne gli occhi,' fol. 7r–v.

23. 'Il conoscere non è altro, che riceuere gli oggetti nella potenza conoscente . . . Ora se la bellezza non è altro, che quella proportione di membra . . . senza fallo ne segue, non altrimenti potersi possedere la bellezza, che riguardando, & contemplando. Imperoche l'occhio, & la mente nostra altro modo non hanno da possedere, che questo . . . la bellezza del corpo si gode col mezzo della vista . . . La bellezza dell'animo col pensare dello stesso animo, & colla vista dello intelletto si gode. Ma perche, mentre che gli animi sono rinchiusi in questa pregione del corpo, non si possono scorgere l'un l'altro da faccia a faccia . . . conuiene che delle parole, & dell'udito, quasi di finestre per veder l'animo, ci vagliamo,' fols 12v–13r, 14r.

24. 'Non senza cagione adunque il gentilissimo Bembo volendo in persona di Lauinello formare uno schietto Amatore di humana bellezza, l'introduce tale, che solo colla vista, & coll'udito, & col pensiere di goder l'amata Donna s'appaga,' fol. 14v.

25. 'A me certamente non è mai auuenuto di conoscere alcun Lauinello, il quale si contentasse di goder la bellezza in quel modo, nel quale propriamente si gode la

NOTES TO PP. 45-6

bellezza, dico col vedere, coll'vdire, col pensare, anzi ho veduto, che tutti . . . vorrebbono sodisfare al tutto: & quel che dice Philone esser fine dell'Amore, il goder la bellezza con vnione, a me non si lascia troppo ben comprendere: Imperoche, se della corporale fauelliamo, a goderla non si richiede unione, ma più tosto giusta distanza tra l'occhio, & lei: se della bellezza spirituale, cio è dell'animo della Donna amata, primieramente in questo mondo con tale bellezza unire non ci possiamo, ne puramente vederla, percioche ci si attrauersanno nel mezzo questi corpi materiali, & grossi; & oltre a ciò, quando puramente la potremo vedere, non in lei ci appagheremo, ma nel Fonte della Diuina Bellezza, vera, & compiuta felicità nostra,' fol. 17r.

26. 'ragioneulomente niegò Platone Amore esser desio di bellezza, non perche nell'Amore non si desideri di veder il bello, che ardentemente si desidera; ma perciò, che questo non era il principal fine del desiderio amoroso, ma bene l'immortalarsi, & propagarsi col partorire,' fol. 17v.

27. 'Aristotele . . . è vusato di penetrare più a dentro, che tutti gli altri, così in questa mi pare, che toccasse molto il viuo, conchiudendo per ferma ragione questo vicendeuole Amore essere il desiderato fine dell'Amore . . . Et lasciamo stare, che la Donna, quasi altro testimonio non ha da assicurarti del suo Amore, la qual certezza è da se ardentemente disiderata, saluo il farti dono della sua persona,' fols 18r, 22v.

28. 'Raccontasi parimente d'Aristotele, che era usato di dire Amore non douer essere ne per lo congiugnimento de i corpi, ne senz' esso; quasi volesse inferire, che principal fine douer essere l'vnione de gli animi, ma pure etiandio quella de i corpi richiederuisi; poiche quegli habitando in questi, tanto più pare che si uniscano, quanto più s'accostano i corpi,' fol. 23v.

29. 'è conceduto il bacio, il quale alla fine è pur congiugnimento di corpi, & comune ancho alle bestie; talche questo congiugnimento non ripugna all'Amore humano (intendendo per Amore humano quello, che è ragioneuole, & honesto) se non segue la violatione delle leggi, ò se non si trapassano le altre conditioni della temperanza,' fol. 24r. It was thought that the lovers exchanged their souls through the kiss; it was for this purpose that this physical union was permitted. See *The Courtier*, pp. 349–50, and my article, '"El pasadizo que hay de un cuerpo a otro": ¿amor mixtus o amor purus en un poema de Quevedo?'

30. 'A questo Diuino Amore no sò già quanto necessaria scala sia la bellezza donnesca; percioche il considerare i miracolosi, & pur ordinati effetti dalla Natura, i muouimenti stabili del Cielo, il vigor della luce, la perfettione dell'vniuerso, mi pare molto più sicura strada per condurci alla cognition della somma Belleza, che il perdersi, & star fisso in un volto,' fol. 25r-v.

31. 'di questo parere auiso, che fosse il Bembo, il quale introducendo quel valente Romito a trattare dell'Amore Diuino, mentione giamai di Donna non fa, ma di quelle Bellezze eterne del Cielo, & sopra tutto della prima, & vltima cagione di tutte le cose, Oceano di bellezza, & di felicità, fol. 25v.

32. 'Certamente, come stimo che Platone ponesse per fine dell'Amor Diuino il goder la vista della Bellezza Diuina, percioche questa naturalmente è forma, & perfettione degli animi nostri, così veggio, come di sopra dissi, che nell'Amor humano espressamente il niega, imperoche ne la bellezza del corpo d'una Donna, ne ancho dell'animo può essere oggetto appagante del'intelletto nostro, il quale è ordinato a felicitarsi in tanto più nobile, & eccellente oggetto,' fol. 27r.

33. 'Ragioneuolmente adunque si dubita, qual sia il sommo fine dell'Amore Humano, ò il goder la Bellezza, ò il generar nel Bello, ò l'esser guiderdonato di pari Amore. Et per cominciare a soluer questo nodo, io per me stimar non posso, che debbia essere, il godere sì fragile, & dentro a sì stretti termini racchiusa bellezza, come quella d'vna Donna; imperoche non veggio come si potesse scusar

la Natura, se per fine sì debole hauesse in noi produtto sì gagliardo mouimento come si vede esser quello del'Amore,' fol. 26v.

34. 'Ne mi è gia mai occorso come altra volta ho testimoniato, di trouare Lauinello alcuno, che si appaghi della Bellezza sola. Adunque confessando, che la Bellezza della Donna amata, all'Amante marauigliosamente piaccia per ordine della Natura, che ha voluto seruirsi di questo piacere ad altro fine, non però concederemo che il goder la bellezza sia lo stesso vero, & principal fine dell'Amor nostro,' fol. 27v.

35. 'Resta, eschiuso il goder della Bellezza, di giudicare tra Platone, il quale assegnò per fine d'Amore il partorire nel bello, & Aristotele, il quale stimò supremamente disidierarsi il vicendeuole Amore,' fol. 27v.

36. 'l'Amante si dona alla cosa amata, & in lei viue, morto in se stesso . . . L'animo è doue opera. L'animo del'Amante opera sempre d'intorno alla cosa amata, in lei colloca tutti i pensieri, e desiderii suoi, e per conseguente si par che diuenti l'animo di lei, & in lei si trasformi; talche vera fu quella sentenza, l'animo esser più doue ama, che doue anima & viuifica,' fols 27v–28r.

37. 'Cosi naturalmente il generare è il principal fine, come volle Platone, ma quasi per accidente, ciò è per quella alienatione dell'animo diuiene principale il vicendiuole Amore, come stimarono Aristotele, é gli Stoici,' fol. 29v.

38. 'Amore humano . . . è gagliardo piegamento dell'appetito, & della volontà nostra, escitato da conosciuta bellezza, & risoluentesi in disiderio di generare nel bello, ò di acquistar la gratia della Donna amata . . . Ma se il vocabolo d'humano prendessimo nel sentimento di conforme alla dritta ragione, all'hora conuerebbe alla diffinitione aggiugnere, che fosse disiderio honesto, ciò è secondante il voler delle leggi, & quelle in niuna guisa violante,' fol. 31r.

39. 'Quindi conchiude, che Amore, ò non sia in modo alcuno per lo congiugnimento de i corpi, ò se pur questo si cerca, non si cerchi per altro, che per chiaro testimonio d'esser amato . . . Adunque secondo l'opinione d'Aristotele il fine dell'Amore sarà in vn Gentilhuomo il vicendeuole amore, dalla quale opinione non s'allontanarono gli Stoici, essendo essi vsati diffinire Amore vno sforzo di fare amicitia per cagion di bellezza; & fare amicitia non vuole inferire altro che produrre nell'amato pare amore,' fol. 18v.

40. D. L. Guss notes that 'Some theorists justify spiritual love by separating it entirely from sexual love, which they denounce; others accept sexuality as an attendant good; many argue that physical love is good when it is limited to the senses of sight and hearing. But virtually all justify amorous enjoyment by its spiritual direction.' However, 'Since their system is eclectic rather than deductive, the theorists usually accept all . . . generalizations, even when they seem incompatible . . . The Renaissance love theorists echo the same authorities and each other. Nonetheless, they are engaged in a fruitful intellectual enterprise: by reinterpreting their literary and philosophic heritage, they seek to discover the ultimate meaning of secular life'; 'Renaissance love theory,' in *John Donne, Petrarchist*, pp. 130–2.

41. 'Malagevoli a comprendere sono gli affetti humani per la doppiezza della Natura nostra,' fol. 5r.

42. This frustration is aptly expressed by Francisco de Aldana in the sonnet, '¿Cuál es la causa, mi Damón, que estando,' in *Poesías*, E. L. Rivers, ed.

43. The Christianization of Eros was achieved much earlier by St Augustine. To the concept of Eros in this context, modern theology/philosophy has added 'agape.' Strictly speaking, Eros is now a love, even of God, that is self-seeking, that is, seeks salvation; agape is the purely disinterested love of God that seeks no reward; see A. Nygren, *Eros and Agape*.

44. Fray Luis de León, 'A Francisco Salinas'; Francisco de Aldana, 'Carta del

Capitán Francisco de Aldana para Arias Montano sobre la contemplación de Dios y los requisitos della.'

45. 'Eran las mujeres antes / de carne y de güeso hechas; / ya son de rosas y flores, / jardines y primaveras. / Hortelanos de facciones, / ¿qué sabor queréis que tenga / una mujer ensalada, / toda de plantas y yerbas?', 717.

3 QUEVEDO AND COURTLY LOVE

1. 'Confieso . . . que advirtiendo el discurso enamorado que se colige del contexto de esta sección, que yo reduje a la forma que hoy tiene, vine a persuadirme que mucho quiso nuestro poeta este su amor semejase al . . . del Petrarca . . . Mucho parentesco habemos de dar en estas dos tan parecidas afecciones, como con que ambos las manifestaron en sus poesías'; in *Obra poética*, I, Blecua, ed., p. 117.

2. See C. Consiglio, 'El "Poema a Lisi" y su petrarquismo,' pp. 79–93; J. G. Fucilla, *Estudios sobre el petrarquismo en España*, pp. 195–209; L. Close, 'Petrarchism and the "cancioneros" in Quevedo's Love Poetry,' pp. 836–55; and D. G. Walters, 'Three Examples of Petrarchism in Quevedo's *Heráclito cristiano*,' pp. 21–30.

3. Cf. 492, 'Laméntase, muerta Lisi, de la vida, que le impide el seguirla': 'pues viendo, ¡oh, Lisi!, que por verte muero, / con la vida me estorba el poder verte.'

4. H. H. Fränkel notes in his doctoral thesis that Lodovico Castelvetro had annotated Petrarch's sonnet, giving the source of the initial quatrain as Psalm 102: 6–7. Fränkel studies the 'split ego' as expressed in the octave of Quevedo's imitation; in 'Figurative Language in the Serious Poetry of Quevedo,' fol. 105.

5. *The Mind's Wit and Art*, I, p. 321, Chambers, trans. 'De las ingeniosas transposiciones. Esta especie de conceptos es una de las más agradables que se conservan. Consiste su artificio en transformar el objeto y convertirlo en lo contrario de lo que parece; obra grave la inventiva y una pronta tropelia del ingenio,' *Agudeza*, I, p. 179.

6. *Dicc. Auts*. The lines would be read: 'El sueño . . . en mí a la muerte vence dificilmente.'

7. W. Sanders, on Donne's 'The Canonization,' *John Donne's Poetry*, p. 22.

8. Warnke, on Donne's 'The Canonization,' *Versions of Baroque*, p. 104.

9. 'Il pensare, & immaginare è come disse Aristotele, una manera di sentirse, quantunque più debole, & all'Amante vale quasi altrettanto, quanto il vedere, & vdire; onde spesso lamentasi del sonno che sottragga il core a quel dolce pensier, che in vita il tene,' fol. 14r–v.

10. 'Es de Museo,' notes González de Salas.

11. A. Terry, 'Quevedo and the Metaphysical Conceit,' p. 213. J. M. Pozuelo Yvanco calls the Leander–ship conceit a prolonged metaphysical conceit, in *El lenguaje poético de la lírica amorosa de Quevedo*, pp. 133–6. Chapters 5 and 6 will discuss the difference between the organic and the metaphysical conceit. Pozuelo Yvanco's study came to my attention when my manuscript was nearing completion.

12. D. Alonso points out that 'hartarse' was used by Garcilaso in his 'Canción II': '¡quién pudiese hartarse / de no esperar remedio y de quejarse!' (ll. 38–9), but reveals that 'el verbo, un siglo después, seguía sin haberse aclimatado en la lengua poética,' p. 545. Quevedo perhaps had Garcilaso's lines in mind when writing this sonnet.

13. 'Dime una hartazga de cielo / en tan altas maravillas; / maté la hambre al deseo, y enriquecí la codicia,' 440.

14. Blecua put a semicolon after this line in his Planeta edition, 1963. The punctuation was changed to a full stop in the Castalia edition, and appears this

way in the Planeta edition, 1971. The sonnet's structure clearly calls for a major pause.

15. Hoover compares sonnet 474 with Donne's 'The Computation,' pp. 95–100.

16. The same expression is found in a letter written during one of Quevedo's incarcerations. Suspected of treason, along with the Duque de Osuna, Quevedo was imprisoned in the fall of 1620 in the castle of Uclés, the seat of the military order of Santiago, of which the poet was a knight. On February 25, 1621, he sent a letter to the Duque, in which he writes: 'estoy *preso y desterrado*, y con más rigor que ha estado un caballero jamás, y cada día se ve peor condición en mi carcelería,' *Epistolario*, pp. 100–01; italics mine. The sonnet cannot be dated on the basis of the letter. The same expression occurs in 439, a *romance* addressed to Floris: 'Yo solo, Floris, preso y desterrado.' A variant occurs in 430, where we find a similarity between its final lines and the sonnet's: 'Ausente, preso y solo . . . / Floris ya está en la villa, / yo peno en Guadalerce; / allá era yo ninguno, / acá no soy viviente.' It is impossible to tell which of these poems corresponds to the poet's imprisonment of 1621. Poem 441, with a reference to Floris, alludes to an imprisonment in late September. Four periods of incarceration include this month, 1628, 1640, 1641, 1642. Poem 430 was written before 1637, the date of *Maravillas del Parnaso*, a *cancionero* compiled by Jorge Pinto de Morales. The earliest poem concerning Flori(s) is 673, 'Floris, la fiesta pasada,' which describes the festivities in honor of the Prince of Wales in March 1623. Poems concerning Lisi are found in the *Cancionero antequerano* of 1627–8; see Crosby, *En torno a la poesía de Quevedo*, pp. 141, 168, 171. But it appears that poems to Lisi may have been written as early as 1615–16; see Ettinghausen, 'Un nuevo manuscrito autógrafo de Quevedo,' and Moore, *Towards a Chronology of Quevedo's Poetry*, pp. 52–3, 56–7. It may be that sonnet 474 alludes to an actual imprisonment, an experience which gives the metaphorical motif a literal basis and allows for the expression of two modes of experience. Either in this prison or in its recollection, the poet possibly had an experiential analogue of the *cárcel de amor*, which contributed to a vivid dramatization of the topic.

17. The 'alma en pena' may also be an expression of the various archetypal beliefs and legends of the soul that has not been admitted to heaven and must roam the earth.

18. Forster uses the term in the sense of topics or categories, p. 8.

19. 'Por alusión o semejanza la sangre, que se derrama para testificar alguna verdad,' *Dicc. Auts.*

20. Because of González de Salas's title, we know that 'cárcel' refers to the poet's ring. Nonetheless, the analysis assumes that it was the poet's intention that this identification should not be made until the final tercet. The identity of the subject, Lisi, is apparent in that the sonnet is of the Lisi cycle.

21. The shaping of this image began in 303, was developed in 339, and culminates here. Another version of the image is given in the poet's 'Poema heroico de las necedades y locuras de Orlando el enamorado,' ll. 465–8.

22. Tuve, pp. 24–5; also in Terry, *Anthology*, I, p. xxi.

23. *The Mind's Wit and Art*, II, p. 759, Chambers, trans. 'La suelta es aquélla en la cual, aunque se levantan tres y cuatro y muchos asuntos de un sujeto . . . no se unen unos con otros, sino que libremente se levantan y sin correlación se discurren . . . La encadenada en una traza es aquella en que los asuntos . . . se unen entre sí como parte para componer un todo artificioso mental,' *Agudeza*, II, pp. 167–8.

24. *Ibid.*, II, p. 781, Chambers, trans. 'Cuando se ajustan todas las circunstancias y adyacentes del sujeto al término de la translación, sin violencia, y con tal

consonancia que cada parte de la metáfora fuera un relevante concepto, está en su mayor exaltación el compuesto,' *Agudeza*, ii, p. 180.

25. 'La "agudeza",' 1952, pp. 331-2. Sonnet 449, which has much the same cause as 465, is not included in my study, because little could be added that has not already been said in Parker's lucid analysis.

26. 'Quevedo es, ante todo, intensidad,' J. L. Borges, 'Grandeza y menoscabo en Quevedo,' pp. 254-5.

27. These are the final lines of a poem that follows the illustration of the muse of lyric poetry, Euterpe, in *Las tres musas últimas castellanas. Segunda cumbre del parnaso español*, 1670, Pedro Alderete Quevedo y Villegas, ed., reprinted in *Obra Poética*, i, p. 146. Following the poem are the initials 'D.M.C.,' which Astrana Marín suspects stand for the 'Duque (de) Medina Celi,' in *Verso*, p. 942. Thus, although not written by Quevedo, these lines, in the *persona* of Euterpe, do synthesize an aesthetic which, as perceived by the anonymous poet, could be assigned to Quevedo. They are also an indication that such an aesthetic was appreciated by the seventeenth-century reader of love poetry: 'Toda pasión amorosa, / aunque es pasión, entretiene, / mas no dura, si no tiene / mucho de gaita golosa,' idem.

28. Forster, p. 8. Other internal conceits are the nature of love, relations between lovers, rejection of the beloved, death motifs.

29. A *romance*, 440, makes this clear: 'No pueden los sueños, Floris, / ofender prendas divinas, / pues permitan a las almas / el mentir para sí mismas.'

30. G. Sabat de Rivers has discovered that the tercets of 337 are an imitation of the tercets of the sonnet of the Jesuit, Pedro de Tablares, ' ¡Ay!, dulce sueño y dulce sentimiento.' The latter is a love poem 'a lo divino,' whose lover's paradox Quevedo reappropriates 'a lo humano'; 'Quevedo, Floralba y el Padre Tablares,' 320-7.

31. *Dicc. Auts.* There is no adequate translation for 'trasgo'; the definition suggests a poltergeist, but its use in the sonnet indicates that it is visible. Lines 3–6 are an imitation of lines 40–4 of Aldana's 'Epístola vi,' 'y con un trasgo a brazos debatiendo / que al cabo, al cabo, ¡ay Dios!, de tan gran rato / mi costoso sudor queda riendo.' The 'trasgo' appears to be a personification of the 'doble trato' of love and war. Quevedo admired Aldana's poetry, expressing a desire to edit it: 'Si alcanzo sosiego algún día bastante, pienso enmendar y corregir sus obras deste nuestro poeta español, tan agraviadas de la imprenta, tan ofendidas del desaliño de un su hermano, que solo quien de cortesía le creyere al que lo dice, creerá que lo es' (*Anacreón*, xix). Assuredly, what appealed to Quevedo with regard to Aldana's love poetry was the latter's 'actitud medio pagana de hedonismo filosófico que asimismo era típica de la Italia renacentista,' and his disregard for courtly decorum: 'no es idealista, sino intensamente realista y apasionado. Le falta por completo el refrenamiento que imponían las leyes del amor cortés; tampoco hay vestigio de la subliminación de lo erótico que se encontraba generalmente en la poesía amorosa de tradición dantesca o petrarquista,' Francisco de Aldana, *Poesías*, E. L. Rivers, ed., pp. xiv–xv.

32. 'To each his own,' but saying literally 'Every madman with his obsession.'

33. 'El poema que con más exclusiva y tajante vehemencia expresa el dolor de amor,' ' "En los claustros de l'alma," apuntaciones sobre la lengua poética de Quevedo,' p. 470. My analysis endeavors to supplement Sobejano's penetrating study.

34. E.g. sonnets 299, 310, 471, 472.

35. On love as an illness, a cerebral inflammation, see Keith Whinnom's introduction to Diego de San Pedro, *Cárcel de amor*, pp. 13–14.

36. In the comparison of this sonnet with Donne's 'A Nocturnal upon St Lucy's day,'

Hoover notes that the poet is physically destroyed in the quatrains, and psychologically destroyed in the tercets, pp. 134–7.

37. The epithet 'negro llanto' and its variants are expressed in other poems, and in each instance it has a particular significance. In his *Lágrimas de Hieremías castellanas*, 1613, Quevedo gives this versified version of Jeremiah's First Lamentation, 2–Beth: 'Bed su dolor inmenso, / pues no pasó ninguna noche enjuta / de lágrimas amargas de sus ojos, / que, del negro dolor perpetuadas, / acen ruido y señal en sus mexillas. / Toda ocupada en desatarse en llanto, / no halló piedad ni cortesía ninguna / la que nunca pensó para consuelo / haberla menester; aborrecióla / quien antes la adoró; burlóse della / el que por más amigo / a su prosperidad fue lisongero. / Y viéndola en las manos de la ira, / boluiéronse enemigos y contrarios.' This 'negro llanto' is a lamentation deprived of any consolation or pity, as Quevedo affirms in his commentary, distinguishing between 'llorar descansando,' in which weeping is akin to a purgation bringing relief, and 'llorar llorando,' which adds to the cause of weeping: 'mas quien llora cautiuo u perdido u castigado, éste con el llanto aumenta la causa del, y eso es "llorar llorando."' The *negro llanto* is also found in poem 192, where the poet describes Christ descending into hell, and requests: 'Enséñame, cristiana musa mía, / si a humana y frágil voz permites tanto, / de Cristo la triunfante valentía, / y del Rey sin piedad el negro llanto.' Of major importance in our consideration of this lament is that it causes additional torment in the literal sense of the word, since every instance of this particular *llanto* motif is associated with the sufferings of hell (see Sobejano, 1971, 481–2). This association has an undeniable correlation with the sonnet where the poet's lament is given no consolation, and, consequently, his heart becomes an infernal reign of fear. Finally, in the above versification we note with interest that the *negro llanto* results in bitterness, which can perhaps be taken as confirmation of the poet's embittered tone in the sonnet. *Lágrimas de Hieremías castellanas*, M. Wilson and J. Blecua, eds, pp. 41–4.

4 QUEVEDO AND NEOPLATONIC LOVE

1. '¿Para qué me amartelas, / déjame vivir; / no sé qué gusto tienes / en verme morir'; *cantar popular*, in A. de Pagés, *Gran diccionario de la lengua castellana*.

2. Sonnet 332, 'Alma es del mundo Amor; Amor es mente,' is a rejoinder to Flora's command, attempting to persuade her that physical union is in accordance with the natural order of things; see Paterson's astute reading of this sonnet in '"Sutileza del pensar" in a Quevedo Sonnet.'

3. Zahareas and McCallum also see this self-deception as a reflection of the Spanish attempt to hold on to the Renaissance ideology of 'idea over matter,' as a cover up for socio-economic failures, a 'distortion of actual conditions,' 'Toward a Social History of the Love Sonnet,' pp. 97–8.

4. Blecua's Castalia edition, 1969, has a comma after 'favores,' line 10. His Planeta edition, 1971, removes the comma, placing it after 'cuerpo.' This later version is an improvement, since the sonnet's structure indicates that 'gozaran' is a transitive verb requiring an object. I question, however, the semicolon in line 6.

5. The expression is Elias Rivers's, in a lecture given on the occasion of the fourth centenary of Quevedo's birth, at Boston University, October 16, 1980.

6. 'Trato y comunicación familiar, y de ordinario secreta entre dos personas,' *Dicc. Auts*.

7. 'Júpiter en lluvia de oro / poseyó de Diana esquiva / los favores,' A. Moreto, in Pagés, *Diccionario*.

8. A comparison of these two poems will be pursued in a separate study.

9. The full range of the pilgrim archetype is studied by S. Chew, *The Pilgrimage of Life*; see also J. S. Hahn, *The Origins of the Baroque Concept of 'Peregrinatio.'*

10. The possible allusion is to the waters of forgetfulness, and not, specifically, to death, which one would ordinarily associate with Lethe. Quevedo's contemporary reader, taking into consideration the pattern of the imagery pointing to the significance 'meant to be seen,' would have been expected to discard irrelevant associations; see Tuve, chaps. II, VII.

11. Literally, *entrañas* refers to the heart as well as to all the internal organs. Metaphorically, 'se toma por el interior del ánimo, sus afectos, passiones e inclinación de la voluntad y del corazón.' The idea of love entering through the eyes and passing to the heart and soul seems to be taking literally the saying 'Ésto me llega a las entrañas,' 'Phrase con que se da a entender y expresa lo grande y vivo del sentimiento y dolor que uno padece: como si dixera, Me llega a lo vivo del corazón,' *Dicc. Auts.*

12. In this period personal relative pronouns were often used to refer to impersonal antecedents. In this case the sonnet's structure and context suggest a personal use of 'a quien,' 'whom' (the beloved 'fuego'), instead of 'which.'

13. 'En las poéticas del Renacimiento la fórmula doble se presenta como un adorno especial . . . Continuamente se nos presentan fórmulas dobles especialmente en la adjetivación: "alta y divina, pura y hermosa, desierta y dura",' W. Kayser, *Interpretación y análisis de la obra literaria*, pp. 154–5. León Hebreo says that the 'intellectual virtues' are 'pure,' and the love of them 'divine,' p. 439.

14. As the cause revealed differs from the cause preconceived, we have an instance of a poem not completely controlled by conscious design. This would seem to indicate that, to some extent, the experience and its expression are simultaneous. In modern poetry this simultaneity of experience and expression is not uncommon, and sometimes leads to self-revelation. Notable examples are Fernando Pessoa's 'A tabacaria,' and Guillaume Apollinaire's 'Cortège.' However, such poetry requires a flexible form to transmit the varying rhythms of thought, to portray the 'movement of thought in a living mind.' These poems reveal a man *having* a thought, but the seventeenth-century poem shows a man who *had* a thought. The latter *re-creates* experience, arranging thoughts in a logical order, and amplifying them in an orderly pattern. Quevedo's sonnet complies with this ordering of thoughts; nonetheless, we have the sensation that he is not re-creating experience, but following the curve of his feeling. Despite the sonnet's rigid form, requiring deliberation prior to formulation, he seems to have become aware of an unconscious intuition, causing him to react against a conscious idea previously expressed. This is a remarkable instance of poetic introspection. See Tuve, p. 43; quote from F. O. Matthiessen, *The Achievement of T. S. Eliot, an Essay on the Nature of Poetry*, p. 16.

15. Employing a different analytical procedure, G. Gullón arrives at the same conclusion; 'En torno a un soneto de Quevedo,' pp. 25–31.

16. This idea finds a striking similarity to Donne's 'The Paradox': 'Love with excess of heat, more young, than old, / Death kills with too much cold . . . / Once I loved and died; and am now become / Mine epitaph and tomb. / Here dead men speak their last, and so do I; / Love-slain, lo, here I lie.' For a comparison of these two poems, see Hoover, pp. 123–8.

17. Warnke, on Donne's 'The Exstasie,' in *European Metaphysical Poetry*, 1961, p. 8.

18. 'Forse ancora sotto il nome di Gratia spesse volte s'intende la proportione delle membra, quando risulta da i mouimenti del corpo; imperoche il mouimento senza fallo è atto a generare in vn corpo diuersa proportione di parti da quella, che haueua nel riposo; talche per auuentura ci diletterà, quando si muoue, & in

164

sedendo ci offenderà, o per lo contrario fermo ci apporterà piacere, & nel muouersi noia. La onde chi la bellezza secondo il sentimento comune chiamasse gratia stante, & la gratia nominasse bellezza mouentesi, a mio giuditio non errerebbe souerchio' (fol. 10v).

19. Reproduced in *Prosa*, Astrana Marín, ed., p. 1356. The marginalia are on fols 9−10.
20. Cf. Donne's 'The Exstasie': 'So must pure lovers' souls descend / T'affections, and to faculties, / Which sense may reach and apprehend, / Else a great prince in prison lies.'
21. 'di acquistar la gratia della Donna amata'; 'disiderio di generare nel bello,' fol. 31r; see chap. 2, n. 38.

5 LOVE AND DEATH

1. See Ettinghausen, *Quevedo and the Neostoic Movement.*
2. *Studies in Human Time*, pp. 10−19; quote from St Augustine (*Civitas Dei*, I, xii, chap. 25), in Poulet, p. 19.
3. See e.g. Paterson, '"Sutileza del pensar" in a Quevedo Sonnet.'
4. 'Gloria. Theologicamente tomada es lo mismo que la bienaventuranza que gozan los Angeles y almas santas en el Cielo: que consiste en ver a Dios, amarle y gozarle . . . Se toma tambien por lo que ennoblece, ilustra y engrandece alguna cosa,' *Dicc. Auts.*
5. 'Metafísicos' here has to do with death and the contemplation of the after life, not with a style or poetics.
6. In S. L. Bethell, 'Gracián, Tesauro, and the Nature of Metaphysical Wit,' p. 30.
7. This syllogism has a double middle term, but the sonnet is also composed of four other witty syllogisms: (1) Love gives birth to death; death destroys life; therefore, love destroys life; (2) Love is a fire which inflames the soul; the soul lives on after death; therefore, the fire of love continues to burn after consuming the body; (3) Love survives death; love is the memory of the beloved's beauty; therefore, her beauty survives death; (4) To love is to find salvation, but my love finds death; therefore, death is salvation. All are logically fallacious but poetically beautiful.
8. See chap. 2, n. 26.
9. Quevedo may also have had in mind Morello's response to Bembo's praise of the virtuous lover content with only the contemplation of the beloved's physical and spiritual beauty: 'The begetting of a beautiful child in a beautiful woman would be an engendering of beauty effectively; and pleasing him in this way would appear to me a much clearer sign that she loved her lover than treating him with the affability of which you speak,' *The Book of the Courtier*, p. 348.
10. Seventeenth-century poetic theory did not make the modern distinction between *form* and *content*; rather, as Tuve says, 'These earlier theorists customarily make or imply a different division, and it is one which fits their poems admirably; it might not fit ours. Their ultimate critical questions are not, "What does the poem say?" and "How is it said?" but "What is the poem for?" and "How has that been accomplished?" That is, they consider a poem with respect to end and with respect to means, a consideration which does not bifurcate it . . . they do not identify *end* with *content* and *means* with *form*. Insofar as there is any division, it cuts across in a different way. When the end of poetry is spoken of, the poem does not seem to be conceived of as a unit made up of "logically stateable structure of meaning" plus "ornament," but as a unit in which "cause" is manifested by "mode of operation" . . . The meaning of the

poem is what-its-ideas-in-that-form-do . . . A poem has in it the germ of a reader's active understanding of what it "says," and any discussion of the poem's meaning must take cognizance not only of what ideas or images it may be said to contain but of what those ideas and images are doing, put together in that form,' pp. 110–11.

11. '"Cerrar podrá mis ojos . . ."'; see also A. Alonso, 'Sentimiento e intuición en la lírica,' in *Materia y forma en poesía*; F. Lázaro Carreter, 'Quevedo entre el amor y la muerte'; M. R. Lida, 'Para las fuentes de Quevedo'; W. Naumann, '"Polvo enamorado." Muerte y amor en Propercio, Quevedo y Goethe.' J. L. Borges gives a possible source for the sonnet's final line as Propertius, Eleg. 1, 19: 'Ut meus oblito pulvis amore jacet,' *Otras inquisiciones*, p. 61.

12. Generalizations and 'loose' definitions of metaphysical poetry are discussed by L. Unger in *Donne's Poetry and Modern Criticism*, pp. 3–21.

13. Most of the attention is centered on line 9, which, following the *editio princeps*, is 'Alma a quien todo un dios prisión ha sido.' Because of the structural correlation between lines 10 and 11, there is a tendency to revise line 9 so as to fit firmly within this correlation; thus, Lida states 'habría que leer: "Alma, que a todo un dios prisión ha sido," y así lo exige el riguroso esquematismo de los tercetos: "Alma, que . . . ha sido" como "venas, que . . . han dado" y "medulas, que . . . han ardido," correspondiendo al paralelismo del otro terceto que encierra en cada verso períodos de idéntica arquitectura,' p. 374, n. 1. Following her lead, perhaps, the analyses of Alonso and Lázaro Carreter take this point of view, although the latter, as well as Blanco Aguinaga, feels that one version should not exclude the other. Blecua retains the version as given in the *editio princeps*, and in this regard it is well to point out that such a construction also figures in sonnet 292, 'Fuego *a quien* tanto mar ha respetado.' He makes a judicious amendment, however, in line 12, changing the verb to the singular to accord with the subject, 'Alma.' It is also worth mentioning that the versions adopted by the aforementioned critics for analysis not only have this verb in the plural, but also have 'mas *tendrán* sentido.' Since Blecua indicates he has only amended 'dejarán' for 'dejará,' it must be assumed that the latter is the version given in the *editio princeps*.

14. Lázaro Carreter believes that the subject of 'dejará' is death, stating,'La muerte no dejará . . . en la opuesta ribera, la memoria de la amada, en la cual el alma ardía enamorada,' p. 149. Grammatically, this impression is given, but the subject, logically, is 'alma–llama.' Furthermore, while the idea that the soul burns within the beloved is an important association, the main idea is that the soul burns in the *poet*, sharing with the *body* the experience of love. Line 12 makes it clear that it is this body which the soul must leave, but taking love's memory.

15. We recall that in sonnet 460, 'De esotra parte' is death, but in 472 it is life.

16. There is some polemic in the studies cited over whether the allusion is to Lethe or Styx. Because of the immediate context of retaining memory, the allusion must be to Lethe; but the latter also functions as a synecdoche to include the river of death. However, with '*nadar* sabe mi llama la agua fría,' Quevedo may have had in mind Dante's *Il purgatorio* XXXI rather than Virgil's *Aeneid* VI, or the imitation of closer predecessors. Arriving at Lethe's edge, Dante's companion, Virgil, disappears, and the poet finds Beatrice waiting for him on the other bank. The poet is assisted by angels across Lethe, but before reaching the other shore, he is submerged in the stream so that his memories will be drowned. In contrast, Quevedo's soul *can swim*, thereby retaining the memory of his corporal passion. In this context Lethe loses its sinister association, and points to the eternal love on the other shore. The river Styx, on the other hand, marks the descent into Nether Hell, *L'inferno*, VII.

17. Naumann confirms this reading, p. 333, n. 3, as does Rivers, from his translation of the sonnet.
18. E.g. '¿Por qué bebes mis venas, fiebre ardiente, / y habitas las medulas de mis huesos? / Ser Dios y enfermedad ¿cómo es decente? / Deidad y cárcel de sentidos presos,' 310.
19. 'Prissiónes. Se llaman tambien los grillos, cadenas y otros instrumentos de hierro, con que en las cárceles se asseguran los delinquentes. Prissión. Por extensión se llama qualquiera cosa que ata ù detiene physicamente,' *Dicc. Auts.*
20. 'Desata de este polvo y de este aliento / el nudo frágil en que está animada / sombra que sucesivo anhela el viento,' 28, variant; 'aguardo que desate de mis venas / la muerte prevenida / la alma, que anudada está en la vida,' 12.
21. It must be pointed out again that Blanco Aguinaga analyzes the sonnet taking the verb 'dejar' in the plural. The change to the singular is dictated by 'alma,' and gives form and meaning to the entire sextet.
22. See J. Frank, 'Spatial Form in Modern Literature,' in *The Widening Gyre*, pp. 3–62; also B. Hernstein Smith, *Poetic Closure: a Study of How Poems End*, p. 27.
23. From *Make it New*, cited in Frank, pp. 9–10. I have applied Pound's own definition of an image in order to vindicate Quevedo from the mediocre estimation that Pound had not only of his poetry but, in general, of all Spanish poetry of the Golden Age. Taking to Spanish literature his peculiar antipathies ('The disease of Spanish literature has been "Elizabethanism"'), he calls Quevedo a 'versifier of the second or third order,' adding that 'A great deal of Spanish 16th and 17th century verse is at about this level. There is no use blinking the fact.' In defense of Quevedo and Golden Age poetry, I would just add that Pound read the wrong poems. See Pound, 'Some Notes on Francisco de Quevedo Villegas, pp. 199–213.
24. Cf. Garcilaso de la Vega, Églogas I and III, 'Cuando me paro a contemplar mi estado,' 'Un rato se levanta mi esperanza'; Gutierre de Cetina, 'Por vos ardí, señora, y por vos ardo'; Fernando de Herrera, 'Dulce el fuego de Amor, dulce la pena'; Lope de Vega, 'Resuelta en polvo ya, mas siempre hermosa,' 'Yo no espero la flota, ni importuno.'
25. 'A veces la pasión lo hunde en la tierra, lo hace más poderoso que la misma muerte y a veces la muerte de todas las cosas invade su loco territorio de pasiones carnales. Sólo un poeta tan carnal pudo llegar a tal visión espectral del fin de la vida. No hay en la historia de nuestro idioma un debate lírico de tanta exasperada magnitud entre la tierra y el cielo . . . ¿A quién puede la muerte conceder después de la partida toda la potencia del amor? Sólo a Quevedo. Y este soneto es la única flecha, el único taladro que hasta hoy ha horadado la muerte, tirando un espiral de fuego a las tinieblas,' 'Viaje al corazón de Quevedo,' *Viajes*, p. 33.
26. I have not encountered any reference to such a practice. It is likely that commercial entrepreneurs sold hourglasses with dust 'pretending' to be the remains of courtly lovers; in other words, these hourglasses were a *fad*. This mockery of courtly love would be appropriate to its decline in these times.
27. 'Este polvo sin sosiego, / a quien tal fatiga dan, / vivo y muerto, amor y fuego / hoy derramado, ayer ciego, / y siempre en eterno afán,' 420; 'Ostentas, ¡oh felice!, en tus cenizas, / el afecto inmortal del alma interno; / que como es del amor el curso eterno, los días a tus ansias eternizas,' 380.
28. For a lucid analysis of this sonnet, see Walters, 'Conflicting Views of Time in a Quevedo Sonnet.'
29. I reiterate that I do not propose that this progression is chronological; rather, it is a gradation of intensity of expression.
30. 'el alma, al dejar el cuerpo, se llevará su cuidado; venas y medulas serán cenizas,

pero nunca ya mera materia, sino poseedoras de un sentido eterno . . . para siempre vivirá el sentido de ser ceniza de aquel fuego,' A. Alonso, pp. 16, 107.

31. Cf. Shakespeare's sonnet XVIII: 'So long as men can breathe or eyes can see, / So long lives this, and this gives life to thee.' Herrera affirms that immortality, in the form of eternal memory, can be achieved through poetry: 'El ingenio humano, que es la fuerza de nuestra alma, como se conozca inmortal, desea también que su mismo cuerpo, compañero y aposento suyo, en cuanto fuere posible, goze de aquella misma felicidad . . . y esta apetencia de inmortalidad . . . nos impele . . . a procurar que viva nuestro nombre perpetuamente en la boca de la fama y en los escritos de los hombres sabios, mayormente de los poetas,' in Gallego Morrell, ed., *Garcilaso de la Vega y sus comentaristas*, p. 429. It is not known where Quevedo is buried.

32. Donne's 'The Relic' criticizes the Catholic practice of venerating relics, calling it a 'mis-devotion': 'If this fall in a time, or land, / Where mis-devotion doth command, / Then he that digs us up will bring / Us to the Bishop and the King / To make us relics.' But, like Quevedo, he protests at the preternatural courtly ideal; instead of loving according to Nature's plans, the lovers had to obey a law imposed on Nature, the law of chastity: 'First, we loved well and faithfully, / Yet knew not what we loved, nor why; / Difference of sex no more we knew, / Than our guardian angels do . . . / Our hands ne'er touched the seals / Which nature, injured by late law, sets free.'

6 CONCLUSION

1. ¿Por qué moviéndose Quevedo en un clima de ideas tan tópicas desde la Edad Media en toda Europa, logra conmovernos? La explicación está en el estilo y en que muchos momentos nos hace olvidar la abstracción teórica para llegar a lo más hondo del alma, a lo particular,' Blecua, 1971, pp. cii–ciii.

2. Although the concept of pure love antagonizes, for Quevedo, the duality of body and soul, this does not mean that *amor mixtus* can provide the solution for their unification. In the love poetry of the Middle Style of this period, reciprocated physical love can give delight and a sense of oneness to the lovers, but it often ends with *desengaño*. See Aldana's Soneto XII for an excellent expression of this disillusion (*Poesías*, pp. 9–10). In the High Style, where only pure love should be treated, Quevedo attempts to experience a solution to this dilemma.

3. Tuve (chaps IX, 4, XII, XIV, pp. 409–10) denies that metaphysical imagery was based on a new poetic. Her assertion has been ably countered by S. L. Bethell, in 'Gracián, Tesauro, and the Nature of Metaphysical Wit'; see also J. A. Mazzeo, 'A Critique of Some Modern Theories of Metaphysical Poetry.'

4. See Mazzeo, 1952; idem, 'Metaphysical Poetry and the Poetic of Correspondence,' 1953.

5. T. Hawkes, *Metaphor*, p. 55; see also Warnke, *Versions*, chaps I–III, and Mazzeo, 'A Seventeenth Century Theory of Metaphysical Poetry,' p. 255.

6. Warnke's observation on Marvell's poem 'The Unfortunate Lover,' that 'is a poem that constitutes an experience – the imaginative experience of the validity of contradictory truths' (*Versions*, p. 59), fits my interpretation of this aspect of Quevedo's poetry.

7. The following discussion of 'Cerrar podrá' incorporates some of Terry's observations on the sonnet, in 'Quevedo and the Metaphysical Conceit,' 218–20; see also R. Price, *Anthology*, p. 113.

8. My reading of the sonnet coincides with Walters's interpretation, in 'Conflicting Views of Time in a Quevedo Sonnet,' p. 156. Lázaro Carreter affirms that the

sonnet expresses 'Un ansia de sobrevivir, típicamente agónica, pertinazmente quevedesca,' in 'Quevedo, entre el amor y la muerte,' p. 160. D. Alonso sees *exasperación* as the center of Quevedo's lyric poetry, *Poesía española*, p. 569. With regard to the sonnet's concluding conceit, Naumann says: 'En esta fórmula no se renuncia a conocer: se renuncia a que el conocimiento tenga sentido. El resumen de lo vivido por la conciencia es un delirio'; '"Polvo enamorado,"' p. 337.

Bibliography

The best bibliography on the criticism of Quevedo is James O. Crosby, *Guía bibliográfica para el estudio crítico de Quevedo*, London: Grant & Cutler, 1976. The following bibliography includes sources used or works mentioned in the study.

Quevedo y Villegas, Francisco de. *Obras completas, verso, prosa*, 2 Vols, Luis Astrana Marín, ed. Madrid: Aguilar, 1932.
Epistolario completo, Luis Astrana Marín, ed. Madrid: Reus, 1946.
Obras completas, poesía original, José Manuel Blecua, ed. Barcelona: Planeta, 3rd edn, 1971.
Obra poética, I, José M. Blecua, ed. Madrid: Castalia, 1969.
Lágrimas de Hieremías castellanas, José M. Blecua and Edward M. Wilson, eds. Madrid: Revista de Filología Española, Añejo LV, 1953.
Obras completas, prosa, Felicidad Buendía, ed. Madrid: Aguilar, 1958.
An Anthology of Quevedo's Poetry, R. M. Price, ed. Manchester: Manchester University Press, 1969.

Aldana, Francisco de. *Poesías*, Elias L. Rivers, ed. Madrid: Espasa-Calpe, 1957.
Alonso, Amado. *Materia y Forma en Poesía*. Madrid: Gredos, 3rd edn, 1969, 11–18, 103–07.
Alonso, Dámaso. 'El desgarrón afectivo en la poesía de Quevedo.' *Poesía española*. Madrid: Gredos, 4th edn, 1966, 497–580.
Andreas Capellanus. *The Art of Courtly Love*, John Jay Parry, trans. New York: Columbia University Press, 1941.
Baehr, Rudolf. *Manual de versificación española*. Madrid: Gredos, 1969.
Baum, Doris L. *Traditionalism in the Works of Francisco de Quevedo y Villegas*. Chapel Hill: University of North Carolina Studies in Romance Languages and Literatures, no. 91, 1970.
Bembo, Pietro. *Gli Asolani*, Rudolf B. Gottfried, trans. Bloomington: Indiana University Press, 1954.
Bethell, S. L. 'Gracián, Tesauro, and the Nature of Metaphysical Wit.' *The Northern Miscellany of Literary Criticism*, I (1953), 19–40.
Bishop, Morris. *Petrarch and his World*. Bloomington: Indiana University Press, 1963.
Blanco Aguinaga, Carlos. '"Cerrar podrá mis ojos . . .": tradición y originalidad.' *Filología*, VIII (1962), 57–78.
Boase, Roger. *The Origin and Meaning of Courtly Love: a Critical Study of European Scholarship*. Manchester: Manchester University Press, 1977.

Borges, Jorge Luis. 'Grandeza y menoscabo de Quevedo.' *Revista de Occidente*, VI (1924), 249–55.
'Quevedo.' *Otras inquisiciones*. Buenos Aires: Emecé, 6th edn, 1971, 55–64.
Bouvier, René. *Quevedo: hombre del diablo, hombre de Dios*, Roberto Bula Piriz, trans. Buenos Aires: Losada, 1951.
Brown, Gary J. 'Rhetoric as Structure in the "Siglo de Oro" Love Sonnets.' *Hispanófila*, 66 (1979), 9–39.
'Rhetoric in the Sonnet of Praise.' *Journal of Hispanic Philology*, I (1976), 31–50.
Castiglione, Baldesar. *The Book of the Courtier*, Charles S. Singleton, trans. New York: Anchor Books, 1959.
Carilla, Emilio. *Quevedo*. Tucumán, Argentina: Universidad Nacional de Tucumán, 1949.
Chew, Samuel. *The Pilgrimage of Life*. Port Washington, New York: Kennikat Press, 1973.
Close, Lorna. 'Petrarchism and the "cancioneros" in Quevedo's Love Poetry: the Problem of Discrimination.' *Modern Language Review*, Vol. 74, No. 4 (1979), 836–55.
Coffin, Charles M. *John Donne and the New Philosophy*. New York: Columbia University Press, 1937.
Consiglio, Carlo. 'El "Poema a Lisi" y su petrarquismo.' *Mediterráneo*, IV (1946), 13–15, 76–93.
Crosby, James O. *En torno a la poesía de Quevedo*. Madrid: Castalia, 1967.
Denomy, Alexander J. *The Heresy of Courtly Love*. Gloucester, Mass.: Peter Smith, 1965.
Donato, Eugenio. 'Tesauro's Poetics: Through the Looking Glass.' *Modern Language Notes*, 68 (1963), 15–30.
Donne, John. *John Donne's Poetry*, A. L. Clements, ed. New York: W. W. Norton, 1966.
Dronke, Peter. *Medieval Latin and the Rise of European Love-Lyric*. Oxford: Clarendon Press, 1965.
Eliot, T. S. *Selected Essays*. New York: Harcourt, Brace and Company, 1932.
Elliot, J. H. *Imperial Spain, 1416–1716*. New York: St Martin's Press, 1977.
Ettinghausen, Henry. *Francisco de Quevedo and the Neostoic Movement*. Oxford: Oxford University Press, 1972.
'Un nuevo manuscrito autógrafo de Quevedo.' *Boletín de la Real Academia Española*, 52 (1972), 211–84.
Forster, Leonard. *The Icy Fire: Five Studies in European Petrarchism*. Cambridge: Cambridge University Press, 1969.
Frank, Joseph. 'Spatial Form in Modern Literature,' in *The Widening Gyre.* Bloomington: Indiana University Press, 1968, 3–62.
Fränkel, Hans H. 'Figurative Language in the Serious Poetry of Quevedo: a Contribution to the Study of *Conceptismo*.' Dissertation, Berkeley: University of California, 1942.
Fromm, Erich. *The Art of Loving*. New York: Bantam Books, 1970.
Fucilla, Joseph G. *Estudios sobre el petrarquismo en España*. Madrid: Revista de Filología Española, 1960, 195–209.
Gallego Morell, Antonio. *Garcilaso de la Vega y sus comentaristas*. Madrid: Gredos, 1972.
Góngora, Luis de. *Poems*. R. O. Jones, ed. Cambridge: Cambridge University Press, 1966.
González de Amezúa y Mayo, Augustín. *Las almas de Quevedo*. Madrid, 1946; reprint in *Opúsculos literarios*, I, Madrid, 1951, 374–416.

González de Palencia, A. 'Quevedo por de dentro.' *Del Lazarillo a Quevedo*. Madrid: Consejo Superior de Investigaciones Científicas, Instituto Antonio de Nebrija, 1946, 273–304.

Gracián, Baltasar. *Agudeza y arte de ingenio*, 2 Vols. Madrid: Castalia, 1969.

'Baltasar Gracián's *The Mind's Wit and Art*,' 2 Vols, Leland H. Chambers, trans. Dissertation, University of Michigan, 1962.

Green, Otis H. *Courtly Love in Quevedo*. Boulder: University of Colorado, 1952.

Spain and the Western Tradition, 4 Vols. Madison: University of Wisconsin Press, 1968.

Gullón, Germán. 'En torno a un soneto de Quevedo.' *Explicación de Textos Literarios*, III, 1 (1974), 25–31.

Guss, Donald L. *John Donne, Petrarchist*. Detroit: Wayne State University Press, 1966.

Hahn, Juergen S. *The Origins of the Baroque Concept of 'Peregrinatio.'* Chapel Hill: University of North Carolina Studies in Romance Languages and Literatures, 1972.

Hawkes, Terence. *Metaphor*. London: The Critical Idiom, No. 25, 1972.

Hoover, L. Elaine. *John Donne and Francisco de Quevedo, Poets of Love and Death*. Chapel Hill: University of North Carolina Press, 1978.

Huizinga, Johan. *The Waning of the Middle Ages*. Garden City, New York: Doubleday, 1954.

Jones, Royston O. 'Ariosto and Garcilaso.' *Bulletin of Hispanic Studies*, XXXIX, 3 (1962), 153–64.

'Bembo, Gil Polo, Garcilaso, Three Accounts of Love.' *Revue de Littérature Comparée*, XL, 4 (1966), 526–40.

Kahler, Erich. *The Tower and the Abyss: An Inquiry into the Transformation of Man*. New York: The Viking Press, 1967.

Kayser, Wolfgang. *Interpretación y análisis de la obra literaria*. Madrid: Gredos, 1968.

Laín Entralgo, Pedro. 'La vida del hombre en la poesía de Quevedo.' *Cuadernos Hispanoamericanos*, 1 (1948), 63–101; also in *Vestigios*. Madrid: Ediciones y Publicaciones Españolas, 1948, 19–46.

Lázaro Carreter, Fernando. 'Quevedo entre el amor y la muerte.' *Papeles de Son Armadans*, 1 (1956), 145–60; also in G. Sobejano, ed. *Francisco de Quevedo*, 291–9.

León Hebreo: *The Philosophy of Love*, F. Friedeberg-Seeley and Jean H. Barnes, trans. London: Soncino Press, 1937.

Lewis, C. S. 'Donne and Love Poetry in the Seventeenth Century.' *Seventeenth-Century Studies Presented to Sir Herbert Grierson*. Oxford: Clarendon Press, 1938; also in A. L. Clements, ed. *John Donne's Poetry*, 144–59.

The Allegory of Love. London: Oxford University Press, 1936; reprint 1971.

Lida, María Rosa. 'Para las fuentes de Quevedo.' *Revista de Filología Hispánica*, 1 (1939), 373–5.

Mahood, M. M. *Poetry and Humanism*. New York: W. W. Norton, 1970.

Martz, Louis L. *The Poetry of Meditation*, 4th edn. New Haven: Yale University Press, 1965.

Mas, Amédée. *La caricature de la femme, du mariage et de l'amour dans l'oeuvre de Quevedo*. Paris: Ediciones Hispano-Americanas, 1957.

Matthiessen, F. O. *The Achievement of T. S. Eliot, an Essay on the Nature of Poetry*. London: Oxford University Press, 1958; reprint 1969.

Maura y Gamazo, Gabriel. *Conferencias sobre Quevedo*. Madrid: Saturnino Callejo, no date.

May, Rollo. *Love and Will*. New York: The Viking Press, 1975.

Mazzeo, Joseph A. 'A Critique of Some Modern Theories of Metaphysical Poetry.' *Modern Philology*, 50 (1952), 88–96; also in *John Donne's Poetry*, 134–43.

'Metaphysical Poetry and the Poetic of Correspondence.' *Journal of the History of Ideas*, 14 (1953), 221–34.

'A Seventeenth-Century Theory of Metaphysical Poetry.' *Romanic Review*, 42 (1951), 244–55; these articles are included in *Renaissance and Seventeenth-Century Studies*. New York: Columbia University Press, 1964, chaps II, III.

Mérimée, Ernest. *A History of Spanish Literature*, S. Griswold Morley, trans. New York: Henry Holt and Company, 1931.

Essai sur la vie et les oeuvres de Francisco de Quevedo. Paris: Alphonse Picard, 1886.

Moore, Roger. *Towards a Chronology of Quevedo's Poetry*. Fredericton, N.B.: York Press, 1977.

Mourges, Odette de. *Metaphysical, Baroque and Précieux Poetry*. Oxford: Clarendon Press, 1953.

Naumann, Walter. '"Polvo enamorado." Muerto y amor en Propercio, Quevedo y Goethe.' *Francisco de Quevedo*, G. Sobejano, ed. and trans., 326–42. First published as '"Staub, entbrannt in Liebe." Das Thema von Tod und Liebe bei Properz, Quevedo und Goethe.' *Arcadia*, III (1968), 157–72.

Navarro de Kelley, Emilia. *La poesía metafísica de Quevedo*. Madrid: Guadarrana, 1973.

Neruda, Pablo. 'Viaje al corazón de Quevedo.' *Viajes*. Santiago de Chile: Nascimento, 1955, 9–40.

Newman, F. X., ed. *The Meaning of Courtly Love*. Albany: State University of New York Press, 1969.

Nobili, Flaminio. *Il trattato dell'amore humano*. Lucca, 1567; facsimile reprint, *con le postille autografe di Torquato Tasso*, Rome: Ermanno Loescher, 1895.

Nygren, Anders. *Eros and Agape*, Philip S. Watson, trans. New York: Harper and Row, 1969.

Olivares, Julián, Jr. '"El pasadizo que hay de un cuerpo a otro": ¿ *amor mixtus* o *amor pursus* en un poema de Quevedo?' *Explicación de Textos Literarios*, VII, 2 (1978–9), 117–83.

Panofsky, Erwin. *Studies in Iconology*. Oxford University Press, 1939; reprint, New York: Harper and Row, 1972.

Papell, Antonio. *Quevedo*. Barcelona: Editorial Barna, S.A., 1947.

Parker, Alexander A. 'La "agudeza" en algunos sonetos de Quevedo: Contribución al estudio del conceptismo.' *Estudios dedicados a D. Ramón Menéndez Pidal*, 3 (1952), 345–60.

Luis de Góngora: Polyphemus and Galatea, a Study in the Interpretation of a Baroque Poem. Austin: University of Texas Press, 1977.

Paterson, Alan K. G. '"Sutileza del pensar" in a Quevedo Sonnet.' *Modern Language Notes*, LXXXI, 2 (1966), 131–42.

Petrarch, Francesco. *Petrarch's Lyric Poems*, Robert M. Durling, ed. and trans. Cambridge, Mass.: Harvard University Press, 1976.

Pfandl, Ludwig. *Historia de la literatura nacional española en la edad de oro*. Barcelona, 1933.

Post, Chandler R. *Mediaeval Spanish Allegory*. Cambridge, Mass.: Harvard University Press, 1915.

Poulet, Georges. *Studies in Human Time*. Elliott Coleman, trans. Baltimore: Johns Hopkins Press, 1956.

Pound, Ezra. 'Some Notes on Francisco de Quevedo Villegas.' *Hermes*, 69 (1921), 199–213.

Pozuelo Yvanco, José M. *El lenguaje poético de la lírica amorosa de Quevedo*. University of Murcia, 1979.

Richards, I. A. *The Language of Poetry*, Allen Tate, ed. Princeton: Princeton University Press, 1942.

Rivers, Elias L., ed. *Renaissance and Baroque Poetry of Spain*. New York: Charles Scribner's Sons, 1966.

Romera-Navarro, M. *Historia de la literatura española*. New York: D. C. Heath, 1928.

Sabat de Rivers, Georgina. 'Quevedo, Floralba y el Padre Tablares.' *Modern Language Notes*, XCIII, 2 (1978), 320–8.

Sainz de Robles, Carlos. *Diccionario mitológico universal*. Madrid: Aguilar, 1944.

Salinas, Pedro. 'La tradición de la poesía amorosa.' *Jorge Manrique o tradición y originalidad*. Buenos Aires: Sudamericana, 1962.

Sanders, Wilbur. *John Donne's Poetry*. Cambridge: Cambridge University Press, 2nd edn, 1974.

San Pedro, Diego de. *Cárcel de amor*, Keith Whinnom, ed. Madrid: Castalia, 1972.

Shattuck, Roger. *The Banquet Years: The Origins of the Avant-Garde in France, 1885 to World War I*. New York: Vintage Books, 1968.

Smith, Barbara H. *Poetic Closure: a Study of How Poems End*, 2nd edn. Chicago: University of Chicago Press, 1970.

Smith, James. 'On Metaphysical Poetry.' *Scrutiny*, II, 3 (December 1933), 222–38; also in *Determinations*, F. R. Leavis, ed. London: Chatto and Windus, 1934, 10–45.

Sobejano, Gonzalo. '"En los claustros del alma . . ." Apuntaciones sobre la lengua poética de Quevedo.' *Sprache und Geschichte, Festschrift für Harri Meyer*. Munich, 1971, 460–92.

(ed.) *Francisco de Quevedo*. Madrid: Taurus, 1978.

Terry, Arthur. *An Anthology of Spanish Poetry*, 2 vols. Oxford: Pergamon Press, 1965. 'A Note on Metaphor and Conceit in the Siglo de Oro.' *Bulletin of Hispanic Studies*, 31 (1954), 91–7.

'Quevedo and the Metaphysical Conceit.' *Bulletin of Hispanic Studies*, 35 (1958), 211–22.

ter Horst, Robert. 'Death and Resurrection in the Quevedo Sonnet: "En crespa tempestad."' *Journal of Hispanic Philology*, 5 (1980), 41–9.

Ticknor, George. *History of Spanish Literature*, II. New York: Gordian Press, Inc., 6th edn, 1965.

Tuve, Rosemond. *Elizabethan and Metaphysical Imagery, Renaissance Poetic and Twentieth-Century Critics*. Chicago: The University of Chicago Press, 8th edn, 1968.

Unger, Leonard. *Donne's Poetry and Modern Criticism*. New York: Russell and Russell, 1962.

Valency, Maurice Jacques. *In Praise of Love: An Introduction to the Love Poetry of the Renaissance*. New York: The Macmillan Company, 1958.

Vilanova, Antonio. 'El peregrino de amor en las "Soledades" de Góngora.' *Estudios dedicados a D. Ramón Menéndez Pidal*, 3 (1952), 421–60.

Walters, D. Gareth. 'Conflicting Views of Time in a Quevedo Sonnet: An Analysis of "Diez años de mi vida se ha llevado."' *Journal of Hispanic Philology*, 4 (1980–1), 143–56.

'Three Examples of Petrarchism in Quevedo's *Heráclito cristiano*.' *Bulletin of Hispanic Studies*, 58 (1981), 21–30.

Warnke, Frank J. *European Metaphysical Poetry*. New Haven: Yale University Press, 1961.

Versions of Baroque, European Literature in the Seventeenth Century. New Haven: Yale University Press, 1972.

Wilson, Edward M. 'Modern Spanish Poems. Guillén and Quevedo on Death.' *Atlante*, 1 (1953), 22–6.

Zahareas, Anthony N. and Thomas R. McCallum. 'Toward a Social History of the Love Sonnet: the Case of Quevedo's Sonnet 331.' *Ideologies and Literature*, 2 (1978), 90–9.

Key to poems studied

First line, number, page

'A Fabio preguntaba' (412), 116
'A fugitivas sombras doy abrazos' (358), 6, 10, 76–80
'A la sombra de un risco' (430), 161 n. 16
'A vosotras, estrellas' (401), 103
'" ¡Ah de la vida!" ' . . . ¿Nadie me responde?' (2), 123
'Al oro de tu frente unos claveles' (339), 65–7
'Alma es del mundo Amor; Amor es mente' (332), 163 n. 2
'Aminta, para mí cualquiera día' (308), 106, 138–9
'Amor me ocupa el seso y los sentidos' (486), 120–1
' ¡Ay, Floralba! Soñé que te . . . ¿Dirélo?' (337), 53, 74–6

'Bastábale al clavel verse vencido' (303), 11–12

'Cargado voy de mí: veo delante' (478), 79, 97–8
'Cerrar podrá mis ojos la postrera' (472), 15, 89, 99–100, 124, 128–41, 147, 151–3
'¿Cómo es tan largo en mí dolor tan fuerte' (451), 9–10, 60
' ¡Cómo de entre mis manos te resbalas!' (31), 114
'¿Cuándo aquel fin a mí vendrá forzoso' (492), 160 n. 3
'Cuando está recién nacido' (439), 161 n. 16
'¿Cuándo seré infeliz sin mi gemido?' (47), 114

'Dejad que a voces diga el bien que pierdo' (360), 60–3, 79
'Después que te conocí' (423), 115–16
'Diez años de mi vida se ha llevado' (471), 139–40

'En breve cárcel traigo aprisionado' (465), 67–74
'En crespa tempestad del oro undoso' (449), 58, 72–3, 127, 148–9
'En los claustros de l'alma la herida' (485), 60, 79, 84–9, 105, 143
'Enséñame, cristiana musa mia' (192), 163 n. 37
'Es hielo abrasador, es fuego helado' (375), 85
'Éstas son y serán ya las postreras' (473), 86–7, 105–8
'Este polvo sin sosiego' (420), 139, 167 n. 27

'Floris, la fiesta pasada' (673), 161 n. 16
'Flota de cuantos rayos y centellas' (311), 57–9, 79, 86, 130
'Fuego a quien tanto mar ha respetado' (292), 99–105, 107–8, 130

'Hago verdad la fénix en la ardiente' (450), 55, 86
'Huye sin percibirse lento, el día' (6), 124

'Lisis, por duplicado ardiente Sirio' (484), 36–9, 90
'Los brazos de Damón y Galatea' (413), 8–9

176

'Mandóme, ¡ay Fabio!, que la amase Flora' (331), 90–3, 133, 154 n. 2
'Más solitario pájaro ¿en cuál techo' (359), 50–7, 75
'Mejor vida es morir que vivir muerto' (488), 116

'No es artífice, no, la simetría' (321), 109–12. 148–9
'No me aflige morir; no he rehusado' (479), 106–7, 118–21, 132, 139, 145, 150
'No pueden los sueños, Floris' (440), 160 n. 13, 162 n. 29
'¡No sino fuera yo quien solamente' (301), 26–7

'¡Oh tú, que, inadvertido, peregrinas' (12), 87, 167 n. 20
'Osar, temer, amar y aborrecerse' (367), 87
'Ostentas, de prodigios coronado' (293), 22–4, 27
'Ostentas, ¡oh felice!, en tus cenizas' (380), 139, 167 n. 27

'Piedra soy en sufrir pena y cuidado' (379), 79, 48
'Por ser mayor el cerco de oro ardiente' (458), 40–2, 90, 101, 108
'Por yerta frente de alto escollo, osado' (480), 10
'Puedo estar apartado, mas no ausente' (490), 31–3, 80, 87

'¿Qué buscas, porfiado pensamiento' (474), 63–4, 80, 161 n. 15
'¿Qué importa blasonar del albedrío' (442), 60
'¡Qué perezosos pies, qué entretenidos' (475), 98
'¡Qué preciosos son los dientes' (717), 49, 160 n. 45
'Que vos me permitáis sólo pretendo' (457), 40, 90
'Quien no teme alcanzar lo que desea' (335), 24–6, 27–8, 62
'Quien nueva ciencia y arte' (387), 86
'Quiero gozar, Gutiérrez; que no quiero' (609), 7

'Salamandra frondosa y bien poblada' (302), 85
'Si en el loco jamás hubo esperanza' (353), 62–3
'Si hija de mi amor mi muerte fuese' (460), 92, 107, 122–7, 138–9, 146, 150
'Si mis párpados, Lisi, labios fueran' (448), 93–9, 109, 138, 148
'Si tu país y patria son los cielos' (310), 167 n. 18
'Si yo tengo de pasar' (441), 161 n. 16
'Solo sin vos, y mi dolor presente' (374), 80–4, 121

'Todo tras sí lo lleva el año breve' (30), 88, 113
'Tras arder siempre, nunca consumirme' (371), 98

'Ven ya, miedo de fuertes y de sabios' (28), 167 n. 20
'Vivir es caminar breve jornada' (11), 64

'Ya formidable y espantoso suena' (8), 115

Index